When the
NEW AGE
GETS OLD

LOOKING FOR
A GREATER
SPIRITUALITY

Vishal Mangalwadi

InterVarsity Press
DOWNERS GROVE, ILLINOIS 60515

Published in the United States of America by InterVarsity Press, Downers Grove, Illinois, with permission from Hodder & Stoughton, England, which published it under the title In Search of Self.

InterVarsity Press® is the book-publishing division of InterVarsity Christian Fellowship®, a student movement active on campus at hundreds of universities, colleges and schools of nursing in the United States of America, and a member movement of the International Fellowship of Evangelical Students. For information about local and regional activities, write Public Relations Dept., InterVarsity Christian Fellowship, 6400 Schroeder Rd., P.O. Box 7895, Madison, WI 53707-7895.

Cover illustration: Roberta Polfus

ISBN 0-8308-1770-0

Printed in the United States of America

Library of Congress Cataloging-in-Publication Data

Mangalwadi, Vishal.
   [In search of self]
   When the New Age gets old: looking for a greater spirituality/
Vishal Mangalwadi.
     p.   cm.
   Originally published under the title: In search of self.
   ISBN 0-8308-1770-0
   1. New Age movement.   2. Jesus Christ—Person and offices.
I. Title.
 BP605.N48M33   1992
299'.93—dc20   92-36926
                                                  CIP

17	16	15	14	13	12	11	10	9	8	7	6	5	4	3	2	1
05	04	03	02	01	00	99	98	97	96	95	94	93	92			

For
Chandrakant & Rebecca Shourie
because the perseverance of
their faith is inspiring
their walk with God is challenging
and their friendship is refreshing

ACKNOWLEDGEMENTS

I am grateful to my friends in the international L'Abri 'family' who continue to help shape my thinking, as reflected in this book.

I would not have had the confidence to undertake this project if Ruth Bradby had not provided the initial practical support in research and Juliet Newport and Dave Adams the initial enthusiasm.

Dana and Judy Crider, along with their children, sacrificed their computer for months and also allowed me to invade their weekends when I needed to learn how to use it.

Joy Caton and Christian Szurko in England, Chris Ramsay and Annetta Whitley in the USA, and Georg Pflüger in Germany provided the practical support structure that I needed for collecting research material, travels, etc.

The support and sustaining structure in India was provided by my friends in the Himalayan L'Abri Resource Centre, including Joe and Marietta Smith, David Hope, and Jose Matthews, and also by various staff members at the Woodstock School, especially John Mihevc and Hugh Bradby. Hugh helped edit some of the chapters and made it possible for my wife Ruth to work at the school, thereby easing the financial pressures at home.

I am grateful for friends who were willing to read various chapters and to help and encourage – Dr Lawrance Osborn, Brian Austin, Dr Peter Deutschmann, Dr Raju Abraham, Stan Rubesh, Joseph Suozzo, Willy Barton and others.

Without the financial support of Deo Gloria Outreach, Howard Ahmanson, South Asia Concern, India Groundwork Trust, Stan and Marilyn Reuter, Doug and Beth Heimburger and others, it would have been impossible for me to travel for research, and for our family to survive with a husband and father who does not earn!

This is my fourth book in English. But because I have continued to give priority to my work as a social-political activist, I still have not learned to write a page of English without making a few mistakes. Earlier Ruth used to help, now my daughters Nivedit and Anandit have become eager helpers. They hope that I will write more. Ruth wishes that I will become a 'normal' person again – not disturbing her sleep night after night, for months on end. Needless to say, Ruth, Nivedit and Anandit provide much more than an emotional and practical support structure, which helps me to grow and continue to find myself as an author and as a person. They have served as my primary spiritual support structure, to help me grow in my knowledge of God.

AUTHOR'S PREFACE

The New Age dawned in our generation in the West – in California – and moved east to Europe and Asia. The established order was reversed. The material universe ceased to be the ultimate reality, people began to seek the spiritual, mystical, occultic, extra-terrestrial reality. Faith in 'intuition' or 'revelation', channelled by spiritual entities, replaced the earlier 'modern' faith in human reason. Historians ceased being important, for people could recall, if not actually relive, their past lives with the help of hypnotists or acupuncture needles. Counsellors and futurologists were replaced by astrologers as more reliable interpreters of the present and guides for the future.

The New Age of environmentalism taught powerfully that the world was not made for man, but man for the world. It claimed that the technological and nuclear powers of the passing masculine age were destructive, while the psychic and sexual energies of the coming feminine age would be potent remedies for human and environmental crises. This was because the human self was no longer viewed as an animal or a machine, but as the divinity itself.

In Search of Self is a sympathetic yet critical study of the New Age world-view. It accepts the New Age's rejection of the old 'secular, materialistic, rationalistic' age as both untrue and harmful. Yet it is not convinced that what is called 'the New Age spirituality' is the answer. Therefore it keeps comparing the New Age answers with the biblical world-view (not necessarily the same as contemporary Christianity), which it claims to be a viable alternative.

This book aims not merely to inform, but to stimulate vigorous reflection, to help the reader to separate the grain from the chaff, to make intelligent choices.

Vishal Mangalwadi

PROLOGUE:
SUE'S SEARCH FOR FREEDOM

Matteya had evolved so much into the image of his deity Shiva that it seemed as if, had he opened his third eye, he could have burned Sue to ashes. His looks were fierce. His language was filthy and abusive. Sue, in contrast, was calm and confident, though sad. As I stood near the Theosophical bookstand at the Festival of Mind, Body and Spirit and watched the two argue, I felt there was pathos in Sue's firm but gentle assertion that Matteya should not have made Sue's girlfriend pregnant and then walked out on her.

Strolling outside the Royal Horticultural Halls in London, where the Festival was taking place, Sue then told me how George, her boyfriend, had walked out on her when their daughter Linda was only two years old. Being both a mother and father to a darling 'terrible two' had visibly damaged Sue's feminine grace. She looked exhausted. Having been a champion of freedom for so long, she hated herself for being a disciplinarian now. But there seemed no other way to parent Linda alone.

Sue would never consider infanticide – sacrificing Linda to the Goddess to preserve her own sanity and freedom, in the hope that Linda would be reborn under more favourable circumstances. Yet she felt strongly that abortion was a better option for her girlfriend than being a single-parent family. And singleness was better than being married to a Shiva-worshipper like Matteya.

Sue hated to see Matteya doing to her girlfriend exactly what George had done to her. Her only source of comfort was her knowledge that Matteya was not only hurting her friend, but also destroying himself. A similar lifestyle had destroyed George too.

Not too long ago, Sue had admired George for his crusade to see a global government set up to ensure a nuclear-free world. Such a government could efficiently sort out the international economic injustices and care for Mother Earth holistically instead of splitting her into artificial political boundaries. Now George had no cause left to fight for, except to champion the rights of AIDS patients. When all his attempts at loving heterosexual relationships failed, he had come to believe that he must 'love' everybody, not just one woman. He became gay and was soon infected with the HIV virus.

Matteya appeared to be going further than George. Along with a few other sannyasins he was a devoted worshipper of Shiva – the male counterpart of the goddess Shakti. They indulged in phallic worship of the Shivalinga to increase their sexual potency and to have mystical experiences, and in occultic rites to gain magical powers to open their third eye like Shiva, who could destroy the world with the eye.

Sue blamed Christianity not only for her own wounds, but for the earth's ills as well. If only the 'Father God' of Christianity had not succeeded in destroying the Golden Age when humankind worshipped Mother Earth, perhaps today we would be facing neither ecological disaster nor the myriad ailments that have resulted from our lack of understanding of nature and our disharmony with it. If only we could learn again to flow with nature instead of struggling against it, what health and happiness we could regain – if not paradise itself.

Having given up physics at university, and having travelled around the world, Sue was now considering a career in alternative medicine. There was no question of her going to work in a factory, a big office or a corporate business where she would be turned into a non-person in exchange for money, security and promotion. She wanted a profession which preserved her freedom and identity.

On her extended travels in India, Sue had encountered the late Osho Rajneesh. She loved him and admired his inner strength to free humankind from the moral shackles imposed by religion. But what Osho's followers such as George and Matteya had done to others and to themselves in the name of freedom was too costly. For a time, therefore, Sue was attracted to the discipline and asceticism of the

Hare Krishna movement. But their vicious attacks on other groups who were sincerely trying to usher in the New Age of harmony, reconciliation and peace convinced her that no group claiming a monopoly on the truth could possibly help bring in the Golden Age.

Therefore Sue, an attractive young woman of twenty-seven, was already getting tired of life. She had largely given up her earlier attempts to create a new world through meditation and psycho-technologies. In fact at present she was not even seeking to become God. Her more immediate goal was to find her soul mate – irrespective of what sex this mate was. The astrologers and channellers she had consulted before going to Egypt had said that she would see her soul mate there. Even if she had met him/her, she felt neither had recognised the other. So she had begun to distrust astrologers for no fault of their own. Now she was more inclined towards trusting her own dreams and inner self than spirit guides and gurus. Nor could she fully understand why people should contact spirits when they were God themselves.

A string of unhappy relationships with idealistic men, utopian gurus, spirit guides and exclusive sects had made Sue a little unsure if a New Age had indeed dawned. Yet she was not a 'quitter'. Her hopes of a New Age were rooted not in her own unhappy experiences with the New Agers, but primarily in the astronomical fact that the Earth's movement of precession had indeed ended the two thousand years of the Piscean Age and ushered in the Age of Aquarius.

True, the general sense of alienation in her society, the increase in mental illness, violent crime, social disruption and bizarre cults suggested that Western civilisation was coming to an end. But she believed that these were in fact signs of a coming inevitable transformation. She believed the Chinese philosophers who taught that a period of Yang is not the end of history, but is always followed by a period of Yin, only to be repeated by Yang and Yin as a cycle. It seemed to Sue that this ancient teaching was confirmed by modern historians such as Arnold Toynbee and sociologists such as Willis Harman, who have also argued that the social crises we are witnessing may in fact be the birth pangs of a new, more humane, culture.

Even though emotionally Sue was not too optimistic about herself, intellectually she still believed that a quantum leap in the spiritual evolution of humankind is just round the corner. Perhaps whatever hope there was for her personally would have to be enjoyed in successive reincarnations. In this life it could be her destiny, as was true of her late guru, to bear the karma of Western society. Had not the West accumulated too much bad karma? No wonder the pioneers of the movement had to suffer, as did the Christ two thousand years ago, for the karma of others.

Sue's optimism also rested on the fact that increasingly, all around her, people are indeed giving up the old adherence to rationality and old-fashioned morality. In principle she had no objection to people like Matteya enjoying spontaneity and naturalness in their relationships with the opposite sex or even the same sex. But more important than being free morally is setting ourselves free from rational consciousness with the help of music and psycho-technologies. For nothing is more untrue than the old rationalistic paradigm that reduced the whole universe, including human beings, to the level of machinery. That reductionistic, mechanistic view is simply foolishness. Sue knew for sure that we are spiritual beings and are literally surrounded by disembodied spirits. The mere fact that the world is rediscovering the supernatural convinced Sue that a New Age is about to dawn. Christianity teaches that human beings are sinners. If one accepts that hypothesis, how can we evolve? The New Age teaches that at least potentially humans are God – evolution to Godhood is at least theoretically possible.

But what kind of a God would someone like Matteya make? As far as Sue was concerned, Matteya's act of making her girlfriend believe that he loved her, making her pregnant, and then just moving on to seek mystical, tantric power through sex with other women was unacceptable behaviour. She had felt compelled to challenge him to his face. But now, instead of repenting of his sin, he was abusing her in filthy language and trying to be Shiva – the God of destruction. Sue was forced to reconsider whether a spirituality devoid of morality could create a New Age, even with the help of a benevolent constellation such as Aquarius.

Happily I found that Sue, who as a young idealist had been willing to be personally wounded in her quest for human freedom, still had the stamina and was willing to journey beyond the New Age to find a better age. This book is therefore dedicated with a deep sense of respect and feelings of human solidarity to people such as Sue. I have struggled with the intellectual issues raised by the New Age more as an observer than as a participant. But this in no way undermines my respect for those inside the movement. I hope that my studies, reflections and conclusions will be of some value to those who are still searching.

1

THE UNIVERSE IN THE HUMAN MIND: THE BACKGROUND TO NEW AGE THOUGHT

*The body was nothing more than a materialized
thought . . . a dream.
The universe is made up of our own mental
images.
I and the universe were one.*

Shirley MacLaine[1]

The New Age movement is breathtaking in its boldness. It postulates that far from being a speck of dust, a machine, a monkey or even an image-bearer of God, the human self is in fact the Divine Self, the creator of the universe. One of the earliest and most coherent articulations of this thesis was in Joseph Chilton Pearce's book, *The Crack in the Cosmic Egg: Challenging Constructs of Mind and Reality*.[2]

If I am not a powerless individual, but the kingpin of my universe, then what I need primarily is not a fuller understanding of the secrets of the physical universe, but of my own self. True spirituality, then, is to realise my own potential.

Echoing Pearce's view, Shirley MacLaine writes: 'I have come to realize that "reality" is basically that which each of us perceives it to be . . . we each live in a separate world of reality.'[3]

This view is becoming increasingly widespread. It takes many forms. It has many consequences. It could change the face of the Western world.

Much of this book is devoted to examining the highly diverse theories and movements which we group together under the broad term 'New Age', and which have as their basis this view of self or consciousness as the creator of the universe. But before we do so, let us look first at the theoreticians who laid the foundations of this philosophy.

The universe – A process in God's mind

The idea that the physical universe may be a process, 'a flux' in the Universal Mind, was developed by the theologian, philosopher and mathematician Alfred North Whitehead (1861–1947) in his book *Process and Reality* (1929). Whitehead was building his philosophy on the discovery of twentieth-century physics that the atom was not substance as such, neither solid nor liquid nor gaseous. It could be described more aptly as a 'process' – a complex rhythmical pattern of energy.

The physicists
The founders of this new science, nuclear physics, include Max Planck (1858–1947) and Albert Einstein (1879–1955). They undercut an important foundation of scientific materialism when they conceded that the material universe is not necessarily all that we perceive it to be. Einstein agreed with Planck that there are at least three different kinds of realities.

First, there is the universe as we perceive it with our senses – the solid wall, the rising and setting sun, the coal and diamond which appear to be different entities even though they are both carbon.

Second, there is the universe as it really is in itself, though not open to direct sensory experience – we see the inert, motionless, solid rock, but we cannot see, touch or hear the tremendous dynamic activity or the non-stop motion within each atom.

The third is the universe of the scientist – the universe captured in mathematical equations, esoteric diagrams and the mind-blowing philosophical theories which keep appearing and disappearing as surely as the moon. These theories, that is, the universe of the scientist, have to be revised each time a genuinely new facet of the second reality, that is the given reality, is understood ... or can no longer be understood in the light of the existing theories of the universe.

The founders of twentieth-century physics did not doubt that a real universe exists outside the scientist's mind. That is, a universe which would still be there even if no human beings existed to examine it. Einstein wrote:

> The belief in an external world independent of the perceiving subject is the basis of all natural science. Since, however, sense-perception gives information of this external world indirectly, we can only grasp the latter by speculative means. It follows from this that our notions of physical reality can never be final. We must always be ready to change these notions in order to do justice to perceived facts in the most logically perfect way.[4]

Scientific materialism, which rejected all notions of spirituality or divinity, had assumed that 'seeing is believing', that is, that what we observe with our senses and interpret with our reason is the final truth. The implication of Einstein's view, on the other hand, is that what we perceive can probably never be the final truth, because our senses do not experience reality directly. It follows from this that atheistic materialism was nothing more than naive ignorance.

Another physicist, Arthur Stanley Eddington (1882–1944), took the thought of Planck and Einstein further when he declared that the world of physical science is only a symbolic world, 'a world of shadow'. The physicist, argued Eddington, begins by abstracting from the world of sense experience only those aspects which are measurable, deliberately ignoring the rest, such as love, morals and thought. In order to interpret his selective and therefore already limited data, the physicist is forced to introduce such 'symbols' as 'electrons', 'quanta' and 'potentials', which are not observed, but assumed.

Therefore we have to agree, reasoned Eddington, that the abstract and symbolic world of physics is only a construction of the human mind. It is constituted by thought. It follows from this, he concluded, that ultimately reality is not material but 'spiritual'. It is wrong to assume that matter is the primary reality and consciousness or spirit merely an accidental by-product or epiphenomenon – like bubbles in boiling milk, which do not have an existence of their own but are a condition of the milk itself. To Eddington, thought or consciousness seemed to be a more basic reality. He wrote in *The Nature of the Physical World* (published in 1928, only one year before Whitehead's *Process and Reality*): 'Recognising that the physical world is entirely abstract and without "actuality" apart from its linkage to consciousness, we restore consciousness to the fundamental position, instead of representing it as an inessential complication occasionally found in the midst of inorganic nature at a late stage of evolutionary history.'[5]

These scientific propositions, which could no longer consider the solid, material universe to be the primary reality (the milk) which created consciousness (the bubbles), led Eddington to conclude that it was more sensible to assume that a Universal Mind was the final reality: 'The idea of a Universal Mind or Logos would be . . . a fairly plausible inference from the present state of scientific theory.'[6]

Eddington's assumption that 'the stuff of the universe is mind-stuff' was admittedly a 'scientific speculation', incapable of being proven by the empirical methods of science – if 'empirical' means only that which is experienced by our physical senses. But scientists had already conceded that our senses do not give us a direct experience of reality as it really is. For example, our senses are obviously dependent on our consciousness for their usefulness. But consciousness itself can neither be seen, heard, touched, smelled nor tasted. Mystical experience, thought Eddington, may be the proof needed to know that the reality behind the universe is consciousness.

It should be clear that Eddington had gone beyond the assumption that the universe may exist independently of consciousness to a view that the universe is dependent on consciousness. A logical step in this sequence was taken by Eddington's senior contemporary, A. N. Whitehead, who believed that if 'matter' was really energy, then it was not necessary to uphold the traditional Western dualism of mind and matter as two distinct categories.[7]

To think of mind and matter as two separate entities creates several riddles. For example, when does a mind or soul come into a baby? Or, what is the mechanism of interaction between the non-material mind and the physical brain? If we were to think of mind and matter as two sides of the same coin we would not have these problems. Whitehead therefore decided that the presupposition of his philosophical system would be that all 'actual entities' are bipolar, with mental and physical processes as their two poles. 'Mental', for Whitehead, does not necessarily imply the brain or consciousness.

God, Whitehead presupposed, is also an 'actual entity' and is therefore bipolar. The mental or conceptual pole of God, which he calls 'primordial nature', is unchanging, complete and the source of all ideals and new possibilities. The physical pole of God, or his 'consequent nature', is the creative, evolving, advancing world. Put simply, Whitehead held that the world is a process in God's mind. This view was strengthened by the famous statement of the astronomer Sir James Jeans, that the universe is like a great thought rather than a giant machine.

The question arises: On the basis of this line of thinking, how did some New Age thinkers reach the conclusion that the universe may be a process in the *human* mind?

The missing link – Pierre Teilhard de Chardin

In her New Age classic *The Aquarian Conspiracy*,[8] Marilyn Ferguson says that a 1977 survey revealed that among those who had embraced New Age ideas thoughtfully the greatest single influence had been the Jesuit palaeontologist Pierre Teilhard de Chardin (1881–1955), followed by Aldous Huxley, Carl Jung and Abraham Maslow.

De Chardin developed his philosophy from his observations of fossil records of evolution. By his time many biologists had accepted Conway Lloyd Morgan's (1852–1936) view that biological evolution was not a resultant phenomenon but an emergent one.

By resultant, Morgan meant something which could be predicted from the factors operational in a process. For example, if we know the proportions in which carbon and sulphur combine, we can predict the weight of the resultant compound simply by adding together the weights of the components at hand. An emergent phenomenon, in contrast, occurs when something entirely new comes into existence; a novelty which could not have been foreseen from the antecedent factors.

Evolution was emergent, Morgan said, because it had produced completely new factors in species which were different from a mere regrouping of pre-existing factors in parent species – the elemental 'particles' had become atoms; atoms had turned into molecules; the inorganic molecules had emerged as living cells; the cells had been transformed into multicellular organisms, culminating in a self-conscious human beings.

De Chardin, who was studying fossils, had a different perspective. The evidence, he argued, goes contrary to the materialist's viewpoint that evolution was random – 'by chance'. A definite pattern or direction was observable in evolution – a direction towards ever higher forms of life and consciousness. If evolution was guided purely by chance, life could not possibly evolve only in a 'higher' direction. There had to be something more than pure chance. We therefore have to conclude, wrote de Chardin, that 'Nothing could ever burst forth as final across the different thresholds . . . (however critical they may be), which has not already existed in an obscure and primordial way.'[9] In other words, consciousness could not have emerged in human beings if it was not already present in the previous 'living' and 'non-living' forms of reality. If 'consciousness' is present in evolution from the beginning, then it is reasonable to assume that it has been guiding the entire process from the beginning.

From this assumption, as well as because of his Christian (eschatological) perspective, de Chardin then extrapolated the evolutionary process into the future. He speculated that the entire process of evolution will converge at an 'Omega-Point',[10] a supra-personal unity of all things in God. This makes God the final cause of evolution, not merely its efficient cause or the Alpha point. Thus, for de Chardin, *Homo sapiens* is like a caterpillar about to become a butterfly – an entity of completely different nature or 'consciousness'.

This was a tremendous gospel of hope to American young people of the 1960s – a generation that was disgusted by the mindlessness of the Vietnam war, which they were powerless to stop, though they lived in a country that claimed to be a democracy; a generation that was depressed by the hypocrisy of the corporate world, which claimed that it existed for people but which was killing them by the hundreds in Vietnam, while not even acknowledging that it was waging a war; a generation that was deeply disillusioned by technology which placed immense power in the hands of a few, but which made the majority feel so helpless that, for all practical purposes, they buried the notion of individual freedom – the essence of the American dream.

These young people were already experiencing an expansion of consciousness by going into a silent cocoon of yogic meditation and by creating an inner world of their own with the help of psychedelic drugs and music. The children of the 1960s counter-culture read de Chardin through the grid of their own experience, and it seemed to them that their intuition was being confirmed by a scientist. They thought that de Chardin's conclusion was that man was indeed in a process of becoming God the creator. Or, as de Chardin himself put it, humanity was about to become the body of Christ. The process of evolution was about to take its final leap, to meet its destiny by transforming consciousness into super-consciousness; utopia was just round the corner.

The fusion of Whitehead's process philosophy with Teilhard de Chardin's mystical optimism was already a potent enough mix for an 'emergent' New Age philosophy. Put this brew into the social bowl of the prevailing Western culture, which is materialistic, optimistic, individualistic and marked by the alienation of people from one another. Now add some or all of the following:

the emergence of the Indian gurus and the Zen masters so popular in the 1960s and 70s;

the paranormal potential of the psychological theories of Carl Jung and Abraham Maslow;

people's experience of the psychic powers of healers;

widely reported encounters with extra-terrestrial beings;

a growing interest in the mystical experience of sex;

the idea of the astrological Age of Aquarius;

a disillusioned youth culture susceptible to cults

and you have integrated most of the necessary ingredients for a powerful philosophical potion. All that is needed for marketing it is to package it in spiritual, ecological, feminist or peace language.

In later chapters we will be examining more carefully the utopian, ecological, feminist and peace claims of the New Age, as well as taking a look at the Eastern journey into the 'inner space', the astronomical influence of the zodiac constellations on human history, the evidence for the human potential to tune in to the collective unconscious wisdom of man, and the powers of the disembodied spirits.

At this stage, however, we need to continue our description of the essence of New Age thought, keeping in mind that we are attempting to systematise a movement which scorns systematic thought and welcomes paradoxes, contradictions and even outright irrationality.

An alchemy of East and West, social and supernatural

The conclusions of Whitehead, Eddington, and de Chardin were only a step away from what the Indian seers, writing 2500 years ago, had already said.

The rejection of reason
Like some of the modern scientists mentioned above, the Hindu seers had grasped the simple fact that our sensory observations, and their 'logical' interpretations, by themselves cannot lead us to truth. Therefore, they too, tried hallucinogenic herbs and consciousness-altering physical, sexual and mental exercises. This route led them to stumble upon the experience of an expanded state of consciousness in which the whole universe appears to be alive, conscious and united. In this mystical experience our sense of individuality appears to dissolve into a feeling of oneness with a larger consciousness. It was this experience which led the Hindu mystics to believe that the spiritual essence in man (self or *atman*) was the same as the underlying essence of the universe (*brahma*).

An essential feature of the New Age is its conscious rejection of reason as the means of discovery of truth. Already in the nineteenth century Western philosophers such as Immanuel Kant and Friedrich Nietzsche were arguing that reason cannot give us knowledge of reality as it really is; and the twentieth-century schools of philosophy such as existentialism,[11] decades before the arrival of the New Age movement, had firmly rejected faith in reason. But in spite of clearly seeing the limits of reason, neither Kant nor the existentialists went on to embrace Eastern techniques of altering consciousness in order to experience truth directly.

It was not until the 1950s and 60s that experimentation with 'mysticism' or artificial alteration of consciousness became a widespread practice in the West, led by Aldous Huxley, Indian gurus and Zen masters such as D. T. Suzuki and their Western popularisers such as Professor Allan Watts. But the New Age had not arrived yet, because while the West was merging with the East, the persistence of the old, materialist world-view, with its insistence on reason as the ultimate source of human understanding and knowledge, still kept the supernatural out of the picture.

Before we discuss the fusion of natural and supernatural in New Age thought, it is important to grasp that the New Age has not rejected the primacy of reason simply because its limitations have been logically demonstrated by the philosophers. Split-brain surgery has also revealed that the human brain has two parts or 'hemispheres'. The left hemisphere is usually the centre of rational, analytical or conceptual activity. The right hemisphere, on the other hand, is primarily responsible for our aesthetic, intuitive, emotive activity. The right hemisphere can often grasp a truth instantly and intuitively long before the left hemisphere is able to figure out the same truth 'rationally'. Therefore it is at best unwise to over-emphasis logic, rationality or left-brain activity at the expense of intuition, feelings or right-brain activity. Yet the West had deliberately made left-brain or logical intellect the foundation of all knowledge and social behaviour.

The acceptance of 'reason' (or left-brain logic) as the sole means of knowledge began with René Descartes (1596–1650). But it is often forgotten by New Age writers that Descartes embraced reason as the ultimate reliable source of knowledge not by rejecting intuition, but by denying supernatural revelation from a personal God.

Before Descartes, in spite of some important exceptions, the Western mind had generally assumed that God's revelation was the real source of our knowledge of truth. There was no antithesis between revelation and reason, because it was assumed that our reason was made in the image of God. Therefore, just as one human being could communicate truth rationally to another human being, so

God could communicate it to us. In fact, it would have been irrational to think that a God who gave us the capacity to think and talk in abstract language lacked these abilities himself. Revelation, in the Judaeo-Christian sense, was not an intuitive, private, mystical, non-rational or 'right-brain' activity – it was a rational communication between one infinite Person and his creation, man, who was finite.

The basic shift which Descartes made was not from right brain (intuitive) to left brain (rational), but from God as the source of knowledge to man as its ultimate source. Thus Descartes' theory of knowledge (epistemology) was humanistic or man-based, although he put emphasis on the rational, logical capacity of man's left brain.

The New Age makes three distinct moves away from Descartes.

The first is the move away from the left brain (logical reason) to the right brain (feelings and intuition). This is not a move away from our ordinary waking or rational consciousness as such, but a recognition that the normal human consciousness is much more than pure reason or logic. Therefore it is, at best, improper to limit our quest for truth to the realm of logic alone.

New Age thought, however, recognises that to depend on the right brain (feelings and intuition) alone is not enough for our voyage of discovery of truth. Therefore, the second shift away from the legacy of Descartes is to go beyond the dethronement of reason (or left-brain logic) to dethrone the normal (waking) human consciousness itself, which functions with the help of both the left and the right hemispheres, in favour of another state of consciousness called 'transcendental' or 'mystical'.

This shift, which began by embracing the Eastern conquest of the normal human consciousness with the help of techniques such as yoga, had taken place in popular Western culture before the arrival on the scene of the 'New Age'. But as the mystics know, a genuine mystical experience is an experience of contentlessness, void or *shoonya*. It gives a feeling of our oneness with the cosmos, but it does not answer any human questions.

This mystical experience, as we will soon see, also implies a more radical loss of self than has resulted from an advance of technology in a competitive economy. Therefore, while this 'trans-rational' experience was adequate for the hermits of the past, it does not fulfil the quest of the New Agers, who seek a better world, not isolation from the world. They are, therefore, forced to make a third, more radical break with Descartes than merely to give up the intellect (left brain) or the normal rational consciousness. In their search for knowledge they choose to go beyond man himself, to contact spirits, disembodied entities who, it is assumed, might know more than we, because they live in a 'spiritual' dimension. The spirits can communicate with us in rational language, using human mediums or channels.

Since it is hard to reconcile the view that real spirit beings exist beyond my own consciousness with the already accepted New Age presupposition that I create my own universe, some New Age apologists such as Shirley MacLaine talk of these spirit guides as our own 'higher selves'. We can create our own spirit guide and project it (him/her) on to the universe, to be available to help and guide us in times of need. Even though the 'higher self' may be our own creation, for all practical purposes it assumes an objective existence of its own and then guides us from its superior position in a 'spiritual' dimension.

At first sight, Shirley MacLaine's idea that 'I and the universe were one' may sound absurd. But Marilyn Ferguson and other New Age apologists defend it by using the analogy of a hologram.

A hologram is a three-dimensional photograph produced by laser beams. One characteristic of a hologram is that, if broken up into pieces, a single part of it can be used to reconstruct the whole picture. This phenomenon, not yet fully understood, suggests that somehow the entire picture is present in each piece. By analogy, the whole ocean may be present in each wave, the whole universe in each individual. Obviously not all New Age thinkers go as far as Ferguson or MacLaine. Dr Fritjof Capra, whom we will encounter again, is one example of a leading New Age exponent who disagrees with the view that the universe is a hologram.

The New Age is thus a struggle to go beyond man as the ultimate source of truth. The movement is not yet able to turn Descartes on his head, to affirm that if spirit beings exist and can communicate with us, then God himself – the infinite, eternal Spirit – may exist and communicate with us, his children. It is not possible for the New Age to reach this Judaeo-Christian conclusion, because it has already accepted and modified the Eastern assumption that man himself is god. Therefore, ultimately, even knowledge received from disembodied spirits becomes humanistic in the sense that these objectively existing spirits are said to be a creation of our own consciousness.

The divinity of man
The view that 'I and the universe are one' is an ancient one. Hindu mystics understood this oneness of the human consciousness and the divine consciousness as the oneness of the wave and the ocean. The ocean is real, but the wave's individuality is only a temporary phenomenon of the ocean. It is not really real. Just as a wave merges back into the ocean, during the mystical experience the individual consciousness also seems to merge into a larger, 'expanded' consciousness. This suggested to the Hindu sages that our individuality was ultimately an illusory, limited experience. The wave seems real while it lasts, but it disappears back into being the ocean.

Anti-individualism and individualism:
Two sides of the same coin
The profound practical consequences this undermining of individuality has had in India dawned on me fully when in 1976 my wife and I left middle-class urban Indian life to live as social workers with peasants in central India. The Hindu peasants did not ask a stranger what their name was, but what their caste was. When we asked their names, usually their spontaneous response was to tell us their caste, as though their own name had no significance.

It is not only the individuality of the peasant which has been made insignificant by Hinduism, but also that of people who in another culture would have been put on a pedestal. We lived only a half-hour drive away from the temples of Khajuraho, famous for their explicitly erotic sculpture. You need not affirm the religious value or the morality of those X-rated 'epics-in-stone' in order to appreciate their aesthetic excellence. Plane-loads of Western tourists who arrive at Khajuraho every day never fail to be impressed by the fact that the names of the sculptors and architects who carved and built these temples only a thousand years ago remain unknown. What many of these tourists do not seem to realise is that in its rush towards the New Age the West is finally catching up with the East. Some of the most influential New Age books, such as *A Course in Miracles*, do not carry their author's names because their own individual creativity has been made insignificant by higher forces, or at least by the new belief system.

The profound, often unconscious, influence the Bible has had on Western civilization for almost two thousand years continues to mould basic features of that culture such as its high view of the individual person, even though a majority in the West has ceased to believe that the Bible is God's revelation.

The assumption that, far from being an illusion, our individuality is precious, is rooted in the biblical teaching that Adam and Eve were created as special and distinct individuals in God's own image, to live for ever with the same personalities in the paradise of the Garden of Eden. Their notion of individuality was not their bondage or *maya* (illusion). Nor were they mere waves in the Ocean of Consciousness or the Mind-at-Large. They experienced themselves as distinct individuals because that is what they were created to be. Adam and Eve did die as a result of sin, but the Bible teaches that just as Jesus rose again from the dead, with his memory intact, in his nail-pierced body, recognisable to his disciples, individual believers will also be resurrected to eternal life.

One illustration of this view of the significance of individuality is that the Bible contains two lists of the genealogies of Jesus – whose father, Joseph, was only a carpenter – and that one of these lists goes right back to Adam! Most of the sixty-six books of the Bible are named after their authors – some of them written more than two thousand years before the temples of Khajuraho were carved.

I am by no means blaming the Bible for the extreme 'individualism' we experience in the West today. It could not teach individualism, because even the biblical God is not an individual. God, the Bible reveals, is triune – three persons (Father, Son and Holy Spirit), bound together by love in such a way that the Bible can simply say 'God is love' (1 John 4:8), or God is one.

A consequence of the biblical view that man and woman
were created in the image of God (Gen. 1:26) is that Adam
and Eve were meant to become 'one flesh', completely intertwined in love. Adam said about Eve:

> 'This is now bone of my bones
>   and flesh of my flesh; . . . '

For this reason a man will leave his father and mother
and be united to his wife, and they will become one flesh
(Gen. 2:23–4)

Not only were husband and wife called to be 'one flesh',
even the disciples of Christ who were promised individual
immortality were commanded to live as 'one body' – the
church – with one another. Therefore, the first church in
Jerusalem practised a radical version of 'communism' –
sharing all material possessions in common, meeting the
needs of widows, orphans and the poor. The New Testament
records that 'All the believers were one in heart and mind.
No-one claimed that any of his possessions was his own, but
they shared everything they had' (Acts 4:32). This oneness
of believers was not limited to liberally sharing material
blessings with one another; the whole ethos of the Bible was
to summon believers to submit to one another in humility,
giving preference to one another (e.g., Eph. 4:1–3; Phil.
2:1–2).

The biblical view of God left no room for individualism, because God sacrificed himself for others; self-denial
therefore became a virtue for 'God's people'. Nevertheless,
because of the high premium which the Judaeo-Christian
tradition put on the significance of each individual, mainstream Christianity could never allow self-denial and the
'taking up of one's cross' to mean asceticism or the denial of one's own fulfilment. The second highest moral
principle enunciated by Jesus was 'Love your neighbour
as yourself' (Matt. 22:39), which justified self-love within
the limits of love for one's neighbour.

As Western culture cut itself off from its biblical roots, the
high view of the individual-in-community degenerated into
individualism. Charles Reich lamented in *The Greening of
America*:

America is one vast, terrifying anti-community. The great

organisations to which most people give their working day, and the apartments and suburbs to which they return at night, are equally places of loneliness and alienation. Modern living has obliterated place, locality and neighbourhood, and given us the anonymous separateness of our existence. The family, the most basic social system, has been ruthlessly stripped to its functional essentials.[12]

The New Age is, in part, a response to this social reality. While the New Age does not seek to produce stable relationships through monogamy and sexual fidelity, it does struggle to replace alienation by 'loving relationships'. The New Age does not have a concept of repentance, but it does emphasise forgiveness and positivity. It even attempts to take you back to the moment of your first breath at birth, to root out completely all negative thoughts from your psyche and to 'rebirth' you into a positive outlook to enable you to cultivate and enjoy 'loving relationships'.

In the seminars and workshops at the Festival of Mind, Body and Spirit, where I met Sue, there were about twenty sessions and workshops on 'relationships'. They used techniques of visualisation (explained later in this chapter) and dreams to find your 'soul mate' and sexual partner. Not one seminar was exclusively devoted to realising Teilhard de Chardin's vision of evolving to Godhead. Sue said that four years ago she was seeking her divinity. But when we met, her dreams and visualisations were now for a partner who could help her cope with the pressures of living as a single-parent family in an inhuman, individualistic West where the Matteyas and Georges care more for their selfish Shiva-hood in a nuclear-free world than for the women they have impregnated. To me, this shift of emphasis from cosmic to private needs seemed to indicate that the Indian gurus, who in the 1960s and 70s offered Godhead at the price of the surrender of one's individuality, have now been sidelined. The leadership of the New Age is often in the hands of single, separated or divorced people, for whom the search for a soul mate has become more urgent than God-realisation – which can await another incarnation.

The privatisation of spiritual property
Hindu mysticism is the private and exclusive experience of

a yogi. But instead of affirming one's individuality, it facilitates its dissolution into a larger universal consciousness, like a wave into an ocean. It is this loss of individuality which is reflected in the loss of private life in the ashram.

The gurus whose popularity peaked in the 1970s were highly directive. The disciple usually had to sacrifice his body, soul and possessions to join a guru's ashram/commune. Not only were spiritual 'techniques' prescribed, but in most ashrams strict rules were laid down about what you could wear or eat, and the time you must sleep or wake up. (In some cases, such as in the Hare Krishna sect, when and how often you could have sex were dictated.) This loss of private rights obviously did not harmonise too well with the Western tendency towards privatisation, or with young people's quest for the 'recovery of freedom'. New Age spirituality is in many ways a reaction to this, and is a process of privatising Eastern religious traditions. The New Age is led not by gurus 'made in India', but by those cast in the Western mould. Rather than surrendering their all to a guru, they now prefer to own and even create their gurus and spirit guides.

Shirley MacLaine teaches that each one of us can create or discover within ourselves a private 'higher self' whom we can summon for help and guidance whenever we wish. Ms MacLaine's neighbour near Seattle in Washington, Mrs Judy Zebra Knight, is said to have gone on to obtain legal patent rights for the exclusive channelling of Ramtha – a spirit being who claims to be thirty-five thousand years old. Mrs Knight has not created Ramtha; he used her body and mind first. So now an alien spiritual entity has become a commercial private property which can be used for the public good only if an adequate fee is paid.

In Hinduism the guru owned the surrendered disciple; in the New Age the disciple owns or even creates his higher self or perfect master. This total privatisation of spiritual experiences, beliefs and rituals, with no inherent checks to ensure their social usefulness or 'orthodoxy', has meant that the New Age has been able to churn out a 'spirituality' that can be considered anything from responsible to bizarre, from ecological to irresponsible.

It is this radical privatisation of beliefs, rituals and 'spiritual' experiences which makes a comprehensive survey of the New Age movement difficult.

A materialistic spirituality

Whitehead, Eddington, de Chardin and others had decisively undercut the scientific and philosophical roots of atheistic materialism. Therefore the Indian gurus who had renounced the world, including the responsibilities of marriage (though not necessarily the pleasures of sex), had little initial difficulty in conquering the Western citadel of ethical materialism, where economic prosperity had become the chief end of life. All they needed was an anti-materialistic rhetoric, even if it was delivered from a golden throne in an expensive and garish temple.

But Western materialism was not rooted simply in atheism. The Bible itself had affirmed the material universe to be a good creation of God; a physical paradise was God's original blessing to mankind. The Bible taught that a life of obedience to God's law usually, though by no means always, resulted in material prosperity even though in the short term, in exceptionally wicked historical circumstances, a commitment to righteousness led to temporary persecution and suffering. But suffering for righteousness was worth it because it was the way to the kingdom of God (Matt. 5:10).

The enjoyment of material blessings is therefore too deeply embedded a value in Western consciousness to yield to the Eastern emphasis on renunciation of the material. It played a role in producing industrial and technological revolutions and has shaped Western history in a fundamental sense.

Hinduism, on the other hand, not only saw the material world as maya or illusion, but attachment to it as bondage. Detachment from materialism was therefore a prerequisite to liberation and a high religious value. A clash between these opposite attitudes to material prosperity was inevitable.

I have seen several examples of this conflict. Sue is one. An intelligent, ambitious, determined enough person who could succeed in the competitive materialism of the West renounces her home, studies and career to follow a guru whose anti-materialistic stance fits in so well with her own idealism as a student. For years she does not see any contradiction between supposed anti-materialism and the fleet of Rolls-Royces her guru cherishes. Later, however, she is bitter that she cannot really afford to spend £25 to attend a seminar to learn the techniques of finding her soul mate. A two-hour session with a channeller might cost £100, and a weekend with a Hollywood guru could cost $2,000 just to learn the techniques of 'going within'.

Did Eastern spirituality conquer the West? Or, did Western materialism succeed in commercialising the anti-materialism of the East? She is no longer sure; but she seeks to become a spirit healer mainly to support her child – who must not be too poor to miss meeting these non-material entities.

Utopia can now be 'visualised'

If the universe does not exist outside of, or at least independent of, my consciousness, then it is not too far-fetched to assume that it can be transformed by my consciousness. This utopian conclusion is another 'resultant' feature of the fusion of Eastern philosophy with the historical optimism of Western thought.

Hinduism and Buddhism never had the utopian expectation of transforming the world. Buddha is one of the greatest Indians of all time. One reason for his greatness is his deep empathy with those who suffer. But Buddha saw the universe intrinsically as a condition of suffering, which cannot be improved. It therefore had to be transcended in *nirvana* or enlightenment. The Hindu goal of *moksha* (liberation) is also an attempt at escaping the wheel of *samsara* – our bondage to the cycle of repeated births and deaths.

Eastern thought has therefore not bred utopian visions or movements. Western religious and political history, on the other hand, is a tale of failed utopias, inspired in part by the biblical teaching of creation, fall and redemption – of paradise enjoyed, lost and restored. Robert Bellah writes: 'The Puritan settlements in the seventeenth century can be seen as the first of many efforts to create utopian communities in America. They gave the American experiment as a whole a utopian touch that it has never lost, in spite of all our failings.'[13]

The biblical vision of the millennium, or the thousand-year reign of Christ at the end of this age, includes the ecological hope of renewal of the earth, as well as the restoration of paradise where God himself 'will wipe every tear from their eyes. There will be no more death or mourning or crying or pain' (Rev. 21:4).

The Bible, which has moulded Western history, sees creation, both 'living' and 'non-living', as very good. Man was made to live in Eden, that is, bliss. Evil and suffering entered history later. They are therefore finite and temporary aberrations, introduced by the 'fall' or the free choice of human beings. Because suffering is not intrinsic to the human condition, it can be overcome and removed. This viewpoint gives a basis of hope for our future. In the West Thomas More immortalised this hope in his book *Utopia* (1516). However, in Western history the hope is often secularised, as in the French Revolution inspired by Rousseau, in the theory of social evolution, and in the dialectical materialism of Engels and Marx.

The East's pessimism, on the other hand, is a logical result of its view of 'creation' as an illusory situation, in which infinite consciousness has somehow forgotten its true nature and has begun to treat its dream of finiteness as reality itself.

This traditional difference between East and West can be stated in another way. In Eastern thought God somehow forgets his divine infinity and becomes the finite man. Man suffers the consequences of God's mistake, and his suffering cannot be eradicated until he ceases to be man and once again becomes the blissful, impersonal divine consciousness (*sacchidananda*).

In contrast, the Bible says that it is *man* who forgot his finiteness in the garden of Eden. He tried to be independent, the master or god of himself and his environment, and therefore ate the forbidden fruit, with catastrophic results. God then suffered the consequences of human sin upon the cross to set right the wrong and to eradicate suffering.

The New Age accepts the Eastern metaphysical theory that the human self is the divine self. But the deeply ingrained optimism of the Western psyche does not permit it to accept the pessimistic implications of that metaphysics. Therefore the New Age seeks to transform the Eastern view by making it mean that because the human self is the divine self, therefore the infinite self of man should be able to transform his universe. But because it is not possible to build such hope on the Eastern view of self alone, the New Age is, in practice, necessarily driven to seek help from astrological constellations, extra-terrestrial intelligences and disembodied spirits from primitive eras.

One practical implication of this attempted conceptual shift from pessimism to optimism is that in the New Age visualisation becomes more important than meditation. Eastern meditation, as we will see in later chapters, was an effort to empty the mind of all thought and imagination, because the 'thinking self' is the self in bondage. The 'pure' consciousness (in contrast to 'gross' consciousness), is beyond thought; it is silence, shoonya or void. These were popular themes in the 1960s and 70s. But now the emphasis is on visualisation, which is an attempt to restructure our thought-produced universe.

If our world appears to be undesirable at the moment, then it is because we have allowed too much negative psychic energy to flow out of ourselves. We need to send out positive energies to transform our reality. That visualisation (or mental energy) affects physical reality is a common experience with all of us, argues Shirley MacLaine: if your sexual fantasy has ever given you a physical orgasm, then you ought to know that thoughts affect material bodies. In a universe which is a process in the human mind, to visualise utopia should indeed be as simple as visualising an orgasm.

A time to hope
If I am walking on a New York street and a mugger comes from behind and clubs me on the head, did I create that reality myself? In her earlier books such as *Out on a Limb* Shirley MacLaine's answer would have been, 'Yes, you created that reality for yourself in a previous life. You get in this life what your karma of an earlier incarnation deserves.' But if being clubbed from behind is what my karma merited, then I could not possibly escape my fate.

This view of karma and reincarnation, then, inevitably breeds fatalism and pessimism, especially when it is assumed our individuality is a passing phenomenon in an endless time ruled by our planets. In India this pessimism was reinforced by the Hindu view that time is a cycle; the universe begins with a golden age of *satyuga* and gradually deteriorates into *kaliyuga*, or the dark age. The world is then destroyed, only to begin again and repeat the cycle of going from bad to worse, until it is destroyed again.

The West, in contrast, has governed or managed time, because of the biblical belief that Adam and Eve were created to live for ever and therefore were above time. Sin, because it resulted in death, made us slaves of time. But since through his death and resurrection Jesus has given us eternal life, we are once again above time. The sun, moon, stars and planets do not rule our times. But they help divide time into manageable parts to assist us in our task of governing.

Because the West has thought of time as linear and manageable, the past has gone, never to be repeated again; the future is not here yet and can be shaped by our present efforts: it is marked by hope rather than pessimism.

However, the earlier simplistic concept of linear time became untenable after Einstein proved that time is not absolute, but is relative to the speed and position of the observer. If time were absolute, it would mean that everywhere in the universe (and for everyone) one hour would mean 60 minutes and each minute would mean 60 seconds. No one could complete one hour, say, in 59 minutes. Relative time means that this is not necessary. Someone might reach one minute in only 50 seconds. C. S. Lewis popularised this idea in his children's stories *The Chronicles of Narnia*. In these stories, a lifetime in Narnia equalled only a moment on our earth.

Let us illustrate this viewpoint further: when we see a supernova, we know that the incident in fact took place ages before we saw it happen. This is because the light from the event took a long time to reach us. If someone much closer in space to the incident could send information to us faster than the speed of light, he could have told us the precise time when we would see the phenomenon as well as the exact spot in the sky where we would see it happen. That is obvious. But Einstein thought this could not happen in practice, because nothing could travel faster than the speed of light.

However, Einstein proved something rather different. According to a New Age interpretation of Einstein, popularised by movie series such as *Back to the Future* and *Star Trek*, one implication of time being relative is this. Suppose you and I are travelling at significantly different speeds. I am at Goa, jogging along the longest beach in India, and you happen to pass by the same place in a spacecraft almost like a 'time-machine' of the kind depicted in science-fiction movies. Imagine now that you overtake me at a point when I am under a coconut tree. The thunder of your flying machine causes a coconut to fall on my head. According to this interpretation of Einstein's theory, you would see the coconut fall before I experienced it. And in theory, you could even inform me in time to save me from being hit.

This means, at least theoretically, that a person in a different space-time dimension or speed could see our future before we do, and predict it to us. We can visualize this geometrically quite easily.

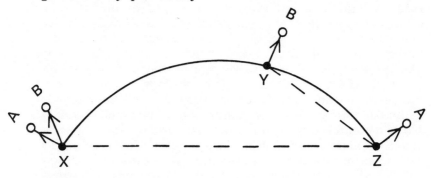

Point
in time

Imagine time as an indefinite curve. Suppose two people, A and B, at point X are moving towards Z. If, somehow, A could go relatively straight, he could reach Z while B was still approaching point Y. A could even send information to B and tell him what will happen when B reaches Z. This would not be possible if time was absolute and everyone got to point Z at the same time.

Our purpose here is not to discuss whether the above actually reflects Einstein's own understanding of his theory. Nor is it to evaluate whether or not it is true. The point is that if that is an accurate understanding of time, then the phenomenon of prophecy is possible. That explains why ancient prophets such as Nostradamus and prophetic books such as Revelation are so popular in the New Age.

But a curve, these interpreters point out, is a part of a circle. If you keep going on a curve, you will arrive at the beginning, or at least get back to the beginning point. This could mean that time is not linear but cyclical. If you keep going forward you will get back to the past. Or, if you go fast enough in reverse gear, you can go back to the future. Time, in other words, is not going anywhere.

That is why the spaceship *Enterprise* in the movie *Star Trek IV* could travel back and forth between the twentieth and the twenty-third centuries and save the whales. Both the twentieth and the twenty-third centuries are *now*. You can go from one to the other, if you can go fast enough.

If the cyclical view of time is understood as *nowness*, Shirley MacLaine argues in her book *Going Within*, one can believe in karma and reincarnation without accepting fatalism and pessimism. If time is going nowhere, my 'previous incarnation' was not in a past century, but I can live it now by visualising or 'recalling' my 'past' life. I can 'progress' to a future life as easily as I can 'regress' to a past life. They are both *now*.

The Eastern mystics, when they reached that state of enlightenment, saw linear time to be an illusion and gave up the notion of reincarnation completely. Reincarnation was real, they said, only as long as you lived in the bondage of *avidhya* (ignorance). By contrast, the New Age retains the notion and fuses it with the idea that the universe of matter in space and time is a creation of my consciousness. This is then made to mean that I can visualise a perfect incarnation – utopia. This discovery by the New Agers makes our age a time of great hope for the world, for utopia is now only a thought away!

One problem with this interpretation of Einstein is so obvious that even Anandit, my eleven year old daughter, could see through it when we were discussing *Back To The Future III*.

'A curve', she said, 'does not necessarily mean a circle. It could begin at a point and end before completing the circle. Time, because it is not God, might have a beginning and therefore be finite. Even if it does not end, a curve still need not be a circle,' she argued. 'It could be spiral, then it would still be linear, in the sense of going forward.'

One can stretch the concept of 'curved time' to mean that time is cyclical only if it is presupposed that time is eternal. Following Newton, many scientists did think that time and space were eternal. In that case a curve could have meant a circle, and a cyclical view of time would be tenable. But the scientific consensus has now moved decisively away from that view. The universe, according to contemporary physics, is neither infinite nor eternal. Its age is calculable. Some say that by the second law of thermodynamics, the cosmos is moving inexorably towards total entropy, when matter as matter may cease to exist. Therefore, unlike in Newtonian physics, space and time are no longer thought of as two different forms of infinity. Space-time is a single finite entity, which begins at a calculable time-distance from the present. It has a limit at which it may cease to exist. This means that time, even if it is 'curved', need not mean a circle. Certainly the idea of an eternally existing cyclical time has no scientific basis.

If time was eternal, then the human self would be under time, unable to have dominion over it, to govern it and shape the future. Only if human beings share God's transcendence and eternal life could they plan, manage and govern time.

I thought that Anandit's argument, that a curve could mean a spiral rather than a circle, was interesting, because the book of Revelation, which is one of the most popular books in the New Age, does suggest that history moves forward as a spiral. When the seven seals that shut the future have been broken, we do not reach the end, we see seven angels with trumpets. When the trumpets end, and we think the climax of history is in sight, we find yet another circle, but this time of the seven bowls. Then there are also the seven words.

The concept of time as linear – whether curved or spiral – unlike that of time as a cycle, implies that each moment of history is unique and cannot be repeated. If that is so, then time is real; it is not dependent on my consciousness. I am dependent on a real history. I am affected by it and I in turn affect it. Human action could then be significant (provided we are not determined by external forces, such as benevolent or capricious constellations). If we are free agents, then there could be hope – though not necessarily utopian, because my consciousness alone does not create history.

What is the ultimate truth about the nature of time (if there is anything like an objective truth)? That question is not our primary concern at the moment. The point here is to note that the current emphasis in some New Age circles on time as *nowness* reflects another attempt by the West to conquer Eastern pessimism, while bowing before its metaphysics and spirituality.

What the New Age person does not seem to understand is that there is no exit that way. If all time is now, then we live in a cosmos where all events are entirely determined. What will be, already is. We can then bid goodbye to free will, goodbye to any sense of meaning, and certainly goodbye to the *raison d'être* of visualisation.

Is this Western victory over Eastern pessimism credible and durable? Or is it built on a concept of time that exists not in the real universe, but only in science-fiction movies?

If the concept is fictitious, then the New Age is a castle built not on sand, nor even in the air, but only in thought.

Can this castle of consciousness withstand the persistent lashes of the mighty tidal waves of dehumanising ideas and social currents that have already brought the lofty humanism of the Enlightenment to such a sorry end?

Or will pessimism, asceticism, escapism, the denial of individuality and private rights – all inherent in the Eastern philosophy – have the last laugh? Perhaps some spirits or extra-terrestrial beings might still come to our rescue. Let us therefore turn to them in the next chapters.

2

'LET US MAKE MAN IN THE IMAGE OF HIS STARS': ASTROLOGY AND THE NEW AGE

When the Moon is in the Seventh House
And Jupiter aligns with Mars
Then peace will guide the planets
And love will steer the stars.

(From the musical Hair*)*

The significance of astrology for the New Age should be obvious from its other name, 'The Age of Aquarius', popularised by the well-known musical *Hair*. Outside the New Age movement, astrology is usually perceived as a tool of divination, used to draw conclusions about future events from the position of the sun, the moon and the planets, in relation to the constellations of the zodiac and one another.

A need for such divination is felt because our self, imprisoned as it is in the confines of time, cannot see the future. This knowledge of the future becomes a means of guidance when we are required to make decisions for which we do not ordinarily have adequate information. For reasons discussed later in this chapter, many in the New Age prefer to look upon astrology not as a means of divination but as a source of answers to metaphysical questions, especially about ourselves. This trend received great impetus when a French scholar, Michel Gauquelin, produced statistical evidence that some personality types or traits seem to have a definite correlation with certain planets in our horoscopes.

Tracy Marks, one of the most influential New Age astrologers, begins her popular book *The Astrology of Self-Discovery* with these statements:

> The astrological chart is . . . a map for discovering who we truly are and who we can become . . . Astrology . . . involves experientially as well as intellectually contacting the planetary personalities within us. By actively using astrology, we can discover our overall life purpose or life direction.[1]

Is there a scientific basis to her claim?

The astronomical meaning of the Age of Aquarius

The astronomical definition of the Age of Aquarius begins with the fact that the earth has three principal motions. First it rotates on its axis, once in twenty-four hours. That gives us our day. Second, it revolves around the sun, once in 365 days, with its axis in virtually the same direction. That is how we get our year. There is also a third motion, a slow rotation of its axis, which makes a complete circle in about 25,800 years. This is called precession. On about 21 March the sun is overhead on the equator. As seen from the earth, the sun then appears to be near one end of the stars of the constellation Pisces. That point is called the Vernal Equinox (VE). Because of the precession of the earth's axis, the VE is slowly moving backwards through the stars, and nearing the stars of the constellation Aquarius (see p.34). The VE remains in one sidereal sign for about 2150 years.[2]

When does the Age of Aquarius begin? Astronomers and astrologers have not been able to agree on the answer. Some believe that it started on 13 March 1781, when the planet Uranus was discovered. Others have suggested dates as varied as 1844, 1900, 1962, 1983, 2000, 2160 and as late as the year 3000.

While there is disagreement about the dates, astrologers are generally agreed that the characteristics of the Age of Aquarius will be harmony, peace, universal brotherhood, joy, freedom (especially in ethics), science, accomplishment, and inspiration (especially in religion). The underlying assumption is that the stars influence, if not actually determine, human behaviour.

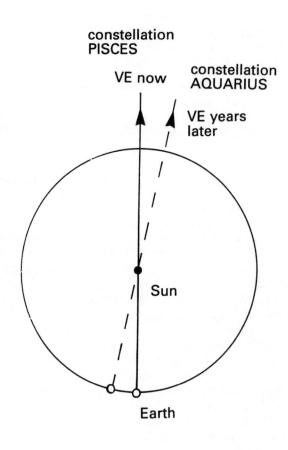

How do the stars influence us?

Three kinds of hypotheses regarding the influence of the stars appear worthy of consideration. The first and most common assumption is that there is a mechanical (cause-and-effect) relationship between us and our zodiac sign, therefore our stars influence all of our life. This implies that astrology is a proper scientific study of horoscopes. Although an ancient science, it is, so the theory runs, often abused and mixed with superstition.

An alternative hypothesis has become associated with the name of Carl Jung. It postulates that astrological (and other) predictions come true neither by chance nor because stars cause them to happen in a physical sense. Some things are related to each other meaningfully though not mechanically. Jung called this phenomenon 'synchronicity'. Others, following this general trend, postulate that we are connected with our stars at some pre-atomic vibrational level, or that planets are in fact 'sub-personalities' within us, with lives of their own, and therefore they are able to influence us. There are several variations of this viewpoint within the New Age, all of them seeking to combine astrology with physical or emotional therapy. A common thread running through these theories is that although astrology is real it is not a mechanistic science.

The third kind of hypothesis rejects the view that astrology has anything to do with stars and planets. Some authors such as Dan Korem, a magician turned psychic detective, argue that psychic and astrological readings are common-sense 'cold readings'. Others, such as Dr Anthony Stone, a mathematics professor turned Sanskrit scholar, and an authority on Hindu astrology, maintain that when there are genuine astrological predictions their source is spiritistic not astrological. We will examine this third kind of explanation of astrology in a later chapter.

A causal relationship: Astrology as a science

Some years ago John H. Nelson, a scientist working for the Radio Corporation of America, was able to predict with an astounding 93% accuracy the days on which radio reception would be poor. This was because he had found that good reception occurred when two or more planets were at angles of 60 or 120 degrees relative to the sun, and bad reception when the planets were at angles of 0, 90 or 180 degrees. He also found smaller effects at various multiples of 7.5 degrees.

Because 90 divided by 12 is 7.5, many intellectuals, including the prominent Indian scientist Dr B. V. Raman, have argued that Nelson's predictions are based on 'astrological data'.[3]

Michel Gauquelin, a French scholar, makes many similar and significant observations in his books *Astrology and Science* and *The Cosmic Clock*.[4] For example, he points out that there is a shellfish which produces eggs only at full moons from January to July. Countries in the northern hemisphere show more than the average number of human births in May and June, and less than average in November and December. The sunspot cycle, of about eleven years on the average, coincides approximately with cycles in climate, plant and animal life, and even in economic and business trends. High tide occurs when the moon is in the fourth and tenth astrological houses, and low tide when the moon is in the first and seventh houses.

In recent decades attempts have been made to study the horoscopes of top people in various professions to arrive at statistical conclusions about the reliability of horoscopes. Gauquelin's conclusion is that while professional success cannot always be correlated with specific planets, certain personality traits do correlate with certain planets. J. A. West and J. G. Toonder maintain in their book *The Case for Astrology* that the statistical results produced by correlating professional success with specific planets are crucial because the probability of obtaining these results by chance is only one in a million.[5] Facts such as these lead many astrologers to conclude that the planets influence our lives directly, and therefore that astrology is a legitimate science which studies and interprets planetary influences on human behaviour.

We know that DNA inherited from our parents has an enormous influence on our physical and mental make-up. The DNA template stores information on what colour our hair will be, long before our skull even exists. There is a cause-and-effect relationship between DNA and our future development. Therefore, it can be studied scientifically.

Some astrologers, anxious to establish their craft as a science, argue that there is a similar cause-and-effect relationship between one's horoscope and one's life. Indeed, a horoscope is a scientific/mathematical chart of the position of various heavenly bodies at the time of one's birth. An astronomer who rejects astrology as nonsense would cast exactly the same horoscope for us as an astrologer. But the question is, from that 'natal chart' how does one arrive at a description of one's personality and at predictions about the future? Or, how do astrologers know what characteristics will be the main features of the Age of Aquarius?

The believer in astrology will often answer that just as Francis Crick and James D. Watson decoded the DNA's 'language' in our generation, so our ancestors had somehow learned to interpret the horoscope. We have lost the record of how the horoscopic language was first decoded, but we know that horoscopes contain information about our lives and that they can be read. It is possible, they would say, that some of our ancestors came from other, more advanced, planets and brought the information with them.

The second relevant question is: How do we know that these heavenly bodies do in fact determine our lives in a cause-and-effect manner, making a scientific interpretation of horoscopes possible?

The proponents of the scientific/causal theory would usually answer this second question by affirming a belief in the interconnectedness of everything in the universe. They may refer to the discovery of the new physics that electrons remain mysteriously 'interconnected' even when separated from each other. They would assert that the interconnectedness of the electrons proves that we are also connected to heavenly bodies. Their movement, therefore, has a direct influence on us, just as the moon affects the tides of the oceans.

Critics' response to this idea is that while it is true that we do not yet understand how electrons remain interconnected, we cannot from that microscopic fact draw a macro-scientific hypothesis that everything in the universe is interconnected. That belief is an extrapolation, not a logical, verifiable conclusion. One could assert that the belief is verifiable in mystical experience. Maybe so, but then we are not talking science.

If everything in the universe is mechanistically interconnected, then it would be logically impossible to single out
a few stars and planets and hope to understand ourselves
on the basis of their influence alone. We would also, for
example, need to know the influence of the underground
minerals at the place of our birth in order to have a fuller
knowledge of ourselves, because they too must influence
us.

There are two kinds of objections to the claim that
astrology is a science that have never been satisfactorily
answered. One concerns the nature of science and the
other the logical implications of a belief in astrological
determinism.

Astrology and the nature of science

We can prove that a medicine that heals a specific disease
works in a cause-and-effect manner. The medicine is the
cause of the healing effect even if we do not always know
'how' it produced the effect. As we will see in chapter 9,
'My Course in Miracles', sometimes a plain distilled-water
injection can cure a fever dramatically. However, from the
observation of a causal relationship between a medicine and
healing, we cannot logically conclude that therefore the
water that worked must also have a causal connection with
its effect. We know that there is no direct cause-and-effect
relationship between water and healing. A magic stone, a
mantra, or a tablespoon full of honey and pepper may have
produced the same effect, because it was the patient's faith,
not the water, which triggered off the production of healing
chemicals in the patient's brain.

This should warn us that just because radio reception is
influenced by the movement of planets, we cannot naively
deduce that everything in our life is caused by them. Nor
can we conclude that because an astrologer's prediction
proved accurate it is thereby scientifically proven that the
stars determine our lives. In the case of radio reception, it is
'planetary magnetic storms' that cause the changes. These
storms are not fully understood as yet. But we know that
to make his predictions Nelson also had to consider factors
other than planetary positions. These included the positions
(relative to the sun) of the nodes of each planet. In their book

Astrology: Do the Heavens Rule Our Destiny? (Harvest House, 1989) John Ankerberg and John Weldon debunk Nelson's statistics.

The following factors make astrology essentially unscientific.

The planets

Astrologers get similar results by using different systems of astrology, each involving different sets of planets. Traditional Western astrology uses seven 'planets' – the sun, the moon, Mars, Jupiter, Mercury, Venus and Saturn. New Age astrology is struggling to incorporate planets such as Uranus, Neptune and Pluto in their systems. The traditional Indian system uses nine planets. Seven are the same as in the Western system, the other two are the moon's nodes.

Different Indian and Western astrological systems also use some additional, unobserved, imaginary planets. These can have no physical influence. The other side of the coin is that in astrology most stars, planets and asteroids are ignored. For that matter, generally, the three-dimensional picture of the planetary and stellar position is ignored. Only the positions of arbitrarily chosen sets of planets are considered in the plane of the zodiacal sign.

If a distilled-water injection, a spoon of honey with pepper, a bitter herb, a magic stone, an aspirin or an antibiotic may all have the same healing effect, then the scientific inference would be that some other hidden factor is the real cause of healing. Our 'medicines' only help that factor get started. Likewise, if completely different systems work equally well, then we have to conclude that even if we are connected to the planets, they play no intrinsic role in astrological predictions; some other factor is at work. Indeed, some Indian astrologers are able to get equally good results by using the time of asking the question, rather than the time of the questioner's birth. Some need to look only at the questioner's posture to be able to make 'astrological' predictions.

The zodiac

The twelve signs of the zodiac, of 30 degrees each, were invented in Babylon in the fourth or fifth century BC. Each sign corresponds to a constellation, and was originally near that constellation. Agreement about this was never exact, because constellations vary in size.

In astronomy, the twelve signs of the zodiac form a reference system for the positions of the planets as seen from the earth. In astrology, the signs are given various qualities and interrelationships.

Astrology does not treat the zodiacal signs any more scientifically than it does the planets. Western astrology uses what are called tropical signs, beginning with the sun's position at the beginning of spring. Indian astrological systems work with sidereal signs, starting with various fixed points among the stars.

Another unscientific aspect of astrology is the arbitrary way in which the zodiac is divided into twelve parts relative to the horizon. Some experts believe that originally only eight so-called 'houses' were used. Some astrological systems now use ten houses, others twenty-four and some even forty-eight houses.

It is possible, but not necessary, to study other factors that contradict astrology's claim to be a science. For example, the method of timing future events. Western astrology uses at least five different methods, Indian astrology forty-five. Genuine science is continually correcting itself by rejecting inadequate theories or methods. Astrology retains all methods because it is an authoritarian system, where rules are not usually explained, examined or defended. In science there is a real and direct connection between a cause and its effect. Therefore it is repeatable and can realistically strive for 100% success. Astrology uses only a symbolic connection between planets and human beings. Therefore it makes free use of chance and intuition, and only hopes for success.

A non-causal connection between the stars and ourselves?

Does every effect have to have a physical and knowable cause? A fundamental presupposition of modern science has been that the 'law of causation' is an absolute and inviolable principle.

When we have a dream and it comes true, did the dream cause the event? Or, if an astrologer makes a prediction of an accident and it occurs, did the stars or the prediction cause the accident? We have already seen that a 'causal' explanation of the influence of the stars is tenable for astronomy but not for astrology.

However, there are effects which have no knowable cause. For example, both theoretically as well as experimentally, radioactive decay is totally unpredictable. It is an effect with no knowable cause. Facts such as this have now raised fundamental doubts about whether physical causation is adequate as a full explanation of reality. Therefore many thinkers have begun to put forward alternative theories to explain how astrology could be true without the stars actually causing or determining events in our lives.

Seriality

Many leading intellectuals in our century have espoused a belief that causation is not the only principle which connects objects and events in the cosmos. In 1919 Paul Kammerer, a Viennese experimental biologist, propounded his 'law of seriality'. For twenty years Kammerer had maintained a log-book of coincidences in his life. His book, *Das Gesetz der Serie*, which has never been published in English, contains one hundred selected coincidences. On the basis of these he defines seriality as the concurrence in space or the recurrence in time of meaningfully, but not causally, connected events.

The essence of Kammerer's theory is that as well as the mechanism of causality, with which science deals, there is also another 'acausal' principle active in the universe. It works like the mysterious force of universal gravity. The main difference is that while gravity works indiscriminately on all matter, this hypothetical factor works selectively, by making two similar things or events converge in space and time. Einstein was sufficiently impressed by Kammerer's book to say that it was 'original and by no means absurd'.[6]

Synchronicity

This idea was developed by the Nobel laureate physicist Wolfgang Pauli and the psychoanalyst Carl Jung, whose essay, 'Synchronicity: An Acausal Connecting Principle', published in 1952, widely popularised the concept and made it a possible justification for belief in paranormal events such as telepathy, clairvoyance and divination, including astrology.

How could stars or astrological predictions 'cause' events in our lives, without any physical influence? Jung says:

> Synchronicity is no more baffling or mysterious than discontinuities of physics. It is only the ingrained belief in the sovereign power of causality that creates intellectual difficulties and makes it appear unthinkable that causeless events exist or could ever occur.
>
> ... Meaningful coincidences are thinkable as pure chance. But the more they multiply and the greater and more exact the correspondence is, the more their probability sinks and their unthinkability increases, until they can no longer be regarded as pure chance but, for lack of a causal explanation, have to be thought of as meaningful arrangements ... Their 'inexplicability' is not due to the fact that the cause is unknown, but to the fact that a cause is not even thinkable in intellectual terms.[7]

It needs to be remembered that the concept of 'seriality' or 'synchronicity' is not a proof that astrology is true, or that the stars do influence us. Jung said, 'Astrology would be a large scale example of synchronism if it had at its disposal thoroughly tested results.'[8]

Since such statistics do not as yet exist, the idea of synchronicity is only an admission that many human experiences suggest the possibility that physical causation or chance are not the only possible explanations of reality. Some other principle, as yet unknown, may also exist and mysteriously make things happen; 'things' that are sometimes called divine or demonic, 'miracles' or extra-sensory perceptions by human beings.

Vibrational connection

The notions of seriality and synchronicity are so vague that they really explain nothing. Jung virtually confesses that in a sense his idea is 'not even thinkable intellectually'. Several New Age astrologers try to clarify the situation by using the concept of vibrations. *The Revelation of Ramala*, a book containing messages received by various channels in an influential New Age group in Glastonbury, England, says: 'Astrology is a science of the vibrations of the Cosmos on the Earth ... The most recognisable influences which are felt on Earth are obviously the vibrations of the planets within your Solar Body.'[9]

Donna Cunningham is another typical example. She suggests that planets vibrate at different frequencies at such a subtle level that it is not possible to measure those vibrations scientifically. Planetary vibrations affect the vibrations of our bodies:

> Astrology is a means of attuning to changes in vibratory state, both personal and collective . . . If astrology works, it is not because of causation but of reverberation. That is, Saturn and Uranus do not cause the problems you meet, but they vibrate to the same frequency as the energies that are entering your life when you get a transit by those planets. They may very well be the lenses through which cosmic energies are focussed.[10]

These energy vibrations are said to be at the root of all that exists. However, they are not to be imagined as something physical, subject to the laws of science. The New Age says they are psychic or spiritual in nature. That is why astrology often implies worship of the stars as deities. Attempts are also made to harness this spiritual energy for benevolent purposes such as healing.

An implication of this view, according to Ms Cunningham, is that astrology can be a short cut to diagnosing your trouble. An hour's chart-reading session can save six months of the exploratory phase of traditional therapy.

Tony Drew, a State Secretary for the Federation of Australian Astrologers, has a national weekly magazine column and is a frequent radio broadcaster. During one of his lectures that I heard, he prescribed dietary, exercise and life-style programmes for natural health on the basis of the above understanding of astrology.

If the essence of the planets and of our own selves is some spiritual vibration, then it is not all that far-fetched to assume that the planets implant our personalities in us. Therefore, many in the New Age use astrology more for psychotherapy than for physical therapy. Instead of assuming that pre-atomic vibrations connect us to our planets, they consider our planets to be characteristics or sub-personalities within us.

Planets as personalities within us

We have mentioned that Gauquelin did find statistical evidence that certain planets correlate with certain character traits much more than can be mathematically explained as a chance phenomenon. Although he did not find effects involving the sun, Mercury, Uranus, Neptune or Pluto, some of his findings agreed with astrological characteristics ascribed to the planets. For example, Mars was relatively more aggressive, Jupiter happy and Saturn silent. His other findings contradicted astrological assumptions. For example, Venus was not found to be significant for musicians and painters!

We are still a long way from confirming the validity of Gauquelin's research, and, if it is correct, from understanding the meaning of his statistics; but as we have admitted, that kind of study is a legitimate science. Some therapists, influenced by Jung and these discoveries, have made an important assumption that the planets of astrology are 'sub-personalities' within us. They govern our lives from within and can be used for therapy.

Tracy Marks says:

> An important principle of depth astrology is that our planets are actually personalities within us, not merely parts or qualities of ourselves, but entities in their own right, with lives of their own. In Psychosynthesis . . . we do directed fantasies and dialogues with subpersonalities within us which are similar to our planetary selves.[11]

According to this school of thought some of our sub-personalities actually correspond to our planets. For example, the rebel in us is our first house Uranus, and the workaholic in us is Saturn in Virgo in the sixth house. The objective of studying astrology is to become increasingly aware of all the personalities within us, so that we do not allow just one or two of these planets to run our lives, but make decisions in consultation with all of the personalities within us.

This understanding of astrology sounds new because it is presented in contemporary psychological language. However, many ancient cultures have thought of heavenly bodies as spirits – *stoicheia* in Greek. The English versions of the New Testament often translate *stoicheia* as 'spirits' or 'principles' (e.g., Gal. 4:3, 9 and Col. 2:8, 20). But as Wim Rietkerk says, 'These "spirits" (and "principles") sometimes were identified with stars and configurations of stars in the same way as astrologers do today.'[12]

Whether our connection with the planets is understood as vibrational or in terms of subpersonalities, it is assumed that this connection lies outside the limits of physical science and rational logic. Therefore the concept is not open to rational discussion. Even if that is true, we can still evaluate whether or not teaching and experience fulfil the objectives of the astrological quest.

The self in astrology: Made in the image of the stars

When we say, 'I am angry because I have a difficult Mars,' or, 'I need freedom and variety in love relationships because I have Venus square Uranus,' we do indeed have a kind of knowledge of ourselves. But this self-knowledge has several inherent dangers, rooted in the fact that the planets are impersonal whereas we are personal beings.

The first danger in defining ourselves in terms of the stars is that we begin to fit the complexity of human personality into a neat system devised by human beings rather than the planets themselves. We are supposed to be made in their image, but since they don't speak, we end up defining them in terms of who we are, rather than explaining ourselves in terms of what they are.

If our quest is, 'What is a human being?', then we are particulars and the planets are supposed to be universals. But the dilemma of astrology is that its universals have to be explained in terms of particulars. This problem is explained in the Epilogue. One of its implications is that if I am angry because of my stars, and I am trying to change, I am struggling against my creators. It is for this reason that astrological self-knowledge tends to become a bondage rather than a truth that liberates.

King Solomon, famous for his legendary wisdom, observed: 'A gentle answer turns away wrath, but a harsh word stirs up anger' (Prov. 15:1). St Paul exhorts us: 'Do not let the sun go down while you are still angry, and do not give the devil a foothold' (Eph. 4:26–7). My father, an extremely patient man, had a problem: when he had a disagreement with my mother he would not talk to her for days. I inherited this trait. I have had to assume that I inherited it from him and not from my planets, because we were born under different signs. With my wife's help, however, I have been finding it possible to replace sulking with communication; to not let the sun go down while I am still angry. That sulking really allows the devil a foothold in our family. Through prayer I have also learned quite a bit about how to bring another's anger to an end with a soft answer.

The philosophical underpinning of this is that I am made in the image of a personal being – God. He has spoken and told us that since the fall of Adam and Eve we are not what we were made to be. But we should repent and seek to become perfect, as our Father in heaven is perfect. The astrological chart only tells us what we are – something that we usually know, if we care to be honest with ourselves. God tells us both what we are and what we should be.

The astrological approach to self-knowledge turns us into objects: Mars or Venus or Saturn has done this, that or the other to me. Human beings, however, are subjects, not objects. Self-consciousness is our essence. It enables us to say, 'I am this, that or the other, but I can change.'

A second danger in seeking self-knowledge through astrology results from the fact that astrology uses highly abstract symbols. The more we attempt to fit ourselves into abstract categories, the less we will be able to know ourselves as we truly are. A better way of discovering ourselves is through in-depth, lasting relationships with real people and by reading biographies.

I have found that reading the Bible every day is a very effective way of getting to know myself. This is because the Bible contains literally hundreds of realistic histori-cal biographies from many different cultures, covering a very long historical period. We can know ourselves better by knowing real people. Abstract symbols can be helpful. But our generation, more than previous generations, is in need of real heroes and models. This is because most of us have only known celluloid heroes and models from the un-real world of high-tech advertising. Discovering ourselves from our horoscopes can be comforting or paralysing, but discovering ourselves by looking at real heroes is always challenging and uplifting.

A third danger in seeking to know ourselves astrologically is that we reduce ourselves to concepts. People can be categorised into personality types, such as sanguine, choleric, phlegmatic and melancholic. But our self-concepts never equal our real self. We are far more complex than any intellectual description or psychological analysis of ourselves. Therefore experience and intuition are more profound means of personal knowledge than self-concepts.

Knowing ourselves implies taking responsibility for ourselves. It includes repenting of what we have been; setting higher goals for ourselves, irrespective of what our horoscope says. It involves growing in faith, hope and love.

Our self-concepts are not realities, but they can shape reality. If I read Christ's parable of the good Samaritan in the morning, I might decide to try and be a good neighbour to the people I meet. At the end of the day I will have made new friends and deepened existing relationships. But if I read my horoscope and find that I am likely to be rejected today, I will assume an aloof and defensive posture. My expectation and manner will make that astrological prediction a self-fulfilling prophecy – I will be rejected.

Astrology and relationships: A finite, impersonal reference point

Most marriages among Hindus are arranged only after an astrologer has established that the horoscopes of the boy and the girl match. As faith in astrology grows in the West, believers are increasingly allowing horoscopes to determine their attitudes to other people. To pigeonhole our complex, dynamic personalities into neat, small and static astrological boxes is bad enough; to prejudge others is certainly worse. It could be more destructive of relationships than allowing first impressions to be the last impressions.

On several occasions I have noticed that if someone is expecting me to be angry, he or she will totally misinterpret some word or act of mine. Instead of judging it at its face value, they judge it in the light of their preconceived idea of how I may be feeling. When we habitually prejudge people astrologically, this misconception is bound to happen more often and harm relationships. Strong relationships are built on love, trust and respect for the other person. St Paul says:

> Love is patient, love is kind. It does not envy, it does not boast, it is not proud. It is not rude, it is not self-seeking, it is not easily angered, it keeps no record of wrongs. Love does not delight in evil but rejoices with the truth. It always protects, always trusts, always hopes, always perseveres. (1 Cor. 13:5–7)

A relationship is worthwhile when it is based on mutual give and take, when each partner makes sacrifices for the other and adjusts to their needs and wishes. The problem with the planets is that our relationship with them is only one way. They influence us, but we cannot change them.

A deeper philosophical problem is that the stars are also finite. So while it does help to have them as a larger reference point, they leave us without any ultimate meaning because, as Jung and Sartre have said (see Epilogue), we have to find an infinite reference point to find real – in contrast to merely existential – meaning.

I therefore prefer to find meaning for myself in my relationship with the infinite, personal God. Because God is personal, he is someone you can talk to and expect to respect you and your needs. Because he is infinite, you can expect him to change your personal, social and natural circumstances, according to your needs.

Astrological power: Can knowledge weaken and enslave?

The experience of being alone in an impersonal universe and a selfish society where others are more adept at using us than serving us is frightening. When we stand at important crossroads, the fear of an unknown future can be paralysing, especially if we feel that we do not have the resources to cope. Astrologers can be a source of power in these settings, if they make positive, comforting predictions.

Paradoxically, however, the very knowledge of the future can be a weakening experience in a deeper way. When we are watching a thriller movie, knowing the end lessens the fear and tension of the moment, but our enjoyment is not as great as when we go through the thrill without knowing what's at the end of the tunnel.

King David, who went through many hopelessly dark tunnels in his life, said:

> Even though I walk
>   through the valley of the shadow of death,
> I will fear no evil,
>   for you are with me;
> your rod and your staff,
>   they comfort me.
>
> You prepare a table before me
>   in the presence of my enemies. (Ps. 23:4–5)

David found strength, not by knowing what the future held for him, but by knowing him who holds the stars. Indeed the stronger men and women are those who persevere in faith, hope and love in the midst of suffering and hardships, without knowing when (if ever) these will end.

Who is better placed to face the evils that come our way: a person who knows that his future is planned by his loving heavenly Father, or a person who believes that a capricious planet like Saturn is in charge of his life?

St Paul faced violent persecution, financial difficulties and horrendous natural disasters such as shipwrecks in stormy seas. Yet he said, 'We know that in all things God works for the good of those who love him' (Rom. 8:28).

Conclusion: Should the stars rule our destiny?

Thoughtful New Age authors do not accept the view that astrology works in a scientific/mechanistic manner, because that implies that the human self is determined by external causes, such as a mechanical movement of the planets. This robs the human self of its freedom and dignity. It implies that we are neither responsible for our past and present, nor able to shape our future. If, as many New Agers say, the human self is the creator, and the universe is made up of our mental images, then we ought to be able to control the movements of the planets, rather than they determining our lives.

What then is the truth? Do the stars govern our lives, or are we the governors?

I feel that the perspective offered by the first chapter of Genesis, the first book of the Bible, is most helpful in striking the right balance on this issue. It says that the heavenly bodies were indeed created to govern certain aspects of nature, but that we were also created as governors.

It says this about the sun, moon and stars:

> And God said, 'Let there be lights in the expanse of the sky to separate the day from the night, and let them serve as signs to mark seasons and days and years . . . ' And it was so. God made two great lights – the greater light to govern the day and the lesser light to govern the night. He also made the stars. God set them in the expanse of the sky to give light on the earth, to govern the day and the night, and to separate light from darkness. (Gen. 1:14–19)

About human beings it says:

> Then God said, 'Let us make man in our image, in our likeness, and let them rule over the fish of the sea and the birds of the air, over the livestock, over all the earth, and over all the creatures that move along the ground.' So God created man in his own image . . . male and female he created them . . .
>
> God blessed them and said to them, 'Be fruitful and increase in number; fill the earth and subdue it.' (Gen. 1:26–8)

The sun, the moon and to a lesser extent the other heavenly bodies do govern our lives. For example, in large measure the sun determines when we sleep and when we wake up; when we sow and when we harvest; when we work and when we take holidays and get married. Usually the sun also determines whether we wear shorts or woollen clothes today.

Because these heavenly bodies are created to govern as well as to be signs to mark seasons, days and years, their movements and influence should be carefully studied. It makes no sense to have signs that people do not read or understand. However, are we to study them because they govern our lives? Or are we to study them because they are created to assist us in our task of governing the earth effectively?

The stars do not study us, because their authority is given. We, on the other hand, are creative beings because we are made in the image of the creator. Therefore, we have to go out and learn to establish our rule. We are commanded to fill the earth and subdue it. We are free to become rulers or to choose to be ruled.

For example, the sun decides when we will go to bed. But we are free to say no. We can use electricity to lengthen the day inside our homes, offices or factories. The sun does determine whether we will wear shorts or woollens. But we are not bound to be ruled by what the movement of our earth in relation to the sun decides. We can turn the thermostat up or down, and choose what we will wear in our home, car or office. We are the rulers, we do not have to flow with nature. It is a part of human privilege and authority to use air-conditioning and central heating.

The biblical statement that the sun, moon and other heavenly bodies are created to mark seasons and years means that they are markers to help us divide our time. For example the week is divided into seven equal and manageable parts, so that we are able to plan our week, complete our work in six days and rest on the seventh. If time was not so divided, we would invariably carry our work over from one week into the next, and from one year into the next. That would make it impossible for us to manage our time, to have dominion over it, instead of being ruled by it.

This biblical understanding of time and our relation to it is one of the most important foundations of the remarkable development of Western civilisation. In astrologically determined cultures such as India, we do not generally plan and manage our time, because we believe that we do not rule over time, but that time rules our destiny.

In parenthesis, we could note that the reality of death, the finiteness-in-time of our personal existence, does imply that time is greater than us. We are born and die, but time continues. However, the biblical teaching concerning eternal life counteracts the apparent finality of death. Adam and Eve were created to live for ever. Thus they were above time. But death came as a result of sin. Since Jesus died for our sins, through his own death and resurrection the Lord

Jesus has broken the power of death over us. He says that he is the Alpha and Omega, the beginning and the end. This means that he is above time. He promises that those who receive him will 'reign with him for ever and ever' (i.e., we too will reign over time).

Thus our choice for or against faith in astrology becomes a choice between looking at ourselves as above time or under it; of governing time or being governed by it.

For those who give astrology an important place in their lives, it increasingly becomes a source of weakness, fearfulness and dependency. That happens because they experience themselves as victims; footballs that are kicked around by forces more powerful then themselves; people who are acted upon, rather than individuals who are created to go out and subdue the earth and govern their environment. Therefore it should not come as a surprise to us that God asks his children not to indulge in divination or fear the astrological signs: 'Do not learn the ways of the nations or be terrified by signs in the sky, though the nations are terrified by them. For the customs of the peoples are worthless . . . ' (Jer. 10:2–3).

The New Testament says to those who once knew themselves by knowing God, but later began to seek knowledge, power and reality through their stars:

> When we were children, we were in slavery under the *stoicheia* [the stars or spirits] . . . But now that you know God – or rather are known by God – how is it that you are turning back to those weak and miserable principles [*stoicheia*]? Do you wish to be enslaved by them all over again? You are observing special days and months and seasons and years! I fear for you, that somehow I have wasted my efforts on you. (Gal. 4:3, 9–11)

St Paul wrote to those who loved God in the city of Colosse that he was struggling for them, so that they

> may have the full riches of complete understanding, in order that they may know the mystery of God, namely, Christ, in whom are hidden all the treasures of wisdom and knowledge. I tell you this so that no-one may deceive you by fine-sounding arguments . . .
> See to it that no-one takes you captive through hollow

and deceptive philosophy, which depends on human tradition and the basic principles of this world [i.e., the *stoicheia*, or the spirits of astrology] rather than on Christ. (Col. 2:2–4, 8)

To summarise, the most important question for anyone thinking about astrology is whether we are made in the image of our stars or in the image of the God who made the stars and rules over them. Our answer to that question will determine whether in a given culture human beings will manage and rule over time, or whether time will rule over them. To put it differently, the issue is whether the stars are created to govern us or to assist us in our task of governing.

3

SPIRITISM: A BALANCE SHEET

As we saw in the previous chapter, through astrology some seek to experience oneness with planets, constellations and galaxies. In this chapter we will examine how, through contact with spirits, others attempt to establish that our spirits continue beyond death, that we have lived before our births, and that 'paranormal' information and powers can be a part of our normal experience.

Even though some astrologers do seem to obtain results which cannot be attributed to chance, unfortunately the stars themselves do not speak. And when astrologers move beyond generalisations to make specific predictions they err a bit too often. They also contradict each other's version of what the stars are saying. The excitement of one of them proving accurate is usually neutralised if we look at the logic of several others turning out to be wrong.

Happily for New Agers, however, spirits do speak. In fact their messages have rekindled a dying faith in astrology. But most of them do not seem to have the power to generate sound waves on their own, even though physical and psychic energies are said to be one. Therefore the spirits have to use the mind and vocal chords of a medium to speak, and their fingers to write, paint, or tap on tables.

Few cultural phenomena are as pervasive and as enduring as communication with spirits. During earlier eras, as well as in traditional communities even today, spirits were contacted mainly for divination. It was believed that by virtue of their location beyond the confines of space and time they could see persons, objects and events in distant places, past and future. In the New Age the spirits have usurped the position of philosophers, gurus and theologians. Most of their contemporary discourses are metaphysical. What are we to make, then, of the claim that spirits have begun communicating with us intensively because we are on the threshold of a New Age?

It will help us decide for or against the significance of the spirits if we can draw up a balance sheet of their contribution to us and our culture. What did the West lose by banishing them in the post-Enlightenment era of rationalism? What does it stand to gain by embracing them again in the lives of its citizens and in its intellectual and cultural life?

Before attempting such a balance sheet, we need to define what we mean by a 'spirit', and also to determine whether there is a difference between the powers of magic, our own psychic powers, and the powers received from disembodied spirit entities.

What exactly is a spirit?

We find two different definitions of a spirit within the New Age movement. A spokesperson can put forward either of the views, depending on the context. One definition is that spirits are real entities that exist in another dimension than ours. The other is that they are products of our own unconscious mind.

Both Dr Bernie Siegel, the founder of ECaP (Exceptional Cancer Patients), and Shirley MacLaine talk about their spirit guides as 'real' persons, who exist objectively in their own right, but only in the mind of the individual they relate to. 'George' and 'Bernie' are, Dr Siegel maintains, two distinct personalities existing simultaneously in his mind. Is he then possessed by another spirit? Dr Siegel would not describe his experience in those terms. He says that if we must have an intellectual label for 'George', then we could call him a 'meditatively released insight from my unconscious'.[1]

What exactly does that mean?

Spirits as a creation of our unconscious minds
In some of his earlier writings, Carl Jung postulates that consciousness is like an ocean without boundaries. This ocean he calls the collective unconscious – something similar to the Hindu concept of Brahma or an infinite,

impersonal consciousness. In this ocean arise tiny, temporary waves of consciousness which we call individuality.

Thus 'Bernie' is one wave of self-consciousness that constituted itself in Dr Siegel's body. The spirit or entity which calls itself 'George' is another wave which also constituted itself from the same ocean of consciousness within Dr Siegel's brain, when he was meditating. Ordinarily Dr Siegel identifies his self as Bernie. But that, he would maintain, is ignorance, for we are much more than our finite self-consciousness. That is why Shirley MacLaine says that she is both Shirley as well as her higher self.

But if spirits are only limited and temporary waves on the infinite ocean of consciousness, then why have only one finite individuality within your body? Why not meditate and be filled with many such spirits?

People who have more than one individual spirit living in their bodies do at times seem to have more consciousness, in the sense of possessing information and power to make predictions and so on.

Suppose one individual has many individualities coexisting in his body. One minute he says he is Bernie, the next minute he says that he is George. Then he claims to be Shirley, then Capra and now he says he is Ferguson. What would he make of it? Would he think he was mad? In relating to so many spirits, he no longer knows who he really is. But if the spirit is in fact only a momentary wave, then the real madness would be for him to identify himself with one particular finite consciousness or spirit. Individuality is an illusion. In any case he is a completely different individual or wave of consciousness each time he reincarnates. If he is Bernie now, he may have been George last time. So why not be both now?

Spirits as real entities distinct from our minds
This interpretation of a spirit as a 'meditatively released insight from the unconscious' still leaves us with a problem. How can such a spirit survive death and continue to communicate with us?

This is when the same spokespersons begin to offer a different interpretation of what a spirit is. This interpretation is also based on the reflections of Jung.

In 1919, after a very careful study of occult phenomena,

he wrote, 'I see no proof whatever of the existence of real spirits.'[2] Half a century later he had this to say about his earlier statement:

> After collecting psychological experiences from many people and many countries for fifty years, I no longer feel as certain as I did in 1919, when I wrote this sentence. To put it bluntly, I doubt whether an exclusively psychological approach can do justice to the phenomena in question. Not only the findings of parapsychology, but my own theoretical reflections . . . have led me to certain postulates . . . [such as the existence of a] transpsychic reality immediately underlying the psyche.[3]

Towards the end of his book *Love, Medicine and Miracles*, Dr Siegel too begins to suggest that spirits are not mere waves released by our unconscious mind, but independent realities:

> I also told Janet I believed her [late] husband's spirit exists. Again she asked, 'Do you really believe that?' And I said, 'Yes, I do.'
> 'Well,' she said, 'I was sitting in the living room. He was late for dinner, and the town fire alarm went off. I knew it was about him. I jumped up, and his voice came to me and said, "Do not leave the room for one hour." So I sat down and waited. When I got to the scene of the accident, they were just lifting his body out of the car. I thought to myself, "If I had been out here for an hour, I would never have survived." '[4]

Magic, psychic powers and spirit powers

It is also necessary to distinguish the power of spirits from what is considered to be extra-sensory perception (or the 'psychic power' of our own subtle, etheric body), and from the ability of magicians to perform incredible feats.

The power of magic
Many in the New Age do not make any distinction between magic and psychic powers. But traditionally these two powers have been considered distinct.

When a magician makes a coin or a rabbit appear and disappear, or when he knows what card you have chosen without his seeing it, he uses his natural powers of imagination and well-practised tricks such as sleight of hand. His objective is to amuse and entertain his audience. He is like a skilful film director who creates illusions on the screen. An effective magician is one who can puzzle, confuse and frighten his audience without their being able to understand how he did it. He makes them think that he has unique superhuman powers which they do not have. This is all part of his entertainment. Anyone with aptitude and determination can learn the same tricks.

Some New Age commentators think that genuine magicians do not use tricks, but a subtle energy which the Hindus called *prana* and the Chinese called *chi*. This alleged energy, which is supposed to underlie everything in the universe, including ourselves, is also called psychic power.

Psychic powers

The phrase 'psychic power' is sometimes used by people unfamiliar with New Age thought to mean their normal will-power, used in a concentrated and assertive way. That use of the phrase is very different to its common meaning in New Age circles today. The phrase has now come to mean that each of us has 'subtle energies' that lie beyond the energies known to science. These energies give us an 'aura', like the 'halo' painted around saints. This aura is visible only to psychics, who can also interpret it and with its help understand even our illnesses because our aura changes with our moods and other bodily states.

It is believed that a method of photography developed in 1939 by a Russian professor of engineering, Semyon Kirlian, is able to capture visual images of our aura. Called 'Kirlian photography', it was popularised in the West by a best-selling book in 1973 entitled *Psychic Discoveries Behind the Iron Curtain* by Sheila Ostrander and Lynn Schroeder.

Scientists have explained that much before Kirlian, Jiri Lichtenburg had already demonstrated that these photographic effects were electrical, not psychic. In many New Age circles, however, the belief has continued that Kirlian photography offers empirical proof that each of us has a subtle ethereal or psychic body besides our physical body, and that this body is able to separate from our physical body and travel anywhere in the cosmos.

Because this psychic energy is said to be at the root of everything and everyone, it is also called 'God-energy'. It is said that crystals vibrate at the same frequency as this God-energy, and can therefore help us develop abilities to see distant things with our mind's eye (clairvoyance), hear distant conversations or communications from the spirit world (clairaudience), and travel in our astral/spiritual bodies. It is said that once this power has been developed, we can affect matter just by looking at it. For example, we can bend metal spoons, or read other people's minds, because the same prana flows through every thing and every mind.

Some magicians have claimed that their feats are not tricks, but the product of real, though paranormal, powers. That is, they claim that when they are bending a metal spoon or moving a clock off a table merely by looking at it, they are not performing tricks (like replacing straight spoons with bent ones or pulling the clock with invisible threads), but are actually using their 'mental' or 'psychic' power to affect matter. Or, when they are telling you about your past or present, they claim they are not making intelligent guesses, using common-sense methods of 'cold reading', but are actually reading your mind.

These claims have received wide acceptance and enthusiastic support in our day. One reason is that many people have had remarkable and unusual experiences which suggest that the human mind is capable of instantaneously knowing events that take place thousands of miles away without using normal channels of communication such as a telephone. This is called telepathy. Since many people believe in telepathy, it is easy for them to believe that another person can also read their minds and perhaps see their future.

There is another, deeper reason why so many people so easily accept the claims of magicians that they are not ordinary magicians/entertainers, but people with 'psychic' powers. That reason is that many people have been inclined to believe that the material universe is a product of the same consciousness which is within each one of us – that there is no difference between God and our spirits. Therefore it is natural for them to expect to find that our consciousness can affect matter outside our own bodies. They also think that our normal experience of being an individual self, distinct from all other individuals, is an illusion. They want demonstrable proof of their belief. A 'psychic' who can read their minds becomes a proof that all minds are connected or that consciousness is really one.

When a scientist examines a magician, an astrologer or a fortune-teller, and fails in his attempts to see through their tricks, and then endorses their claim that their feats are genuine instances of the power of the human mind over matter, or of the ability of one mind to connect itself to another mind, and to predict the future, what that scientist is doing is not performing a scientific experiment, but seeing in magic or 'cold reading' a confirmation of his own theoretical presupposition that matter is consciousness and that all consciousness is one.

All forms of energy that science knows of can be detected directly and measured. Their existence can be demonstrated outside the imagination of the perceiver. Admittedly no scientist claims that everything that can be known about different types of energy is already known. Nevertheless, to claim that another form of universal energy exists in everything, that it can be obtained from crystals, and that it is subject to such mundane things as laws of photography is a very radical claim. The claim is worth presenting not just on TV shows, it merits a Nobel prize!

Radical claims require radical evidence. It is not enough to base our faith in 'The Force' simply on the testimony of movies such as the *Star Wars* saga, which uses special effects to create an illusion, as do magicians.

Whenever those magicians claiming to be psychics have allowed themselves to be tested by people who know magic (rather than only science), their claims have always been exposed as fraudulent. Dan Korem's book *Powers: Testing the Psychic and Supernatural*[5] provides concrete evidence of this. He explains how so-called 'psychics' use tricks and common sense to move objects or 'read minds', while making us think that they are using 'psychic energy'.

The simple fact is that there is no conclusive evidence that human beings possess mental powers to affect matter or read another mind by directly connecting their own mind to it. Take the claim that a 'psychic' has tuned into the universal energy or collective consciousness that is said to flow through each one of us. One normally goes to a psychic to have a 'reading' because he or she reads your mind, your past and your future with surprising accuracy. The psychic says that this is not intelligent guesswork, but that he or she has psychic powers actually to read your thoughts because their own mind is now directly telepathically connected to your mind. Yet suppose that for some unforeseen reason the psychic has to change the appointment with you, they cannot communicate with you telepathically, but would have to use your telephone number!

In the light of all the research carried out both by believers and by sceptics, we have to conclude that instances of spontaneous 'telepathy' have to have explanations other than a belief in the connectedness of human minds through some subtle energy. Our normal experience of possessing a distinct, private and exclusive individual self-consciousness has not been disproved as an illusion by any research into meditation, yoga or extra-sensory perception. All attempts by the police and intelligence agencies to draw on psychics in solving crime have not yielded any conclusive proof of ESP. The only exceptions to this seem to be instances of spirit-possession, such as the ones to be discussed in the chapter on miracles, and cases of 'spontaneous past life recall', discussed in the chapter on reincarnation. In these experiences one mind does seem to take over or connect itself to another mind.

The main difference between magicians and those claiming to have mental power over matter is ethical. Suppose a TV producer shows us a very convincing programme, using actors, informing us that the entire royal family has been wiped out by an extremist group during a family re-union. We would admire and enjoy the producer's skill at creating an illusion if we knew that we were watching a fictional movie. But if we knew that we were watching a news programme, in which we expect that only truth will be reported, we would be angry at the deception. Those who use tricks but who claim to have special powers fall into the second category, unless they are actually using the powers of another spirit.

The exposés of magicians who pretend to be psychics show that we do not have any experimental basis for the belief that the cosmos is a creation of the consciousness within us. They also serve as a salutary warning that while we all see data through our preconceived notions of what is true, we must also be objective enough to allow the data to change or modify our theories and philosophical assumptions.

Spirit power

We do not have any evidence that our own soul or psyche is connected with other minds or physical objects. But our mind is obviously connected with our own bodies. The non-physical core of our being – our spirit – is able to influence our brain and our body. Is it possible for another spirit to use our brain and affect our body?

The New Testament records many instances of spirits possessing and empowering individuals. The following is especially instructive:

> They went across the lake to the region of the Gerasenes. When Jesus got out of the boat, a man with an unclean spirit came from the tombs to meet him. This man lived in the tombs, and no-one could bind him any more, not even with a chain. For he had often been chained hand and foot, but he tore the chains apart and broke the irons on his feet. No-one was strong enough to subdue him. Night and day among the tombs and in the hills he would cry out and cut himself with stones.
>
> When he saw Jesus from a distance, he ran and fell on his knees in front of him. He shouted at the top of his voice, 'What do you want with me, Jesus, Son of the Most High God? Swear to God that you won't torture me!' For Jesus had said to him, 'Come out of this man, you unclean spirit!'
>
> Then Jesus asked him, 'What is your name?'
>
> 'My name is Legion,' he replied, 'for we are many.' And he begged Jesus again and again not to send them out of the area.
>
> A large herd of pigs was feeding on the nearby hillside. The demons begged Jesus, 'Send us among the pigs; allow us to go into them.' He gave them permission, and the evil spirits came out and went into the pigs. The herd, about two thousand in number, rushed down the steep bank into the lake and were drowned.
>
> Those tending the pigs ran off and reported this in the town and countryside, and the people went out to see

what had happened. When they came to Jesus, they saw the man who had been possessed by the legion of demons, sitting there, dressed and in his right mind; and they were afraid. Those who had seen it told the people what had happened to the demon-possessed man – and told about the pigs as well. Then the people began to plead with Jesus to leave their region. (Mark 5:1–17)

Two significant things need to be noted concerning this account. The first is that the spirits had given superhuman physical powers to the man they had possessed; the second is that people had two verifiable proofs that spirits had come out of him: his restored sanity and the dead bodies of the pigs in the lake.

In another incident, which we will consider later in this chapter, St Paul cast out an alien spirit from a slave-girl at Ephesus. The spirit had given the girl powers of divination. When the spirit was gone, these powers also disappeared, and her owners, who had had a roaring trade in fortune-telling until then, were mad at Paul.

Such instances, in which people exhibit unusual physical and predictive powers, also occur today. These powers are often accompanied by undesirable or bizarre physical, emotional and social handicaps or behaviour. The powers seem to disappear when the spirits causing the trouble are exorcised. That is why scholars such as Dr A. P. Stone (referred to in the previous chapter), believe that when an astrologer makes an accurate prediction, despite using astronomically unscientific data, it can only be explained in terms of the astrologer's mind being used by another spirit.

In *Truth and Social Reform* (London: Hodder & Stoughton, 1989) I've narrated my own experiences of dealing with spirit-possession, and in the chapter on reincarnation, I will refer to the research done on the subject by Dr Ian Stevenson. Here it is sufficient to state that while I see no conclusive evidence of 'psychic power', I do believe in supernatural power given to us sometimes by God and at other times by finite spirits.

We can now turn to the main concern of this chapter, to see the gains and the losses in the new spiritism. I will attempt to present the case both from the point of view of believers in the New Age and from the point of view of Christian believers.

The loss in Christianity

Over the last few centuries Western culture had managed to suppress the supernatural, not because of its adherence to secularism but, ironically, primarily because of its allegiance to Christianity – itself a supernatural faith. So-called 'Christian' campaigns of witch-hunting were indeed barbaric, and their effect was to drive witches, mediums and other practitioners of the occult underground.

The exorcism of spirits from the Western world-view seems to have been an outworking of Christianity in that culture. From the New Age point of view, this meant that for the first time in history a great and unfortunate divorce took place. Medicine was separated from magic, mathematics from numerology, astronomy from astrology, chemistry from alchemy, religion from ritual, and the divine from the demonic. Secular humanism also denied and opposed the supernatural, and although its roots go back to the Enlightenment, it held sway in a country like America for only a relatively brief period. It had barely succeeded in winning the intellectual high ground from Christianity when its main weapon – rationalism – was weighed in the balance and found wanting. The decline of Christianity and disillusionment with Enlightenment principles – at least in terms of their influence on the Western mind – seem to have set the stage for a remarriage of these disciplines.

For the sake of convenience, let us examine the loss and then the profit of spiritism under the three categories of the quest for knowledge, for relationships and for power, first under Christianity and then in the New Age.

Knowledge: Loss of sorcery and magic

One major effect of Christianity in the West was the loss of traditional respect for sorcery and magic.

In a given situation, medicine and a magic crystal may work equally well. The witch doctor may believe that the medicine and the stone cause the healing in the same sense of the word 'cause': that is, through their inherent qualities. He might teach that his mysterious stone should be worshipped during the full moon, because its spirit vibrates at the same frequency as the moon goddess. Do we have a right to assume that there should be a more rational explanation for the power of the stone than that? Why? How can you assume that the physical universe is always rational, especially if it is either a product of blind (irrational) chance or a dream of the divine spirit? Do dreams follow rational logic? What if the whole universe, including the stone and our bodies, consists of psychic vibrations of a spirit?

Most traditional cultures have never been able to distinguish medicine from magic; they always merged into each other. Western culture separated them because of the biblical insistence that the creator and his creation, spirit and matter, were fundamentally distinct, even though when God breathed into Adam, physical matter and spirit were fused in a unique way, to make man.

This meant that matter was determined by physical laws, therefore its behaviour could be predicted and controlled. Human beings, on the other hand, did have a degree of personal freedom. Their mental acts could not be fully predicted or controlled. This is not because human freedom equals randomness in a sub-atomic sense, but because the non-physical dimension of human beings is ruled by personal/moral laws. If there were no such personal/moral laws, and matter and human beings were qualitatively the same, then matter could also behave in a free, unpredictable and magical way.

The Bible also taught that God continues to care for his creation. He sustains it and at times acts in it. However, those acts are not normal, but are special or miraculous events. The cosmos usually runs according to rational laws which are the words of God.

This meant that what was not normal and rational was either a misunderstanding, a fraud, or a demonic or divine action. An implication of this view of reality was that while human beings could perform magic tricks, they could not make matter behave contrary to rational laws by some 'psychic' power. Miracles, on the other hand, were possible. They were to be welcomed when done by God, and shunned when done through a sorcerer's contact with the demonic powers.

Scientists of the Christian era therefore assumed that a stone could not heal because it has neither therapeutic ingredients nor psychic/spiritual vibrations. If it does heal, then there has to be another rational explanation. It is the patient's faith which starts chemical reactions in his brain, thus producing healing substances. For the New Age, the important thing to note is that the Western mind, shaped by the Christian world-view, rejected faith in magic stones before it was known how the stone heals. It was assumed that physical matter must work according to chemical laws. If healing was taking place without any reference to those laws, then there had to be a non-physical (human, demonic or divine) explanation for it. If the explanation was neither human nor divine, then it must be shunned.

This attitude deprived the West of faith in sorcerers' magic.

Loss of subjective revelation

According to the New Age world-view, by exorcising spirits Christianity inflicted another loss upon Western man. It denied him private, subjective and unverifiable revelations. Not that Christianity rejected the reality of communications from the spirit world – it affirmed the reality of the supernatural, but rejected the necessity or the validity of private revelations. It made them unnecessary by offering a historically objective yet supernatural revelation of God in the Bible. And it questioned their validity on the grounds that a spirit is not omniscient, unlike God. Why enquire from the dead, when the living God himself speaks? God says through the prophet Isaiah, 'When men tell you to consult mediums and spiritists, who whisper and mutter, should not a people enquire of their God? Why consult the dead on behalf of the living?' (Isa. 8:19).

For the New Ager the biblical revelation suppressed Western spiritism by offering objective criteria to distinguish God's Holy Spirit from demonic spirits, and warning of the possibility that Satan himself may appear as an angel of light. That made it possible for Christians to discern God's Spirit and to identify and condemn what was fraudulent and/or demonic.

Biblical faith also created a philosophical problem for spiritism. By presupposing a holy, infinite and personal God as the ultimate reality, Christianity postulated a large enough universal which made sense of everything real and imaginary, mechanical and mysterious, natural and supernatural.

Happily for the believer in the New Age, the demise of that biblical absolute now makes it difficult for secular intellectuals to determine whether the Exorcist II is healing a mental disease or casting out a demon, whether 'Robocop' is a man or a machine, or whether Arnold Schwarzenegger's trip to Mars, or any other holiday that he could have chosen, was real or only a 'total recall'.

Loss of relationship to the spirit world
In the Christian era the average Westerner missed the richness and diversity of relating with spirits from many ages, cultures and planets, because Christianity presented a personal God who was seeking to reconcile a rebellious mankind to himself at the great personal cost of his Son's self-sacrifice.

God is love, but he also demands exclusive allegiance. Therefore the biblical God was jealous when his children sought other gods and goddesses. He equated idolatory, including devotion to other spirits, real or imaginery, with adultery (Jer. 3:6–25). His worshippers also found that he was sufficient for them. Therefore they did not need to hop from one channel to another, and from one spirit to the next.

He proved sufficient not because he was an abstract 'infinite reference point', but because he gave them his Spirit to make them the sons and daughters of the Almighty. For that reason they did not need other spirits. St Paul said:

> You did not receive a spirit that makes you a slave again to fear, but you received the Spirit of sonship. And by him we cry, 'Abba, Father.' The Spirit himself testifies with our spirit that we are God's children ... I am convinced that neither death nor life, neither angels nor demons, neither the present nor the future, nor any powers ... will be able to separate us from the love of God that is in Christ Jesus our Lord. (Rom. 8:15–16, 38–9)

Because the Bible offered reconciliation with the creator himself, it banned relationships with other spirits in the strongest possible terms. God commanded:

> Let no-one be found among you who sacrifices his son or daughter in the fire, who practises divination or sorcery,

interprets omens, engages in witchcraft, or casts spells, or who is a medium or spiritist or who consults the dead. Anyone who does these things is detestable to the Lord . . . (Deut. 18:10–12)

Again, God is grieved when his children turn to spirits instead of turning to him:

> They made him [God] jealous with their foreign
>   gods
> and angered him with their detestable idols.
> They sacrificed to demons, which are not God –
>   gods they had not known,
>   gods that recently appeared,
>   gods your fathers did not fear.
> You deserted the Rock, who fathered you;
>   you forgot the God who gave you birth.
> The Lord saw this and rejected them . . . (Deut.
> 32:16–19)

Loss of power

For the New Ager, Christianity also deprived the West of the power of spirits. It never denied the power of magicians, sorcerers and witches, it just made it unnecessary by demonstrating a greater power and banned it on ethical grounds. The Bible's contention was that spiritual power is to be used for God's glory alone. Therefore manipulation of spiritual powers for oneself is wrong.

For the committed New Ager, the worst aspect of the Christian tactic in the New Testament was that it rejected the monopoly of the priesthood over God's power. Jesus was a carpenter, not a priest, but he displayed awesome power. He picked up ordinary people, such as fishermen, and endowed them with extraordinary spiritual powers. Christ's apostles taught that every believer was called to be a priest. God, as Father, wants to bless each of his children with the Holy Spirit and his supernatural gifts. Since everyone, priest as well as housewife, can have God's power by prayer and faith, no one needs to contact mediums and sorcerers. This teaching and the reality of its experience naturally undermined the harnessing of the power of spirits.

For example, the book of Acts says that in the city of Ephesus

> God did extraordinary miracles through Paul, so that even handkerchiefs and aprons that had touched him were taken to the sick, and their illnesses were cured and the evil spirits left them.
>
> Some Jews who went around driving out evil spirits tried to invoke the name of the Lord Jesus over those who were demon-possessed. They would say, 'In the name of Jesus, whom Paul preaches, I command you to come out.' Seven sons of Sceva, a Jewish chief priest, were doing this. One day the evil spirit answered them, 'Jesus I know, and I know about Paul, but who are you?' Then the man who had the evil spirit jumped on them and overpowered them all. He gave them such a beating that they ran out of the house naked and bleeding.
>
> When this became known to the Jews and Greeks living in Ephesus, they were all seized with fear, and the name of the Lord Jesus was held in high honour. Many of those who believed now came and openly confessed their evil deeds. A number who had practised sorcery brought their scrolls together and burned them publicly. When they calculated the value of the scrolls, the total came to fifty thousand drachmas [a drachma was roughly a day's wage]. (Acts 19:11–19)

Having briefly seen what the West lost when Christianity exorcised spirits, we should now look at what it stands to gain in the New Age.

The gain in spiritism

Let us now assume that the claim by mediums that their minds and bodies are being used by spirits to channel their messages is at least sometimes true. In this section we will look at the advantages of spiritism over against the experience of the supernatural in biblical Christianity.

The Bible does not contain some of the specific 'truths' which spirits teach today such as karma and reincarnation, nature intelligences (*devas*) and vegetarianism, Brahma and maya, astrology and the power of sex. Because some of these are discussed in detail in other chapters, here we will focus only on more general and basic gains.

Subjective knowledge: Freedom from reason

For the New Ager, the biggest advantage of spiritism is that revelation from spirits finally frees the West from the restricting influence of logical reason. Not many people today realise that modern Western confidence in human reason began with the acceptance of the Bible as God's revelation. The Bible taught that the cosmos, including human beings, were made by the *Logos* – God's Word, Wisdom or Reason (John 1:1). God's own revelation thus provided a strong foundation for assuming that human reason could discover scientific truth. Even before the Enlightenment Western intellectuals insisted on the necessity of human reason in the search for true knowledge. This confidence in reason was not destructive so long as it was still under the superior authority of God's revelation.

St Thomas Aquinas (1225–74), one of the greatest Roman Catholic theologians of all time, thought that when Adam and Eve fell into sin, the human will had fallen but not the human intellect. Therefore our intellect was capable of discovering truth on its own, and a 'natural theology' was possible (i.e., a theology which was a product of human reasoning without revelation). Aquinas never denied the truth of God's revelation; he just opened the way to a significant change in the Western attitude to reason.

Later, after Descartes, the biblical concept of the 'necessity of reason' was changed into a fully fledged belief in the 'sufficiency of human reason'. That belief was not all that harmful when only a few intellectuals adhered to it in the isolation of their ivory towers. But gradually it filtered down.

The limitations and undesirable historical consequences of that superstitious clinging to reason had been carefully examined and rejected before the New Age began. In fact, Western disillusionment with faith in reason is the matrix of the birth of the New, non-rational Age. Faith in reason is superstitious because finite reason can neither explain nor justify itself. Earlier God's revelation had explained reason, and our experience with science had begun to give justification for it. But as revelation was denied, reason's justification disappeared. Now, therefore, it appears more rational to believe in the irrational.

The New Age spirits have resolved to banish reason. The biblical world-view, on the other hand, is rational. The biblical God said to those who did not believe in him, 'Come now, let us reason together . . . ' (Isa. 1:18), and Jesus invited his critics and sceptics to weigh the evidence and see if he was indeed the Messiah – the Son of the living God (John 5:31–47).

The biblical writers often claimed that their revelation was based not on some private, esoteric experience, but on observable historical events. St John, for example, writes:

> That which was from the beginning, which we have heard, which we have seen with our eyes, which we have looked at and our hands have touched – this we proclaim concerning the Word [Logos] of life. The life appeared; . . . and we proclaim to you the eternal life . . . We proclaim . . . what we have seen and heard. (1 John 1:1–3)

John, whose contribution to the writing of the New Testament was second only to that of Paul, was talking about what he had seen and heard with his physical eyes and ears; that which could be touched, examined and witnessed to by others independently. Such a revelation is rational.

In contrast, when Shirley MacLaine sees her higher self and talks to it, it is all in her mind. When she sees her higher self (H.S.) stop the swaying branches with its outstretched arms, others are not able to see anything:

> I heard the words inside my mind. The visualization I was seeing was above me . . . I opened my eyes and looked up at the tape recorder, realizing that it was impossible to record all of the two-way conversation. What was happening . . . [was] ethereal conversation.
>
> 'Chris?' I said, 'are you hearing any of this?' I asked.
>
> 'Not in detail,' she said. 'I just feel an intense communication with your higher self . . . '
>
> I looked up at H.S. in my mind . . . [6]

Let us compare this with the revelation St Paul had of Christ, when he was converted from being an enemy of the Christian faith to its most outstanding advocate. Luke, a physician and a close friend of Paul, gives us this report of Paul's (who was then called Saul) first spiritual experience:

> Meanwhile, Saul was still breathing out murderous threats against the Lord's disciples. He went to the high priest and asked him for letters to the synagogues in Damascus, so that if he found any there who belonged to the Way, whether men or women, he might take them as prisoners to Jerusalem. As he neared Damascus on his journey, suddenly a light from heaven flashed around him. He fell to the ground and heard a voice say to him, 'Saul, Saul, why do you persecute me?'
> 'Who are you, Lord?' Saul asked.
> 'I am Jesus, whom you are persecuting,' he replied. 'Now get up and go into the city, and you will be told what you must do.'
> The men travelling with Saul stood there speechless: they heard the sound but did not see anyone. Saul got up from the ground, but when he opened his eyes he could see nothing. So they led him by the hand into Damascus. For three days he was blind, and did not eat or drink anything. (Acts 9:1–9)

Years later, when Paul was explaining to King Agrippa his experience and the reasons for his conversion, the governor Festus interrupted him:

> 'You are out of your mind, Paul!' he shouted. 'Your great learning is driving you insane.'
> 'I am not insane, most excellent Festus,' Paul replied. 'What I am saying is true and reasonable. The king is familiar with these things, and I can speak freely to him. I am convinced that none of this has escaped his notice, because it was not done in a corner.' (Acts 26:24–6)

The argument of Luke and Paul in the above passages is that Christian revelation is open to rational investigation because, even though it has a strong subjective side to it, it is objective and public. Paul's vision was not in his mind. Nor was it a product of meditation and visualisation.

When other disciples saw the resurrected Jesus, they were not visualising. Thomas, one of the twelve disciples, was not present when the others first saw the risen Lord. When they told him, 'We have seen the Lord!' he dismissed it as incredible. 'Unless I see the nail marks in his hands and put my finger where the nails were, and put my hand into his side, I will not believe it' (John 20:25). Although the Lord Jesus reprimanded Thomas for his doubt, he honoured his insistence on the need for empirical verification of a claim of such gigantic proportions, that death had finally been defeated in human history. Therefore Jesus appeared again to his disciples when Thomas was also present. And he publicly invited Thomas to verify the claim: 'Put your finger here; see my hands. Reach out your hand and put it into my side. Stop doubting and believe' (John 20:27).

The subjective, non-rational visualisations of the New Agers have to be accepted as true once we concede that our intellect and senses keep us in bondage to a dream world of maya. Saint Kabir, the fifteenth-century mystic poet of India, has exerted much influence on the New Age, through the guru-movement of the 1960s and 70s. He believed and taught that the subjective visions of the soul were visions of reality. But Kabir himself told an instructive anecdote:

A 'holy man' (sadhu) sincerely believed that whenever he closed his eyes and meditated, Lord Krishna appeared to him, dancing with the gopies – milk-maids – of Vrindavan. Kabir asked the holy man to sit in front of him and visualize. When the holy man began to enjoy the dance, Kabir said, 'When Krishna happens to come near you during the dance, catch hold of his hand and don't let it go.'

At the first opportunity the holy man caught hold of the hand of his Lord, who tried to release himself from his devotee's grip to be able to grasp the gopies. In the struggle the holy man's eyes opened and he was amazed to see that he had firmly grasped his own hand. Bewildered and upset, the man looked at Kabir inquiringly.

Kabir said, 'My good friend, do not be upset. What you have been looking at is nothing but a projection of your own mind. It is good that the illusion is broken.' The holy man wanted to understand more. So Kabir explained, 'Mind is a powerful entity. Within moments it can cover distances far and wide. It can project the picture of whatever object or person one thinks of. More than the waves in the ocean are the waves of the mind.'[7]

What is real – that which is visualised in a state of pure

consciousness, free from the limitations of the senses and
the intellect, or that which is verifiable by these human
means?

For the New Ager, spirits are setting Westerners free
from the ordinary reality of everyday experience to which
Christianity had tied them down. To sum up, the first advantage of receiving knowledge from the spirits is that it
is completely separated from our finite reason. You are
assured that if your intellect tells you that this book in
your hands is real, then you must not believe it. For reality
is mental not physical. By contrast, Francis Schaeffer, one
of the foremost Christian thinkers of this century, said:

> I live in a thought world which is filled with creativ-
> ity; inside my head there is creative imagination. Why?
> Because God who is the Creator has made me in his
> image, I can go out in imagination beyond the stars. This
> is true not only for the Christian, but for every person.
> Every person is made in the image of God; therefore, no
> person in his or her imagination is confined to his or her
> own body. Going out in our imagination, we can change
> something of the form of the universe as a result of our
> thought world – in our painting, in our poetry, or as
> an engineer, or as a gardener. Is that not wonderful?
> I am there, and I am able to impose the results of my
> imagination on the external world.
>
> But notice this: Being a Christian and knowing God
> has made the external world, I know that there is an
> objective external reality and that there is that which is
> imaginary. I am not uncertain that there is an external
> reality which is distinct from my imagination. The Chris-
> tian is free; free to fly, because he had a base upon which
> he need not be confused between his fantasy and the
> reality which God has made . . . As a Christian I have the
> epistemology that enables me not to get confused between
> what I think and what is objectively real. The modern
> generation does not have this, and this is the reason why
> some young people are torn up in these areas.[8]

Knowledge without accountability
A second and related advantage for the New Ager of receiving knowledge from the spirits is that we do not have to

take the trouble to hold channels and their spirit guides accountable.

By contrast, St Paul said that when some Christians claim that they have the gift of prophecy or a special prophetic message from God, then in a given meeting 'Two or three prophets should speak, and the others should weigh carefully what is said' (1 Cor. 14:29).

The Bible says that prophecy can and must be tested because of the abundance of false prophets. One obvious test is to examine whether its predictive aspects come true (Deut. 18:21–2). Another test is to see whether the content of a prophet's teaching, both in the area of morals (what is good?) and metaphysics (what is true?) conforms to God's objective revelation in Scripture and nature (Deut. 13:1–4; 1 John 4:1–3).

The New Age spirits emphasise that the above teaching of the Bible is wrong. It is another Christian attempt to isolate fake from genuine and divine from demonic, when in fact such distinctions do not exist: because God is spirit, therefore every spirit is God. Spirit is consciousness, therefore all imagination or visualisation is spiritual and divine truth. In any case they believe that the finite human mind has no reliable means of receiving information, leave alone examining it. For example, David Icke says that we cannot test messages from spirits because

> Communication between other planes and dimensions and ourselves is not like picking up the telephone. The thought forms have to be processed by the physical brain, and in so doing some of the sharpness of the message can be lost – not the general meaning, but the fine detail can get distorted ... It should be remembered what I have said earlier about the difficulties the other [spirit] realms have sometimes in judging our time, and the timescales are often changing anyway ... [9]

Icke is saying that precisely those aspects of spirit messages which can be tested empirically, such as the dates of various events they predict, should not be taken seriously. A typical statement is 'A message from Attaro in October 1990 predicted serious economic difficulties [in England] even before this book is published, although, I repeat, we should be careful about precise timings.'[10]

This caution against testable predictions and communications has become a standard feature of the New Age after 'Harmonic Convergence' failed to take place in August 1987. That event was highly publicised in books such as *The Mayan Factor: The Path Beyond Technology*, by an art historian, Jose Arguelles. Thousands of people had gathered before dawn at the earth's various 'psychic points' such as the Niagara Falls, to see the UFOs that were supposed to swarm through the skies and to experience the predicted surge in psychic phenomena such as telepathy. But unfortunately nothing happened.

Another illustration of this subtle change from rationally verifiable to completely unverifiable knowledge, is in the kind of spirit-channelling that intelligent spokespersons such as Marilyn Ferguson endorse. She is not excited about Tom McPherson, the spirit from Elizabethan England channelled by one of Ms MacLaine's channels, Kevin Ryerson, because a historian could easily check the authenticity of the information the spirit gives. Nor is Ferguson excited about the 35,000 year old spirit Ramtha channelled by Ms MacLaine's neighbour J. Z. Knight, lest scientists question Ramtha about the physical set-up of the earth in that Atlantian age, or its fauna and flora. Ferguson prefers Lazaris. Jack Pursel has exclusive rights to channel it. Lazaris is safe because it has never been incarnated on earth, so you cannot ask it questions that can be checked against history and science.

This stance stands in sharp contrast to the supernatural knowledge given in the Bible. The Bible is above all else a book of history, and it makes innumerable scientific pronouncements. Thus it opens itself to rational scrutiny. Jesus himself says that he should be believed not because he is in touch with superior intelligences, but because he is true.

A noteworthy feature of the New Age rejection of reason is its consistency: the knowledge given by spirits must be believed because it is not open to rational verification. This view is best expressed by a Sunday school student. His teacher had asked, 'What is faith?' The student replied, 'Faith is believing something you know ain't true.'

David, Shirley MacLaine's spiritual guide in *Out on a Limb*, put the Sunday school student's view slightly differently. MacLaine asked:

'You mean you believe [reincarnation] is that firmly established as a fact?'

[David] shrugged his shoulders and said, 'Why, yeah, I do. It's the only thing that makes sense. If we don't each have a soul – then why are we alive? Who knows if it's true? It's true if you believe it and that goes for anything, right?'[11]

Later, in another context, David says: 'Well, there's no question about it to me. I believe it. I know it. That is all. Of course there's no proof. So what?'[12]

Relationships at the expense of self

For the New Ager the experience of the supernatural has a third advantage over the Christian experience of the fullness of the Holy Spirit: it enables you to relate to higher spirits by completely losing your very notion of being a finite self, a specific individual. Instead of finding meaning for yourself, through a relationship with a higher universal, you can get rid of the problem of meaning by getting rid of your notion of self. If your unconscious mind can produce many different individualities within your mind, each existing in its own right, then you do not really exist as a specific individual.

Thus, from a New Age perspective, the disadvantage of Christian teaching on the fullness of God's Spirit is that it shackles us to our finite individuality. St John remained John when he was filled with the Holy Spirit and received and imparted to others 'the revelation of Jesus Christ' (Rev. 1:1).

The advantage of spiritism is that when Shirley MacLaine goes to her channeller, Kevin, and he goes into a trance, three and a half minutes later it is no longer Kevin but another spirit 'John' who is talking to her. 'In a raspy whisper,' writes Ms MacLaine, 'which didn't sound in Kevin's vocal range, I heard, "Hail. I'm John. Greetings. Please identify yourself and state purpose of gathering." '

After Ms MacLaine's conversation with John (speaking through Kevin) had gone on for some time, she reports:

Kevin shifted his position in the chair. His arms rearranged themselves. His head swiveled to the other side ... I got up on my knees trying to understand what was going on.

'Tip o' the hat to ya' said a completely new voice. 'McPherson here. Tom McPherson. How are you doing out there?'[13]

If many different entities use and control 'my' body, then what is 'I', 'me' or 'mine'? Thus an advantage of spiritism is that it can solve the problem of finding meaning for ourselves without having to find an infinite reference point or a universal which makes sense of what an individual person is. It simply gets rid of our finite individuality – I am no longer Kevin, but also John as well as Tom McPherson. All these spirits or individualities are merely passing waves in the ocean of consciousness, or rather unconsciousness.

If you do not wish to go as far as annihilating your self-consciousness, then spiritism at least allows you to hand over your control over yourself to other spiritual entities.

Dr Bernie Siegel first met his spirit guide, George, in his mind, during a meditation session. Dr Siegel says that George is his most invaluable companion in his practice of 'self-healing', doing all the hard work.

If George is a real spiritual entity that existed before Dr Siegel's psyche was formed, and if it entered Dr Siegel's brain during meditation and has lived there ever since, then spirit-possession is the most appropriate phrase to describe his experience.

In the chapter on miracles we will note the testimony of psychic healers such as Matthew Manning and of psychic surgeons such as Alex Orbito that they have become mere conduits for another spirit to work through them. One cannot criticise the good that these men may do to others. But mediums who genuinely channel other spirits also hand over their work, and the control of their minds and bodies, to another being. Their own personality is overshadowed. Is it safe or desirable for another being to take control of my self? Should another personality take over my vocation, house or family just because I am inadequate?

Mediums have no control even if a spirit is lying through them or doing destructive and immoral things. In India rarely a month goes by without the newspapers reporting human sacrifices that have been demanded by spirits. This month one report said that a man had cut off his tongue and offered it to the goddess. The amazing aspect of the report was that he sat in her temple for more than an hour, bleeding profusely. It seems that a superhuman power had indeed demanded that sacrifice and was in control of his mind and body. Another newspaper report said that a mob put a 'holy man' (*sadhu*) to death because he was found carrying a five year old girl on his back. During the previous weeks several children had disappeared in that region, and the mob suspected that he had been behind the kidnapping and sacrificing of children to the goddess.

The real point is not just that some spirits make some people sacrifice others' lives. My point is that all spirits make us sacrifice either our notion of self, or at least our control over ourselves.

If there are any spirits that don't do this, they still leave us with a fundamental difficulty: our dependence on other spirits implies that far from evolving towards divinity, our own spirits are finite and ignorant. If you were God, would you need other spirits to tell you so? Or would you then channel other finite spirits?

Power without moral restraints
A fourth advantage of spirits is that unlike Christianity they give us power without moral restraints.

A problem with the Christian experience of the supernatural is that the power of the Holy Spirit is available only to do God's will. The New Age spirits have no such hang-up because they set people free from moral restraints.

For example, the higher self not only gives Shirley MacLaine power to still the swaying branches of a tree, it also emphasises that we must be delivered from our notion of good and evil: 'Until mankind realizes there is, in truth, no good and there is, in truth, no evil – there will be no peace. There is only Karmic experience with which to eventually realize that you are each total love.'[14]

Another spirit popularised by Ms MacLaine is Ramtha. A questioner asked it: 'So you're saying that even murder is not wrong or evil?' Ramtha replied, 'That is correct . . . The slain will come back again and again. For life is perpetual; it is continuous . . . I do not abhor the act. I have reasoned it. I have understood it. I am beyond it.'[15]

In her own case, the karmic experiences of previous incarnations lead Ms MacLaine to the beds of many married men, with no notion that adultery is morally evil. Spirits and their channels confirm to her that in these love affairs she is working out the karma of her previous lives.

Chris, who put Ms MacLaine in touch with her higher self, instructs her that every soul chooses the incarnation it gets. If a child is abused, he 'Has to take the responsibility for his fate ... his soul intuitively knows that he can't legitimately blame the parent for his situation, whatever it might be. A damaged child chose to experience that.'[16]

An implication of this is that human beings are God, not creatures bound by moral obligations. Therefore they should neither be held morally accountable, nor punished for what they do. Therefore, the higher self, says, 'Put spiritual understanding in the prisons, not punishment.'[17]

'Spiritual understanding' here does not mean that certain things are morally right and others wrong, and that we are accountable before a Holy God. It is to know that God does not judge us, because each soul is already perfect and full of love. Souls judge themselves: Jews did under Hitler and peasants did under Stalin. According to the law of karma:

> You reap what you sow. It is a manifestation of the cosmic law of cause and effect which is administered by the souls themselves, not by the authority of the penal code or a government or even by God. The God energy is no judge of persons. In fact, there is no judgement involved with life. There is only experience from incarnation to incarnation until the soul realizes its perfection and that it is total love ... [18]

For the New Ager, the disadvantage of a Christian's experience with the Holy Spirit is obvious. He is too holy. Jesus says that when the Holy Spirit comes he will judge and convict the world of its sin (John 16:8–11). That is why when there is a revival of genuine Christianity people repent of their sins, they cry, seeking forgiveness from God and each other.

The Bible says that the power of the Holy Spirit is given primarily to make people holy and to empower them to make their world holy. What changes does the Holy Spirit effect in us individually? St Paul says:

> Live by the [Holy] Spirit, and you will not gratify the

desires of the sinful nature. For the sinful nature desires what is contrary to the Spirit, and the Spirit what is contrary to the sinful nature . . .

The acts of the sinful nature are obvious: sexual immorality, impurity and debauchery; idolatry and witchcraft; hatred, discord, jealousy, fits of rage, selfish ambition, dissensions, factions and envy; drunkenness, orgies, and the like . . .

But the fruit of the Spirit is love, joy, peace, patience, kindness, goodness, faithfulness, gentleness and self-control . . . Those who belong to Christ Jesus have crucified the sinful nature with its passions and desires. (Gal. 5:16–17, 19–24)

And what does the Holy Spirit do in the social arena? The Lord Jesus said:

'The Spirit of the Lord is on me,
    because he has anointed me
    to preach good news to the poor.
He has sent me to proclaim freedom for the prisoners
    and recovery of sight for the blind,
to release the oppressed,
    to proclaim the year of the Lord's favour.'
(Luke 4:18–19)

Jesus promised the power of the Holy Spirit to his disciples, not for their power or glory, but to make them instruments of God's righteous power, soldiers for God's kingdom; to judge their societies by God's yardstick of holiness, to resist evil and proclaim justice and rest. The Bible says that even the power to perform miracles is given to build up the community of saints whose head is not a guru, but God himself. Once in his life Moses tried to use his God-given power for his own glory – by creating an impression that he (rather than God) could get water out of a solid rock. This abuse or manipulation of power cost him dearly. He was not allowed to enter God's promised land of freedom and rest (Num. 20:1–12).

The biblical perspective is that the responsibility and moral accountability of an individual increases in proportion to the power he or she is given. The New Age sets us free from such limitations. Because spiritism sets people free from moral restraints, those who believe the teachings of these spirits do not get entangled with conventional notions of good or bad. They pursue power for its own sake.

The history of spiritism is literally littered with groups and individuals who have drifted into ever-deepening rituals of sexual perversion, animal and human sacrifice, and the bringing down of curses upon their neighbours. That is why mediums and witches were so often feared, banned and persecuted.

Christians must admit that the ecclesiastical power of the church has also been abused often enough, even though Christianity makes an absolute distinction between good and bad. But one advantage of having moral absolutes is that when moral norms are broken, evils can be challenged and reforms sought. When moral distinctions do not even exist, no one can even demand that what is good and right should be pursued.

So while the Christian church has been (and should) be held guilty by its own standards, the same cannot be said about the power of the Holy Spirit. Whenever a community has acknowledged the lordship of the Holy Spirit, it has always resulted in a renewal of holiness in individual and social living.

4

UFOs
– A RELIGIOUS EXPERIENCE?

The knowledge that there are billions of beings in our galaxy, and in other galaxies, infinitely more enlightened than our poor, sick selves, may lead to that humility and self-transcendence which is the source of all religious experience.

Arthur Koestler[1]

Today many people prefer to turn to extra-terrestrials for help rather than to spirits. This is partly because of the negative social and moral baggage that spiritism has brought with it historically. Extra-terrestrials have several advantages over spirits. First, they do not bring with them fraud, deception, destruction of lives and other moral problems. Where there are cases of fraud or self-deception they are comparatively mild in terms of their effect.

Also, while spiritism can support a belief in the continuation of our soul beyond death, it does not prove that souls are eternal, except through the thoughts that spirits allegedly implant in the minds of mediums. That proof is too subjective – inside a medium's head – for Western man, who has grown up believing that a 'proof', by definition, is objective, open to sensory verification and/or rational discussion.

By contrast, 'flying saucers', or unidentified flying objects (UFOs), have been the subject of official scientific studies, because it is claimed that over 200,000 sightings have been reported by air-force pilots and other 'normal' people, including dignitaries such as ex-president Jimmy Carter.

UFOs have been tracked on radar and photographed. If they objectively exist and their origin is indeed non-human, then they prove the existence of a life superior to our own, and a possible source of objective information (revelation) and power. It will be easier to see the religious nature of contemporary UFOlogy if we glance at its history.

Historical waves of UFO sightings

Interest in UFOs started as a popular phenomenon in the 1940s and became an exciting live scientific possibility. Gradually, as extra-terrestrials failed to satisfy the curiosity of our scientists (who must prove rather than believe), UFOs started to appear mainly to New Age groups, for many of whom 'religion' means to believe what cannot be proved.

Richard Hall is an expert in UFOlogy and a committed believer in UFOs. In his well-documented study of UFOs, *Uninvited Guests*, he claims that the Air Technical Intelligence Center of the US Air Force had reached the conclusion in 1948 that the UFOs were spacecraft carrying alien intelligent beings. But that report was rejected by the then Air Force Commander, General Hoyt S. Vandenberg, on the ground that it lacked 'proof'.

The phrase 'UFOlogy' was coined by Air-Marshal Sir Victor Goddard in 1946. He represented the Royal Air Force on the combined Chiefs of Staff advisory committee in Washington, and he initially considered that UFOs were a hoax. Arthur Koestler, who hoped that UFOs would provide a solid scientific basis for our quest for meaning and religious experience, claims that it was Goddard who persuaded President Truman to call off the search for UFOs by the US Air Force. The search had been inaugurated by the President to investigate the rumours of intruders in American air space.

Later Goddard changed his mind, and in his 1975 book *Flight Towards Reality* he wrote:

> In nearly thirty years there must have been two hundred thousand claims of UFO sightings recorded in one hundred countries at the least. That is the kind of basis

of UFO statistics now available in North and South America. Reports upon ten thousand thorough-going checks have furnished evidence which leads to two conclusions: The first is that only six percent of so-called UFO sightings remain unsolved and unexplained; the second is that, of the unsolved residue – twelve thousand unidentified by now – some surely were quite rightly held to be what they were claimed to be – objects of reality but unknown in origin and technicality . . . So, they were UFOs – nothing else.[2]

Those rumours of the late 1940s and early 50s, and the investigation and its termination mark the first important wave in the modern history of UFOs.

The first wave: 1946–52 – First sightings of flying objects
During 1949 Major Donald E. Keyhoe contributed an article to *TRUE* magazine which became a bombshell. Some claimed it was the 'most widely read magazine article ever' up until that time. Keyhoe had a military/aviation background. He claimed that through his personal contacts in the Pentagon he had learned that extra-terrestrial beings were observing the earth. His argument, developed in some detail in his 1950 book *Flying Saucers are Real*, was that these beings were attracted by the series of A-bomb explosions that had begun in 1945. The argument carried much weight, because stories such as the following were circulating:

On October 1, 1948, at about 9 p.m., Lt. George F. Gorman was preparing to land his Air National Guard F-51 at Fargo, North Dakota. The control tower said that there was no other aircraft in the vicinity besides a Piper Cub below him. Gorman was watching the Cub when a 'light' passed him on the right. He pulled up close to 1000 yards to investigate and saw a somewhat flattened round object. It was small, clear white, and blinking on and off. As Gorman closed in on it, the light became steady. Then it pulled into a sharp left bank. Gorman dived in an attempt to catch up, but couldn't. Then the UFO climbed and banked left again. Gorman turned sharply to try to cut it off.

The object seemed to change its mind. It took a sharp turn right and came straight toward the F-51. Gorman dove to avoid collision and went about 500 yards under it. The object kept circling above it, so Gorman decided to chase it again. This time the object came straight at him and a collision seemed imminent. But suddenly the UFO shot straight up into the air in a steep climb out and disappeared.

The 'dogfight' lasted 26 minutes. Both the F-51 and the rapidly moving lighted object were seen by Dr. A. E. Cannon and his passenger in the Piper Cub. Lloyd D. Jensen and H. E. Johnson in the airport control tower saw a round, lighted, unidentified object speeding away.[3]

Reports such as the above forced the US government to examine them carefully, because it was argued in official circles that these unidentified craft could be Russian efforts to spy on US military and nuclear capabilities. The 'extra-terrestrial hypothesis' (ETH) was Keyhoe's contribution, and it captured the popular imagination. Scientists and governments, however, were not impressed.

Their first problem was that these repeated 'fly-by' encounters made no sense. Why would these beings take the trouble of coming all this distance from outer space and not establish contact with us openly? If we went to their planet, would we behave that way?

The second problem was that the reported behaviour of these UFOs suggested an unimaginable propulsion technology. Their speed, their ability to shoot straight up in the air without a thundering noise, their incredible manoeuvrability, and their ability to appear and disappear at will seemed too magical to be true. Their reported behaviour suggested that they were more like weightless thoughts than material bodies, since gravity seemed to have no effect on them or on their passengers. The scientists said that any life form even remotely resembling ourselves could not survive the physical shocks which their reported turns and twists implied.

The third and greatest problem was that these UFOs left no verifiable physical evidence behind them – no flags, no junk, no gadgets and no marks – there were only eyewitness accounts. And psychologists already knew that perfectly sane people were capable of seeing things that do not exist.

Carl Jung is a good example of such a psychologist. He thought that the possibility that UFOs were extra-terrestrial spaceships was still wide open. Therefore his book *Flying Saucers: A Modern Myth of Things Seen in the Sky* (first published in 1959) appeared to endorse the possibility of the phenomenon. He said:

> There are on record cases where one or more persons see something that physically is not there. For instance, I was once at a spiritualistic seance where four of the five people present saw an object like a moon floating above the abdomen of the medium. They showed me, the fifth person present, exactly where it was, and it was absolutely incomprehensible to them that I could see nothing of the sort. I know three more cases where certain objects were seen in the clearest detail (in two of them by two persons and in the third by one person) and could afterwards be proved to be non-existent. Two of these cases happened under my direct observation. Even people who are entirely compos mentis and in full possession of their senses can sometimes see things that do not exist. I do not know what the explanation is of such happenings ... I mention these somewhat remote possibilities because, in such an unusual matter as the UFOs, one has to take every aspect into account.[4]

The scientific/political establishment did not deny that UFOs were being seen. It aired the idea that these sightings could be misunderstandings, optical illusions or even hallucinations produced by some kind of mass hysteria. In any case, it was said, we do not have any evidence that unidentified flying objects are spaceships from outer space. Simply because people claim to have seen peculiar objects flying about, we have no basis for arriving at such a gigantic conclusion.

We do not know if it was this official expression of disbelief which caused people to stop seeing UFOs, or whether they just went away, having completed their mission, whatever it was. What we do know is that this denial started a feud between the establishment and believers in UFOs, the end of which we have not yet seen. Some believers, such as Hall, are convinced that the government has in its possession conclusive evidence that UFOs have visited America, but that for some reason it is hiding this information from the public and is lying about the facts.

Believers ridiculed the scientists' first objection, pointing out that scientists had no business to prejudge the motives of the alien visitors. How could you possibly decide that they should behave the same way as we would if we went to their planet? Is it scientific to refuse to study them until we know the motives behind their 'fly-by' behaviour?

The believers' response to the scientists' second objection was that any technology which is thousands of years ahead of ours is bound to appear magical to us, just as our technology appears magic to primitive tribes. What was there to prevent more advanced civilisations from inventing techniques for overcoming the force of gravity? If the UFO passengers had built around their crafts and themselves an 'anti-gravity' field, then their reported movements were conceivable. As Carl Sagan, himself a sceptic, put it in the 1971 conference on Communication With Extra-Terrestrial Intelligence (CETI):

> Such [advanced extra-terrestrial] civilizations will be inconceivably in advance of our own. We have only to consider the changes in mankind in the last [ten thousand] years and the potential difficulties which our Pleistocene ancestors would have in accommodating to our present society to realize what an unfathomable gap [a hundred million] to [ten thousand million years] represents, even with a tiny rate of intellectual advance. Such societies will have discovered laws of nature and invented technologies whose application will appear to us indistinguishable from magic.[5]

The third objection – the lack of physical evidence that we have been visited by alien spaceships – has been answered in two ways by believers.

First is the belief that some flying saucers have in fact crashed and have been retrieved by the US government. Therefore the government already has in its possession the ultimate proof that UFOs exist. Consider the following FBI memo on crashed 'saucers', reproduced by Richard Hall:

TO: DIRECTOR, FBI   DATE: March 22, 1950

FROM: GUY HOTTEL, SAO, WASHINGTON

SUBJECT: FLYING SAUCERS
         INFORMATION CONCERNING

Flying Discs or Flying Saucers (handwritten)

The following information was furnished to SA _____.
An investigator for the Air Force stated that three so-
called flying-saucers had been recovered in New Mexico.
They were described as being circular in shape with
raised centers, approximately 50 feet in diameter. Each
one was occupied by three bodies of human shape but
only 3 feet tall, dressed in metallic cloth of a very fine
texture. Each body was bandaged in a manner similar to
the blackout suits used by speed flyers and test pilots.
    According to Mr. _____ informant, the saucers were
found in New Mexico due to the fact that the Government
has a very high-powered radar set-up in that area and
it is believed the radar interferes with the controlling
mechanism of the saucers.
    No further evaluation was attempted by SA _____
concerning the above.[6]

Because many such memos have become public, suggesting to believers that the US government is already in possession of conclusive proof that UFOs exist, groups such as
Citizens Against UFO Secrecy (CAUS) have been formed to
force the government to reveal what it is hiding and why.
    Later waves of UFO sightings took care to answer the
criticisms about (a) the inexplicable reasons for the lack
of contact with human beings, and (b) the possibility that
sightings could be hallucinations. However, it seems (for
reasons which will become apparent) that one result of this
controversy was that when they reappeared, UFOs (or was it
the believers?) resolved to bypass unbelieving governments
and their official representatives.

The second wave: 1954 – Europeans follow the leader
It seems that during their first trip the extra-terrestrials

discovered that this was indeed an American century. Most new religious movements seem to originate in America and are then exported to Europe. The rest of the world follows the leader. Likewise, in 1954, during their second trip (sceptics might be happier to call it the second wave of UFO sightings), the extra-terrestrials decided to follow suit and visit Europe, especially France and Italy. This time observers reported seeing humanoids piloting UFOs. Some were only three or four feet tall, others as tall as fifteen feet. Some were like human beings, others very different. It was assumed that they had come from different planets.

The media were quick to see that either the UFOs or the Europeans were simply following the American craze. Publications such as *LIFE* magazine treated the European reports with scepticism, referring to them as 'the Continental madness'. The sightings stopped. It was hard to tell if Europeans were unwilling to see them any more, or unwilling to talk about them publicly for fear of ridicule. Or had the UFOs themselves decided that it would be a better tactic to consolidate a firm following in the US before venturing out into Europe?

That particular wave of sightings of UFOs did not add much to the knowledge of UFOlogy already available in the US. It does seem, however, that the activity of UFOs has remained consistent, except that they have become more circumspect. Now, in Europe, they appear only to people with psychic vision. For example, after Shirley MacLaine revived faith in them in North America in the 1980s through her books such as *Out on a Limb* and *It's All in the Playing*, UFOs have begun to be seen in England as well – but this time mainly by psychics.

David Icke, for example, narrates the following experience, when he was sent to the Welsh border with two psychics, John and Joan, to clear some energy blockage in the earth's leylines (discussed in the chapter on ecology):

> At the same site, Joan had to convert some energy coming into the earth from above into a frequency the earth could absorb. Her body's own energy pattern is designed to act as a filter for very powerful energies, and this is why she is on such a frequency herself. She manipulates the energy with a series of movements, words and sounds

which lower the frequency to the earth vibration and direct it to where it must go, usually to the earth spirit at the core. On this occasion there were some beings from other planets in the area working on the earth's etheric body, the Gaia, and to do that they needed the energy that Joan was filtering. We couldn't see the extra-terrestrials, because they were operating on a non-physical plane.[7]

The third wave: 1957 – Sightings by citizens
It seems it took five years for the UFOs to analyse the data they had collected mainly in America during 1948–52. They reappeared in 1957. At that time the Air Force had officially stopped studying them. The general public, however, was still interested. Therefore UFOs also decided to interact only with ordinary Americans, usually in their automobiles, instead of pilots in their jets. If they interacted with planes at all, it was generally not with American pilots (who may have become arrogant in their scepticism), but with pilots in far away places such as Pan de Azucar in Uruguay on 5 May 1958 and Bougainville Reef, Australia, on 28 May 1965.

On this third trip the UFOs seem to have decided to take care of the 'fly-by' criticism, as well as of the theory that people could be hallucinating. They made their presence known by concrete and physical effects on the automobiles of the people they encountered, because machines do not hallucinate. Because most of these encounters took place late at night (when drivers are not at their most alert), the main impact of the UFOs was to cause electromagnetic failures in the vehicles they encountered – typically failure of headlights and/or engines.

One of the most spectacular extravaganzas involving automobiles, reported in most UFO surveys, is called 'Levelland (Texas) Sightings'. On the night of 2–3 November 1957, citizens in and around Levelland saw multiple landings by UFOs on roadways between 11 p.m. and 1.30 a.m. Witnesses are said to have included Sheriff Weir Clem. A typical witness was Ronald Martin, who saw a glowing red UFO land in front of his truck at 12.45 a.m. It turned to bluish green upon landing and the truck's electrical systems failed. The UFO turned reddish again as it took off.

Most of the UFO reports from that period did not contain any mention of intelligent communications from the

UFOnauts. Therefore, writing in 1958, Carl Jung, like other researchers such as Edward I. Ruppelt (one-time chief of the American Bureau for observing UFOs), had to conclude that we did not have any convincing evidence of visitors from outer space. All that can be concluded from the reports, he said, is that 'Something is seen, one doesn't know what.'[8]

During the next wave, UFOs seem to have responded to this specific challenge. Obviously it is difficult to say whether the UFOs themselves had accepted the challenge, or the believers in UFOs. But the fourth wave seems to have been intended to convince believers that the unidentified flying objects were indeed spaceships from outer space.

The fourth wave: 1964 – Seeing extra-terrestrials

During the seven years from 1957 to 1964, public interest in UFOs had begun to decline. A 'trigger' case, reported widely in the mass media, revived the interest. On 24 April 1964 Lonnie Zamora, a police officer in Socorro, New Mexico, saw an elliptical object resting on stilt-like legs in an arroyo. Two small humanoid figures were standing near it. While he was watching, the craft emitted a loud roar, a blast of flames and smoke, and took off. Investigators claimed that they had found four rectangular imprints in the sand as well as scorched foliage beneath the take-off spot.

The reports of sightings including humanoids this time continued for some time and built up to something of a climax during 1966–7. One result of this wave was that the University of Colorado and the US Air Force collaborated in an infamous study called 'the Condon Report', which ultimately led to the Air Force winding up its own 'Project Blue Book' in 1989. The worst aspect of the Condon Report was that later it was revealed that the study had been biased: that the scientists undertaking the study had made up their minds even before commencing the research that their report would dismiss the claim.

The Condon Report did seem to have compromised scientific integrity. But the other difficulty was that UFOs, too, made matters difficult for their champions. Once again, UFOs seemed to have carefully avoided the Air Force and focused on private automobiles. Most reports said that they saw humanoids in or near the spacecraft. But for some reason the humanoids shied away from communicating with the people who saw them. They also seemed careful not to leave tangible evidence behind that they had truly landed and had been seen. These factors could easily be used by sceptics to dismiss the reports as a hoax. Why would UFOs keep coming, landing, making themselves visible, but not communicating?

It was for this reason that even those scientists and intellectuals who desperately wanted to believe in UFOs and were trying hard to communicate with extra-terrestrial intelligences could not take these sightings seriously. Arthur Koestler says that UFOs were mentioned only in passing in the 1971 conference on Communication With Extra-Terrestrial Intelligence (CETI). Carl Sagan completed his statement referred to earlier thus:

> There is a serious question about whether such [advanced] societies are concerned with communicating with us, any more than we are concerned with communicating with our protozoan or bacterial forebears ... I therefore raise the possibility that a horizon in communications interest exists in the evolution of technological societies, and that a civilization very much more advanced than we will be engaged in a busy communications traffic with its peers; but not with us and not via technologies accessible to us. We may be like the inhabitants of the valleys of New Guinea who may communicate by runner or drum, but who are ignorant of the vast international radio and cable traffic passing over, around and through them.[9]

It could have been sheer coincidence, but an amazing fact was that once again, as in every other previous wave, UFOs stopped appearing once disbelief in them was officially expressed. Predictably, UFOs (or at least believers in them) decided that the main feature of the next wave had to be communication between humanoids and human beings.

The fifth wave: 1973 – Abductions
Night, 16–17 October 1973, a midwestern state, USA. Patty 'Price', a divorced woman with seven children, had just moved into a new house. The tired family had settled down

to sleep. A young boy's scream woke everyone up. He had seen a 'skeleton'. The cat was yowling, a dog was barking furiously. Patty too felt vaguely that she had seen a prowler. So she took her children to sleep at a friend's house.

UFOs were in the air, because on 11 October they had abducted someone in Mississippi and the news had spread. Therefore seven year old Dottie's story next morning seemed perfectly credible. The sister of the boy, she announced that the prowler was actually a 'spaceman'. She had seen the craft and the creatures on it, two of whom came into the house.

Since no one else remembered seeing them, Patty was hypnotised to see if that would help her remember. It did. She recalled seeing two figures standing over her. They were slender, and wore uniforms. They abducted her and four of the children on board a craft. Its large, round and bright room had computer-like machines, displays and buttons.

Patty was on a table with one leg and arm fastened. Four or five aliens, over four feet tall, with large slanted eyes, long arms and clawlike hands were examining her. A taller, normal human being wearing glasses was with them. Her examination included gynaecological aspects, inserting a needle in her abdomen and elsewhere, and 'taking her thoughts'. Finally she was floated back to her house and children.

Betty, the oldest daughter, recalled seeing her mother naked on the examination table. She also saw the human being with the aliens. Dottie saw other people from the neighbourhood also abducted like themselves.

The above story forms part of the second chapter of 'Patty Price's Ordeal' in Coral and Jim Lorenzen's book *Abducted*. It is a typical example of that wave in which the UFOnauts seem finally to have decided to study human beings themselves, rather than their aircraft, automobiles or nuclear installations.

In the New Age, Shirley MacLaine's characters spend days talking to extra-terrestrials and report their teachings in perfect detail. But during this fifth wave the UFOnauts for some reason resolved to erase the memories of abduction. Therefore, along with the UFO wave came a wave of amateur hypnotists attempting to help people recall their experiences. Many of the people abducted were, as usual, travelling in their cars at night. Sometimes the main clue that they had been abducted was the fact that on reaching their destinations they found that they had missed a significant amount of time, such as an hour or two, for which they could not account.

Hypnotists would help them recall that lost time. Needless to say, fascinating stories emerged proving that human beings were now the 'biological test subjects of beings from outer space'. Women would report their breasts being examined. Whitley Strieber, in his best-selling book *Communion* (for which his publishers were willing to risk a $1 million cash advance, calculated on the basis of a massive wave of public interest), described how female UFOnauts were interested in his male sexual organs.

Some reporters, such as Bud Hopkins in his book *The Missing Time*, tried to limit themselves to respectable professional hypnotists. But the amateur hypnotists produced so much literature 'replete with abduction stories of dubious pedigree',[10] that even the extra-terrestrials seem to have become embarrassed.

What kinds of evidence did careful researchers like Bud Hopkins unearth? Shirley MacLaine mentions one:

> In Washington, D.C., I sat in my hotel room with Senator Claiborne Pell (chairman of the Senate Foreign Relations Committee), the Duke of Liechtenstein, Bella Abzug, and several people from Congress as we listened to Whitley Strieber (*Communion*) and Bud Hopkins (*The Intruders*) talk about their experiences with UFOs. Hopkins had brought a girl with him who claimed that she had been impregnated invisibly by an extraterrestrial. She said she had brought the baby to term, only to have it dematerialized by the ETs before she could see it.[11]

The issue here is not that such a thing could not have happened, but that the fact that the foetus disappeared before we could see an 'inter-planetary' baby is a typical pattern of UFO/extra-terrestrial behaviour. They do not leave behind them tangible, verifiable evidence. Astronauts left signs of their visit to the moon on its surface. But perhaps that is a part of our primitive clinging to rational proofs. Extra-terrestrials seem to want us to believe rather than to know. Naturally, their behaviour makes it possible for the critics to say that these are not instances of real encounters with extra-terrestrials, but instances of wishful thinking. Even incidents of 'false pregnancy' have been documented, where the imagination produces physical symptoms.

Our habit of seeking evidence is disliked by extra-terrestrials, as should be obvious by the fact that they stopped abducting Americans when the critics pointed out to the general public that hypnosis was not a reliable means of accurately recalling events that have allegedly been suppressed from the conscious mind. The central phenomenon in hypnosis, according to the *Encyclopaedia Britannica* (1969) is 'Suggestibility, a state of greatly enhanced receptiveness and responsiveness to suggestions and stimuli.' Therefore the process that takes place under hypnosis is not pure 'recall' of previous memories, but 'confabulation' – an attempt by the subject to please the hypnotist. The subject fills the gaps in memory with unrelated memories, fantasies and fabrications. The very questions that a hypnotist asks become suggestions, prompting subjects to fabricate 'memories'.

The New Age wave:
1983 – UFOs as a 'religious experience'
Arthur Koestler was undoubtedly one of the most articulate intellectuals of our century. His incisive mind probed every important facet of knowledge. His lifelong intellectual voyages were concluded with a final appendix in a defence of UFOs entitled 'UFOs: A Festival of Absurdity'. In concluding this appendix he wrote:

> Granted that even the best-documented UFO cases resemble a 'festival of absurdity', we must also realize that when we approach the borders of science, whether in ESP or quantum physics or ufology, we must expect to counter phenomena which seem to us paradoxical or absurd.[12]

To a cat, who can find good food in a dustbin and excellent shelter under a car, it would appear absurd that human beings go to such lengths as they do for food and homes. Similarly, Koestler says, we must not be surprised if the behaviour of superhuman UFOs appears absurd to us.

We should note the following distinctive features of New Age UFOlogy.

UFOs should be believed in not because they are true, but because it feels good to believe in them

Koestler obviously realised that human reason was not sufficient to know the truth. But did he mean that reason must be discarded in the search for truth? Or a claim must be believed only if it is absurd, as long as it feels good to believe it? That is how many in the New Age understand him, because in the New Age truth is not what is known by our logical left brain, but by our intuitive-emotive right brain.

Shirley MacLaine recalls a conversation with Kevin, a channeller:

'Have you ever seen a UFO?' I asked.

'No,' said Kevin. 'I have not yet had that pleasure.'

'But you believe it anyway?'

'Of course. It feels comfortable to me.'[13]

The point is not that Kevin believes what he has not verified, but that for him – and for the New Age in general – objective truth does not exist. As Ms MacLaine puts it, 'Reality was only what one believed it to be anyway.'[14] Therefore we are free to believe whatever gives us good and comfortable feelings, irrespective of whether or not it is true.

Koestler wanted to believe in UFOs for the same reason. To think that we are alone in the universe and we might annihilate ourselves is a terrible feeling, because in that case the wonderful drama of the cosmos will have to go on meaninglessly, without a spectator. So, he says,

> It is nice to know that we are not alone, that we have company out there among the stars – so that if we vanish, it does not matter too much, and the cosmic drama will not be played out before an empty house. The thought that we are the only conscious beings in this immensity, and that if we vanish, consciousness would vanish from it, is unbearable. Vice versa, the knowledge that there are billions of beings in our galaxy, and in other galaxies, infinitely more enlightened than our poor sick selves, may lead to that humility and self-transcendence which is the source of all religious experience.[15]

Thus, in presenting extra-terrestrials as space-age saviours, the New Age is not presenting something which it believes to be objectively true, but something which feels good, even if it has been repeatedly exposed as a misunderstanding, a hallucination or an outright hoax.

The optimism for an Aquarian future rests on extra-terrestrial help
The tragedy is that New Agers build their castles of hope for the Age of Aquarius on such sandy foundations. David Icke writes:

> The extra-terrestrials are arriving on earth in such large numbers, to help us . . . make the giant leap in evolution into the Aquarian Age, when humankind, or those who are evolved enough to meet the challenge, will rise out of the abyss at last. They are here to guide us through tremendously difficult times with love, wisdom and understanding, and we ignore them and reject what they say to our cost.[16]

According to Icke UFOs now visit England invisibly and work through psychics. Ms MacLaine, on the other hand, uses reams of paper in her books to suggest that extra-terrestrials have been coming to Peru openly in their spacecraft for years, and living in the high, inaccessible mountains there.

Mayan, an extra-terrestrial woman, spent hours upon hours giving metaphysical discourses to David, MacLaine's guru. She claims that all residents there have seen UFOs and many have had extensive contacts with them.

Did this overt contact make any difference in Peru, as Icke says it would make in England or as MacLaine suggests it would make in the US? MacLaine seasons the metaphysical discourses of Mayan and David with descriptions of oppressive Peruvian politics, its runaway inflation, its suffocating ecology and technological bankruptcy!

Even the lessons in physics which these extra-terrestrial intelligences give to David seem inferior to what a university textbook could teach. From all that we are told about the teachings of these extra-terrestrials, it is clear that, far from being able to share their higher technology with us, they are not even able to improve upon the 'spiritual' teachings of the spirit channellers of Hinduism and Taoism.

A religious experience: Self-transcendence

Why are UFOs not exposing themselves to us any more? *The Revelation of Ramala* answers that: 'It was their intention to make themselves known generally all over the Earth but, owing to the hostility of Man [notwithstanding that at one point UFO-believers were in the majority in America], this has not been possible.'[17]

These beings are now living 'within the aura of this Earth', but

> This does not mean that they will descend in their space-ships and automatically help Man to avoid that which he has created. It means that they will help only those who send out the thoughts that attract them ... It is by your individual thoughts that they will know you, that they will contact you.[18]

Why would they not seek to help people who do not believe in them? After all, Jesus prayed for those who were murdering him. 'Father, forgive them, for they do not know what they are doing' (Luke 23:34). And the New Testament says that Jesus suffered and died for us while we were still God's enemies, so that he might reconcile us to God as his children (Rom. 5:8).

The New Age answer is that UFOs will not help us individually because, after all, our individuality is not real. If we think we are the most important beings on earth, the centre of God's concern, then we are conceited. The earth itself is a person, Gaia, and is infinitely more important than ourselves. Therefore the extra-terrestrials are here to look after the earth, they are not bothered about satisfying our curiosity. Ramala says:

> That beings from other planets come to this Earth at all is not out of idle curiosity or even out of a desire to ease Man's burdens as he walks his path on the surface of the Earth. They come solely for the preservation of the Earth, for Man with his intellect, his technology, but without the balancing emotion of love is destroying this planet ... They have come and have helped Man, not to interfere with his free choice, but to preserve the Earth. They have held the Earth in balance so that Man in his stupidity would not interfere with the final great move forward in

the evolution of the whole of this planetary system.[19]

If the concern of the extra-terrestrials is primarily with the earth rather than with us, then why would they respond to our 'individual thoughts' that we send out to them? Ramala answers that they will respond to individuals to help them get rid of their individuality:

> [Man] is totally resigned to, and blinkered by, the concept of the importance of the individual ... he has yet to discover that the purpose of life on this Earth is to evolve beyond the individual and to recognize the greater whole and, indeed, to sacrifice the individual for that greater whole.[20]

Angels – Visitors of another kind

The New Age search to rediscover a meaning and role for our self begins with the great hope of putting self at the very centre of the cosmos, but with monotonous predictability it ends with a negation of self. What UFOs finally offer to an individual, burdened and weakened by modern technological society, is the very opposite of what another Saviour, who visited the earth two thousand years ago, offered. He said: 'Come to me, all you who are weary and burdened, and I will give you rest' (Matt. 11:28). And again, he said: 'All who ever came before me were thieves and robbers ... The thief comes only to steal and kill and destroy [including your most precious possession – your self]; I have come that they may have life, and have it to the full' (John 10:8–10).

The Lord Jesus does not deny that, being finite, we need help from outside. He promised us the help of angels in times of our need. The Bible has many examples of angels ministering to God's people. But four features of these angelic visitations should be noted.

Visions and visits
The Bible records many instances when people had subjective visions of angels, who appear and disappear as if from another dimension rather than from another planet. The apostle John records several such visions in the book of Revelation. He does not make us think that he was actually visited by these beings, except in his mind (Rev. 22).

The Bible also records incidents when angels were sent by God to visit specific individuals for specific purposes. For example in Genesis 18 we read about three angels visiting Abraham in person. In Judges 6 an angel visits Gideon and in Luke's Gospel we read of angel visiting Zechariah, the father of John the Baptist (Luke 1:8–22), and Mary, the mother of Jesus (Luke 1:26–38). According to the Bible these were not visions, but actual visits that made concrete physical and social changes in and through the people who were visited

The angelic guests did not demand blind belief

The second thing we must notice is that these angelic visitors did not give metaphysical discourses which people had to believe. They made brief and pointed announcements which called for obedience by faith.

Abraham was a hundred years old, and Sarah, his wife, was ninety – way past the age of bearing children. The angel said that God was going to enable Sarah to get pregnant and bear Abraham's child. Sarah laughed in disbelief. The angel rebuked her. Then the angels told Abraham that Sodom, where his nephew Lot lived, was going to be destroyed. Abraham prayed for mercy. Sodom was destroyed that night, though Lot escaped – dragged out of town forcibly by two angels. The next day Abraham had tangible evidence that he had been visited by the Lord's angels:

> Early the next morning Abraham got up and returned to the place where he had stood before the Lord. He looked down towards Sodom and Gomorrah, towards all the land of the plain, and he saw dense smoke rising from the land, like smoke from a furnace. (Gen. 19:27–8)

The following year Sarah did give birth to Isaac, Israel's patriarch.

Gideon was not meditating when he was visited, but threshing his wheat in a winepress, hiding it away from the Midianites who had occupied his land. The Israelites were crying out to the Lord for salvation. The angel came to Gideon and commanded him to go and rescue his people. Gideon wanted physical evidence that he was in fact being visited by God's messenger. So he asked for several signs. The best-known one is the fleece:

Gideon said to God, 'If you will save Israel by my hand as you have promised – look, I will place a wool fleece on the threshing-floor. If there is dew only on the fleece and all the ground is dry, then I will know that you will save Israel by my hand, as you said.' And that is what happened. Gideon rose early the next day; he squeezed the fleece and wrung out the dew – a bowlful of water.

Then Gideon said to God, 'Do not be angry with me. Let me make just one more request. Allow me one more test with the fleece. This time make the fleece dry and the ground covered with dew.' That night God did so. Only the fleece was dry; all the ground was covered with dew. (Judg. 6:36–40)

The public demonstration that Gideon had indeed been visited and commanded by an angelic being came when he defeated the mighty army of the Midianites with just three hundred unarmed men.

Zechariah, the father of John the Baptist, was visited by an angel when he was burning incense to God in the temple. The angel told him that his prayers for a child had been answered and his wife would have a son who would prepare the way for the arrival of the Saviour. Zechariah thought that the news was too good to be true. He asked in disbelief:

'How can I be sure of this? I am an old man and my wife is well on in years.'

The angel answered, 'I am Gabriel. I stand in the presence of God, and I have been sent to speak to you and to tell you this good news. And now you will be silent and not be able to speak until the day this happens, because you did not believe my words, which will come true at their proper time.' (Luke 1:18–20)

When Zechariah came out of the temple, much later than normal, he could not speak. He made signs, and the people realised that he had had some unusual experience. Nine months later, when he was asked to name his child, his mouth opened up again – and the people were amazed when he told them what had happened. They had two concrete evidences before them that he had been visited: the child born to a very old woman, and his father, who had been dumb for nine months!

We can multiply these instances, but those details are not necessary here. What is extremely important today (and deserves repetition), is to see that the biblical teaching on visits by angels is very different from what UFOlogists, as well as even some Christian teachers, are saying.

In incidents such as the ones above, when the Bible talks about actual visits by angels it implies that these were not visions or visualisations. There was physical and social evidence of real visits. In contrast, when the Bible describes visions, it does not imply physical visits have taken place. As an example, we could look at a biblical case which is immensely popular with many UFOlogists and Christian spokespersons. That is, the vision of the prophet Ezekiel, when he says:

> The heavens were opened and I saw visions of God . . .
>
> I looked, and I saw . . . an immense cloud with flashing lightning and surrounded by brilliant light. The centre of the fire looked like glowing metal, and in the fire was what looked like four living creatures. In appearance their form was that of a man, but each of them had four faces . . . (Ezek. 1:1–6)

Was this a visit by a UFO? No, because every time the Bible uses the phrase 'The heavens were opened . . . ' in association with a vision, it describes a subjective vision, and not an actual visit. For example, in Acts 10 we read this about the apostle Peter:

> Peter went up on the roof to pray. He became hungry and wanted something to eat, and while the meal was being prepared, he fell into a trance. He saw heaven opened and something like a large sheet being let down to earth by its four corners. It contained all kinds of four-footed animals . . . Then a voice told him, 'Get up, Peter. Kill and eat . . . ' (Acts 10:9–13)

This is a description of a vision during an altered state of consciousness, called a 'trance'. It was (like Ezekiel's own vision) a very powerful experience which changed Peter, preparing him to break with his tradition of associating only with the Jews and to open the doors of the church to the Gentile converts. Nevertheless, it was only a vision.

Peter could not live on the food which he saw on that sheet. When he came down from the roof, he would still be hungry and eat the food cooked by his hosts. Similarly, there is no suggestion that Ezekiel was actually visited by some superior beings in a UFO.

The Bible does not of course offer an explicit discussion of the distinction between a vision and a visit. That is because during biblical times, as in most other ages in history, there was not the present-day confusion between reality on the one hand and imagination, fantasy, visualisation or vision on the other. The Bible assumes that the reader will make the necessary distinction according to the context.

The New Age makes no distinction between vision and visit. Not necessarily because it is dishonest in its scholarship, but because it believes that there is no final distinction between reality and visualisation. But it would be unfair to the Bible to read it with today's mentality, with no respect for the context in which it was written – the mentality of its own authors.

Visions and visualisations

In the mentality of the biblical writers even subjective experiences such as visions and visualisation are distinct. In a vision the initiative is with God. He speaks in an audio-visual way to a person, usually a prophet. No one else sees or hears it. Therefore the prophet is responsible for making sure that it is indeed the word of God that he is speaking. He is accountable for what he says. If a prophet has said something which God did not send him to say, his prediction will turn out to be false. Because he has then lied in the name of God, he is guilty of a crime deserving capital punishment.

In the Bible visualisation can be as powerful an experience as a vision. But in it the initiative is with the human subject. What he sees and hears is generally a product of his own unconscious mind, and sometimes demons can delude him. The 'prophets' who speak what is merely a product of their own minds are called 'false prophets' in the Bible. Ezekiel says:

> The word of the Lord came to me: 'Son of man, prophesy against the prophets of Israel who are now prophesying.

Say to those who prophesy but of their own imagination: "Hear the word of the Lord! This is what the Sovereign Lord says: Woe to the foolish prophets who follow their own spirits and see nothing! Your prophets, O Israel, are like jackals among ruins. You have not gone up to the breaks in the wall to repair it for the house of Israel so that it will stand firm in the battle on the day of the Lord. Their visions are false and their divinations a lie. They say, 'The Lord declares,' when the Lord has not sent them; yet they expect their words to be fulfilled. Have you not seen false visions and uttered lying divinations . . . ?

" . . . Because of your false words and lying visions, I am against you, declares the Sovereign Lord. My hand will be against the prophets who see false visions and utter lying divinations . . .

"Because they lead my people astray, saying, 'Peace', when there is no peace, and because, when a flimsy wall is built, they cover it with whitewash, therefore tell those who cover it with whitewash that it is going to fall. Rain will come in torrents, and I will send hailstones hurtling down, and violent winds will burst forth. When the wall collapses, will people not ask you, 'Where is the whitewash you covered it with?' " ' (Ezek. 13:1–12)

Western civilisation today is indeed rapidly moving towards ruin. It does need wisdom from outside itself. But the prophets of UFOlogy, because they are deliberately and openly presenting the imaginations of their own minds as wisdom from above, are 'false prophets'. They are proclaiming a New Age of peace while, like the false prophets in Ezekiel's day, they are not lifting a finger to repair the ruins. The flimsy walls of imagination that they are whitewashing with metaphysical jargon borrowed from quantum physics or mystical philosophy will not stand the trying tests that certainly lie ahead for a culture which no longer knows such simple things as whether marriage is valuable, or motherhood is precious, or a baby's murder is a murder.

The angelic visitors are 'ministering spirits'
The reason biblical angels never came in flying machines is that they are not more highly evolved beings from another planet, but beings from another dimension. Comparing the

greatness of Christ with the smallness of angels, the Bible says: 'To which of the angels did God ever say, "Sit at my right hand . . . "'? Are not all angels ministering spirits sent to serve those who will inherit salvation?' (Heb. 1:13–14).

The Bible does not portray angels as teachers, because they are in fact messengers and ministering spirits. The Bible says that it is the Holy Spirit himself who leads us into all truth (John 16:13). Therefore, although we are asked to seek him, nowhere does the Bible exhort us to seek visions or encounters with angels.

Unlike contemporary UFOlogy, which looks upon these visitors as saviours, the Bible prohibits the exaltation of angels. After the apostle John had his 'revelation of Jesus Christ', he says:

> When I had heard and seen them, I fell down to worship at the feet of the angel who had been showing them to me. But he said to me, 'Do not do it! I am a fellow-servant with you and with your brothers the prophets and of all who keep the words of this book. Worship God!' (Rev. 22:8–9)

In fact, some passages in the Bible clearly suggest that human beings are at least in some respects greater than the angels. Paul says that at the end of this age those who are 'in Christ' will rule with Christ and judge angels (1 Cor. 6:3). In Psalm 8, where some translations say that God has made man 'a little lower than the angels', the New International Version correctly translates the verse. 'You made him a little lower than the heavenly beings' (Ps. 8:5). In the text note it says that the alternative reading of the term 'heavenly beings' is 'God'.

It is for this reason that Paul says that seeking visions of angels and worshipping them is a spiritual disqualification:

> Do not let anyone who delights in false humility and the worship of angels disqualify you for the prize. Such a person goes into great detail about what he has seen, and his unspiritual mind puffs him up with idle notions. (Col. 2:18)

The Bible gives these serious warnings not simply because visions can be hallucinations, but also because the devil, Lucifer, is himself a fallen angel. The Bible says that many other angels 'fell' with him from the presence of God. They attempt to deceive people, appearing not as demons with tails, hairy chests and claws, but as 'angel[s] of light' (cf. 2 Cor. 11:14).

The Saviour himself will return

The final thing that we must notice about the heavenly visitors is that the Bible asks Christians to expect not extra-terrestrials or angels in spaceships, but to look out for the Saviour who died, rose again and ascended into heaven in the presence of his disciples. He has promised to return not in a spaceship, nor invisibly, but in full view of everyone. The apostle John prophesied in the book of Revelation:

> Look, he is coming with the clouds,
>   and every eye will see him,
>   even those who pierced him . . .

'I am the Alpha and the Omega,' says the Lord God, 'who is, and who was, and who is to come, the Almighty.' (Rev. 1:7–8)

5

TANTRIC SEX:
A CELEBRATION OF LIFE?

As we have seen, New Age thought generally assumes that ultimately the universe does not have an existence independent of our consciousness. If that is so, then any claim that astrology, spiritism or communications from extra-terrestrials are objectively true automatically disproves New Age doctrine. For example, if a UFO exists outside my imagination, then no matter what its passengers say, it proves that I do not create my universe or truth. On the other hand, if an 'alien' spaceship is in some mysterious sense only a part of my imagination, then it does not offer objective, verifiable proof of New Age thought.

For many New Agers, therefore, sex and the *chakras* (the psychic points in our bodies) provide better proofs and experiences than stars, spirits or flying saucers.

If sexual experience can open hidden (occult) dimensions of psychic powers within ourselves, then perhaps we can all have proof that 'yin' and 'yang' or 'Shiva' and 'Shakti', the ultimate masculine and feminine energies that created the entire cosmos, lie within us. At the very least we would then transcend our normal limited experience of being either male or female, and would instead see ourselves as 'divine' wholes, incorporating within ourselves the God-energy which is said to be both male and female. This would be evidence of both a subjective and an objective kind, being at least experientially verifiable.

Johannes Agaard, a professor of religion at the Aarhus University in Denmark, is one of Europe's leading authorities on Eastern religious influence in the West. He has often asserted that Tantra lies at the root of virtually all

6

forms of yoga and other Eastern religious practices adopted by the West. Undoubtedly it has influenced some forms of New Age thought. Let us first examine the history of Tantra, and then its philosophy and practice, in both the East and the West.

The historical roots of Tantra

The term Tantra has many meanings. It is used as the collective name of certain Indo-Tibetan scriptures, as the name of the religious practices and yogic techniques taught by those scriptures, and it may also refer to the religio-philosophical tradition that results from those scriptures, teachings and practices.

In Indian history Tantra seems to have emerged around AD 600. By AD 900 at least sixty-four scriptures were already in circulation. And by the year 1000 tantric art had begun to dominate the cultural scene in India. But historians believe that Tantra's roots reach back into Indian pre-history – in pre-Aryan, magical, mystical fertility cults that seem to have worshipped the goddess and the female power of generation.

Dr Fritjof Capra begins his influential book *The Tao of Physics* by narrating his mystical experience in which he 'saw' the essence of the material universe as a 'dance of Shiva'.[1] What Capra does not tell us explicitly is that, when the creator and the creation are perceived as one, not only is creation worshipped as divine, but also the procreative process – sex – is worshipped. Sex is logically looked upon as a possible key to unlock the mysteries of the universe. Most life forms begin in sex. If the distinction between living and non-living beings is unreal, and the earth and the cosmos are also alive, then they too might originate in cosmic sex, and could be understood through it.

In one sense the heart of Capra's argument in *The Tao of Physics* is that the philosophical conclusions of some modern physicists come close to what Hindu and Buddhist tantrics experienced through sex. The first photograph in his book reproduces, 'Self-realization in the experience of sensual love; stone sculpture from the Citragupta temple at Khajuraho. Circa A.D. 1000.'[2] This sculpture, only thirty kilometres from my home in Chhatarpur district in Madhya

Pradesh, is an explicit scene of sexual intercourse.

Capra's book, though widely read, is for scholars who can understand the philosophy of physics. The idea that we can have spiritual experience through sex was introduced to millions of people through the 1984 thriller movie *Indiana Jones and the Temple of Doom*. The hero rescues the 'Shankara stone' from a tantric sect to deliver it to its rightful possessors. The Shankara stone is 'Shiva-lingam' (i.e., the god Shiva's phallus), more worshipped than understood by the Hindus. In the movie the villains had found three primeval Shiva-lingams, and were searching for the other two so as to unite them with Kali (Shakti), the female consort of Shiva. Long before that movie, books such as *Sexual Secrets: The Alchemy of Ecstasy* had presented the tantric world-view powerfully to Western readers. The authors, Nick Douglas and Penny Slinger, write:

> By exploring the sexual potential of ourselves and others, we can come to consciously know the alchemy of ecstasy ... This is a book for those who wish to use the sexual bond as a means to liberation and who desire to transcend the limits of the individual self.[3]

Mircea Eliade, the author of the influential work *Yoga: Immortality and Freedom*, suggests that Tantra might represent the spiritual counter-attack of an indigenous mother-cult, suppressed earlier by the invading Aryans.

Amurey de Riencourt sees in Tantra a human, if not a historical or racial counter-attack: a manifestation of the human instinct for self-preservation, an attempt to save India from the destructive consequences of Hindu and Budhhist outlooks, which view life as suffering, if not illusion.[4]

This fundamental opposition to mainstream Hindu thought was responsible for Tantra's persecution by the Aryan establishment. Its morally suspect practices, sometimes indistinguishable from black magic, also invited fierce Muslim opposition. The persecution drove Tantra underground. Because until fairly recently it existed underground, an eminent scholar such as Dr S. Radhakrishnan (India's ex-president) did not devote even one sentence to Tantra while compiling *A Source Book in Indian Philosophy* along with Charles A. Moore.[5] For Tantra to become the main

Indian influence in the West, in spite of this marginalisation at home, is indeed a remarkable achievement.

The philosophy and practice of Tantra

Creation as the insanity of God

Tantra accepts the classical Hindu view that reality is one. Our normal (rational or sensory) perception of duality – of male and female, living and non-living, force and matter, right and wrong, good and evil – is a perception of unreality, maya or *lila*. Tantra understands lila to be a play of divine consciousness or illusory magic. Before the beginning, beyond time, was pure consciousness, existing in perfect unity or equilibrium, having no polarity, no form, no thought, no distinction.

Something disturbed this primeval, pure and still ocean of consciousness. The divine stability then turned into an oscillating instability, imbalance or insanity. God was divided. The first duality to appear as a result of this 'insanity' was male and female. The consciousness of this original duality produced a series of waves, further disturbing the tranquil surface of the sea of bliss. A criss-crossing of these waves created elaborate patterns. The farther these waves were removed from their original state (as divine consciousness), the 'grosser' they became; appearing finally as condensed matter, the world of sense experience. The cosmos, then, is divine devolution – densified frequencies or compacted waves of consciousness that can conceal their divinity because they are convoluted divine emanations. Thus the original polarity of male and female manifests itself finally as the polarity of mind and matter.

Physicists such as Fritjof Capra find this tantric view of the ultimate oneness of mind and matter to be a mind-blowing insight for scientists. He thinks that it is utterly remarkable that after centuries of painstaking research scientists should arrive at the same conclusion, that matter and energy are one! But is the energy of physics the same as the consciousness of the mystics? Capra recognises that he cannot answer that question in the affirmative, because so far 'Mystics understand the roots of the Tao but not its branches; scientists understand its branches but not its roots.'[6]

The problem is simple but profound: unless someone understands both the roots and the branches he cannot conclude that the roots the mystics claim to see are indeed the basis of the cosmos that appears to our senses. Physics has indeed transcended the polarity of energy and matter, but as Capra himself admits, consciousness still defies its equations. Therefore the tantrics are more honest in confessing that they are talking metaphysics, not physics.

Because the finer 'consciousness' and the grosser 'body' coexist in a human being, we are, according to tantric thought, microscopic versions of the cosmos. Polarity is therefore the key to existence. The gender division of male and female, being the basic polarity in the human race, is therefore the key to our human existence: its reunification in sexual intercourse is our point of contact with the cosmic powers.

In defining our sexual function as the means of our direct connection with the divine, Tantra uses duality as the surest path to cosmic unity. Reality is to be reached by embracing illusion – our own bodies.

This is not to suggest that Tantra is a logical, sophisticated philosophical thought system. In India these teachings are usually sung as mythological stories such as the story of Yama and Yami, the 'he-twin' and the 'she-twin'. They were the primordial male and female formed from the division of God. Yami desires to be reunited with Yama in sexual intercourse. There are metrical dialogues, ballads consisting of entreaties and refusals between them. Yama shrinks from the sin of incest, and Yami remains unfulfilled. Yama dies, but instead of attaining liberation he ascends to the abode of the dead and, being the first deceased mortal, becomes the king of the realm of the dead.

If creation is divine insanity, then sanity has to be left outside the temple of God.

Enlightenment as embracing insanity

Few people realise that a sophisticated version of Tantra entered America in the last century with Swami Vivekanada, at the Parliament of World Religions in Chicago. But many have heard of the late Bhagwan (or Osho) Rajneesh's teaching, contained in his books such as *From Sex to*

Superconsciousness, which made headlines because of what went on in his ashrams at Pune in India in the 1970s, and then in Antelope, Oregon, in the USA.[7]

Those who have watched, whether in person or on film, the meditations practised by the followers of Rajneesh must have wondered how such insanity can lead to God. The answer is that if you were to understand that creation itself is the insanity of God, then you would cease to depend on the sanity of reason. For reason can only keep you in the bondage of maya and karma. As Capra puts it:

> To free the human mind from words and explanations is one of the main aims ... As long as we try to explain things, we are bound by karma; trapped in our conceptual network. To transcend words and explanations means to break the bonds of karma and attain liberation.[8]

Rajneesh taught that the human mind is our 'chief villain', for it acts like a prism, dividing one ray into many. The mind is the source of bondage because it can only see an object by separating it from others, by labelling or categorising it. Therefore, according to Rajneesh, the aim of our religious quest should be to 'kill the mind', in other words to choose insanity.

As has been pointed out by a number of scholars, the shocking uniqueness of Tantra is that while with the rest of Hinduism it admits that this world is maya, it does not scorn it as a source of temptation, but embraces it as the raw material of enlightenment; for Tantra the realm of maya is the only available context of liberation. Brooks Alexander, a Berkeley based researcher, says: 'The tantric thus accepts lila, the play of consciousness, as an arena for knowing the power of consciousness, then uses those powers as a vehicle of enlightenment, thereby transcending lila altogether.'[9]

Mantra: Severing sense from sound

In Tantra, as in the New Age, the Logos or the Word that creates the cosmos is not God's wisdom or reason, but vibrations. These can be tapped into by the practice of mantra – the use of a word, or rather a sound, separated from meaning or reason. It is, as Maharishi Mahesh Yogi says, 'chanting to produce an effect in some other world, [to] draw the attention of those higher beings or gods living there'.[10] But mantra is not prayer, at least as the Christian understands it. For prayer is a meaningful personal conversation with our creator. Mantra is a deliberate annihilation of meaningful language by mechanical, non-personal repetition of a word or sound. As Eliade says, 'All indefinite repetition leads to destruction of language; in some mystical traditions, this destruction appears to be the condition for further experiences.'[11]

The significance of mantra is justified by a belief in occult correspondence. The cosmos is nothing but vibration. And what is sound? Pure vibration, once it is severed from reasoned communication or language. Language keeps us entangled at the level of maya or illusion. Sound can take us to the source of cosmic vibrations. Capra sees here a profound parallel between Tantra and modern physics:

> The Eastern mystics [i.e., tantrics] affirm that . . . a union of one's male and female modes can be experienced on a higher plane of consciousness where the realm of thought and language is transcended and all opposites appear as a dynamic unity.
>
> I have already asserted that a similar plane has been reached in modern physics. The exploration of the subatomic world has revealed a reality which repeatedly transcends language and reasoning, and the unification of concepts which had hitherto seemed opposite and irreconcilable turns out to be one of the most startling features of this new reality . . . Modern physicists should therefore be able to gain insights into some of the central teachings of the Far East by relating them to experiences in their own field.[12]

Yantra: The diagram of divinity

In Tantra the gods and goddesses are the mythological representations of divine forces, the mantras are their audible representations, and yantras their visual depictions. Yantras are not pictures of divinity, but geometric symbols and complex designs that are drawn, painted or engraved on a flat surface.

In Tantra, the yantras become substitutes for idols. The Shiva-lingam in *Indiana Jones and the Temple of Doom* is a three-dimensional yantra, perhaps worshipped more than any other idol in India. An equally popular three-dimensional symbol is the 'Yoni-lingam' – male and female symbols united.

In the West mandalas are more popular than yantras – thanks again to the writings of Carl Jung. 'Mandala' means a circle. It represents wholeness, Jung says; the coming together of yang and yin. While yantras are simple geometric figures, the mandalas are complex paintings. The Hindu mandalas often contain a square within a circle; within that are smaller shapes and spaces depicting deities and demons, heavens and hells, creation and destruction. The overall impression created by a mandala is to suggest diverse emanations within wholeness.

Chakras and Kundalini: The serpent power

The belief that the material body is consciousness is given concrete description in Tantra, which asserts that the body is a network of channels for cosmic (divine) consciousness. Where these channels interact they create pulse points or psychic centres called 'chakras'. Though there are about 88,000 such chakras, seven of them are most important for tantric practice. These seven are situated not in our physical body, but in the 'subtle' body, along the central axis that runs from the tailbone to the skull.

The divine polarities of male and female lie at the opposite ends of these seven chakras. Traditionally it has been taught that the female, called Kundalini, or the serpent power, lies dormant at the base of the spine, separated from her divine lover Shiva, the masculine counterpart who dwells in the crown chakra in the head. Some New Age mystics consider this to be a patriarchal perversion of mysticism.

Now, according to Shirley MacLaine, the top three chakras are yin – feminine or spiritual energy. The lower three chakras are yang – masculine or physical energy. The central heart chakra is the most important one, because it is androgynous. The heart chakra, MacLaine claims,

is the seat or the home of the soul, or Higher Self, and it is perfectly balanced in its yin and yang expressions. The Higher Self is connected and interfaced with God energy, which also is perfect in its balance of creating and manifesting the yin and the yang.

Therefore, the more we each resonate to the perfection of the Higher Self, the more we are reflecting perfect balance in ourselves, the more androgynous we are.[13]

In other words either all Eastern mystics so far were mistaken, or the anatomy of the 'subtle' human body has undergone a fundamental change to facilitate the New Age understanding of femininity.

Later in this chapter we will discuss further why the New Age tantrics reject the traditional psychic anatomy of chakras. Here it is enough to say that in contrast to Shirley MacLaine, traditional Hindu Tantra did not focus on the heart chakra or the higher self. The goal of the tantric mystic (usually a celibate) was to awaken the dormant (female) Kundalini through secret practices borrowed generally from various yogic traditions such as Hatha Yoga. As Kundalini rose to meet her lover in the crown chakra, it gave the tantric intense psychic experiences as it passed through the different chakras. The enlightenment occurred not when an androgynous higher self was discovered in the heart chakra, but only when the god and the goddess were united in a psychic-sexual embrace. The veil of illusion then vanished and the unity of all polarities was perceived.

Maithuna: Sexual oneness within oneself

Sexual ritual in Tantra is called maithuna. The 'right-hand' tantrics, also called white tantrics, believe that the maithuna passages in the tantric scriptures are to be understood figuratively. The 'left-hand', or red, tantrics advocate a literal enactment of the rites. But even they reserve it only for very advanced practitioners.

One has first to find an experienced guru, because the deepest tantric traditions are oral, not written. Even the written texts use ambiguous and symbolic language called *sandha-bhasha*, which cannot be understood without a guru's help. One purpose of such language is to discourage the non-initiate. But it also encourages an enlightened tantric to remember that the reality he seeks is beyond logical language.

During a secret ceremony of tantric initiation, the guru

connects a disciple to the spiritual tradition he embodies. The ceremony may consist of the worship of the guru, the receiving of a mantra, and instructions for meditation and visualisations. It may also involve a 'purification of chakras' by the handling of a disciple's genitals.

During maithuna a male disciple usually favours having a female tantric who takes over the role of the guru. But it is not essential for a man to have a woman companion for tantra. For the objective of maithuna is not to achieve physical release through ejaculation and orgasm. It is to seek psychic experiences by the 'threefold immobility' of semen, breath, and consciousness. Tantric transcendence takes place when the mind is completely still but focused, breathing has ceased and sexual arousal is arrested at the point of maximum tension. Thus maithuna first stimulates and then traps the energies of sexual arousal to be able to release them through the channel of a still mind. This 'spiritual orgasm' does not seek to make a man and a woman 'one flesh'. On the contrary, its aim is to help fuse a tantric's own inner polarities into one; that is, to give him the mystic experience of oneness.

Most Hindu/Buddhist tantrics practise celibacy or *brahmacharya*. They do not seek an abiding, growing, fulfilling love-relationship with a member of the opposite sex because, as Rajneesh says, Tantra treats sex as 'Simply a door. While making love to a woman, you are really making love to Existence itself. The woman is just a door; the man is just a door.'[14]

Once you have learned to reach samadhi or superconsciousness through sex, Rajneesh says, you do not need a woman (if you are a man), for you can have sex with the whole universe – 'with a tree, with the moon, with anything'. Or you can simply shut yourself in a room and reach superconsciousness using the female Kundalini within you.

Samadhi: Powers of the psyche or of spirits?
Tantra gives tremendous psychic experiences of powerful visions, often accompanied by physical tingling sensations. Does it simply unleash the power of our unconscious mind? Timothy Leary, Ralph Metzner and Richard Alpert, who played a decisive role in promoting the drug culture of the 1960s, discovered that Tantra-induced psychic experiences

closely resemble the psychedelic experiences produced by drugs such as LSD. Therefore they published their final interpretation of the 'psychedelic experience' in 1984 as a commentary on the *Tibetan Book of the Dead* – an important tantric scripture.

Tantra was revived in India in the nineteenth century by the powerful psychic experiences and visions of Ramakrishna Paramhamsa, the guru of Swami Vivekanada. The nature of his psychic experiences throws more light on the source of tantric visions. Ramakrishna once said that 'The Divine Mother revealed to me in the Kali temple that it was She who had become everything.'

And who really is the Kali described by the tantric texts? This is how she is presented to her devotees:

> One should adore with liquors and oblations that Kali who has a terrible gaping mouth and uncombed hair; who has four hands and a splendid garland formed of the heads of the giants she has slain and whose blood she had drunk; who is as black as the large clouds and has the whole sky for her clothes; who has a string of skulls round her neck and a throat besmeared with blood; who wears earrings (consisting of two dead bodies); who carries two dead bodies in her hands; whose form is awful and who dwells in burning-grounds (for consuming corpses).[15]

This Kali is the Divine Mother, both of the gentle Ramakrishna, as well as of the criminal 'Thugs', who, in devotion to her turned random murder into an act of worship.

As mentioned earlier, Tantra had been eclipsed in India because of the intense opposition of Brahmanism and Muslim rulers. Even today left-hand tantrics are often the victims of brutal mob-lynching because they are the prime suspects when children begin to disappear from an area. It is suspected, with good reason, that tantrics are sacrificing them to the Mother Goddess (Kali or Shakti) to obtain some special favour or power. Philosophically that is possible, because tantrics have to transcend not only the polarity of male and female, but also that of good and evil. A commitment to goodness, according to Tantra, is a commitment to metaphysical bondage.

What that means in practice can be further illustrated by the well-known case of Swami Muktananda Paramhamsa, who took Tantra to the West overtly in our generation. Muktananda's 'spiritual' journey (like that of Ramakrishna Paramhamsa in the nineteenth century) began when he met Ziprauna, a naked sadhu, or 'holy' man. Ziprauna was 'holy' because as an ascetic he used to sit on a refuse heap – which can be really filthy and stinking in India, where casteism has not allowed sanitation to become a priority. We are told that this naked ascetic made Muktananda sit on his lap and licked his head. That was the initiation. After eight years of intense 'religious' practices such as this, Muktananda's Kundalini finally awoke.

The last link in the chain of his 'spiritual' pilgrimage was Swami Nityananda. One day Nityananda gave a fruit to Muktananda and sent him to meditate. We do not know if the fruit had some consciousness-altering chemical properties, but the following is Muktananda's own account of his experience:

Once Nityananda gave me a fruit and asked me to go to Yeola and continue my sadhana there. I carried the fruit with me to Yeola. On reaching my destination I ate it and then sat for meditation. Soon I started feeling restless and uneasy. Within moments things were happening to me. I could not understand it. I was perturbed mentally and emotionally. My mind seemed deluded. By the time evening came this delusion became worse ... I felt I would soon become insane ...

As I sat again for meditation, I felt there was great commotion around. My entire body started aching and I automatically assumed padmasana, the lotus posture ... I felt severe pain in the knot [the manipur chakra] below the navel. I tried to shout but could not even articulate ... Next I saw ugly and dreadful demon-like figures. I thought them to be evil spirits.

I then saw blazes of fire on all sides and felt that I too was burning. After a while I felt a little better. Suddenly I saw a large ball of light approaching me from the front; as it approached, its light grew brighter and brighter. It then entered unobstructed through the closed doors of my kutir [hut] and merged into my head. My eyes were forcibly closed and I felt a fainting sensation. I was terrified by that powerfully dazzling light. Finally

I saw a blue flame of light which first grew larger and
then diminished to the size of a small pearl.[16]

These experiences greatly perturbed Muktananda. He
was reassured only when the next day another ascetic,
Harigiri Baba, came to him and said, 'Good times have
come for you not bad. You are going to be better off soon.
You will attain Godhead.'[17]

So Muktananda sat again for meditation. The experiences
of 'divinity' restarted: 'I felt the same pain in the chakra
below the navel, and a variety of visions appeared before
me. I even saw naked men and women.'[18]

At first Muktananda thought that he had made a serious
mistake. But later, on reading a book, he learned that these
experiences meant that his Kundalini had been awakened.
The blue pearl of dazzling light that he saw was God.

The interpretation of Tantra

Are tantric experiences divine, or could they be inspired
by the demons whom Swami Muktananda says he saw?
Or are these simply abnormal mental experiences induced
by excessive meditation, austerities, fasting, drugs or the
unnatural distortion of sexual experience?

Naturally the interpretation of tantric experience depends on one's world-view. If one takes a completely secular
(naturalistic) perspective, then, like Charles S. J. White,
one can legitimately ask 'whether they [the experiences] are
not hysterical or other types of psychologically abnormal
states'.[19] This interpretation of Kundalini and chakras is
supported by Muktananda's own statements. He confesses
that he 'frequently found himself in a condition bordering
on madness or complete physical breakdown'.

Intellectuals such as Fritjof Capra cannot seriously dis-
count the possibility that the mystic experience they advocate is simply an experience of madness, since they are, on
their own account, seeking to go beyond normal rational
human experience. John Custance, who suffered from acute
bouts of mania and was certified as insane, gives the following report in his book *Wisdom, Madness and Folly:
The Philosophy of a Lunatic*. He describes his experience

in words which could be (and are being) uttered by New Age spokespersons such as Shirley MacLaine:

> I feel so close to God, so inspired by His Spirit that in a sense I am God. I see the future, plan the Universe, save mankind; I am utterly and completely immortal; I am even male and female. The whole Universe, animate and inanimate, past, present and future, is within me. All nature and life, all spirits, are co-operating and connected with me; all things are possible. I am in a sense identical with all spirits from God to Satan. I reconcile Good and Evil, create light, darkness, worlds, universes.[20]

The actual experience of Custance seems identical with Muktananda's experience of Kundalini and chakras, though it is not derived from tantric tradition. He says:

> At the onset of phases of manic excitement, I have sometimes noticed the typical symptoms, the pleasurable tingling of the spinal cord and warm sense of well-being in the solar-plexus, long before any reaction in the mental sphere occurred. I had the excited shivers in the spinal column and tingling of the nerves that always herald my manic phases.[21]

If at the physiological and psychological levels Custance's experience is the same as that of the tantrics, then was he really experiencing his divinity? He answers:

> Of course, it is all a dream, a vision, pure imagination if there is such a thing. I know perfectly well in fact that I have no power, that I am of no particular importance and have made rather a mess of my life. I am a very ordinary man and a miserable sinner . . . [22]

It is tempting to dismiss Custance's sad interpretation of his own experience as a Westerner's inability to understand authentic spiritual experience. But the problem is that the tantrics themselves understand their experience as insanity, chosen deliberately:

> Shiva is also the god of ecstasy, of divine madness. He personifies lila as the insanity of god. Tantrics worship Shiva, and they accept their existence as the insanity of god with no questions asked. The tantrics' novel response is to get gleefully insane along with god, as god, in

the midst of existence, and thereby penetrate beyond existence altogether.[23]

However, insanity does not appear to be a complete explanation of the tantric experience, because it does not account for the experiences of thousands of Muktananda's devotees who also experienced the awakening of Kundalini, but without practising any psychotechnologies.

For example, at Muktananda's ashram at Ganeshpuri, near Bombay, I had a long conversation with Frank, an American devotee. He reported that his Kundalini began to rise up automatically while he was sitting in the guru's presence reading a book. He started feeling the pain and had all the other usual mystical experiences associated with Kundalini.

If we rule out the possibility that the disciples were secretly given a diet which included some hallucinogenic chemicals, then an alternative or at least a supplementary explanation would be that when Muktananda saw evil spirits, and a light associated with them, coming to him and entering into him, he really was possessed by them. That would explain how tantrics could see Kali as divinity, and rape or brutal murder as acts of worship.

For a long time many of Muktananda's disciples tolerated his habit of raping young girls on the pretext of checking their virginity or initiating them into Tantra. Finally Mrs Chandra Dinga, one of his most important American devotees and head of the food services, could no longer rationalise his attempt to rape a thirteen year old girl who had been entrusted to the ashram by her parents.

Mrs Dinga started to pull out the skeletons from the god-man's cupboard, an action which greatly contributed to the destruction of the foremost tantric empire of our times. More to the point is her repudiation of tantric sex. As Mrs Chandra said: 'Whether or not you actually ejaculate does not make a fundamental difference. If you are going to be celibate, and you're going to preach celibacy, you don't put it in half way, and then pull it out, you live what you preach.'[24]

The attraction of tantric sex in the West
Despite Mrs Dinga's rejection of tantric sex, many in the

West still find elements of its philosophy and practice attractive for a variety of reasons. In particular, many sensitive young people coming out of a Christian and especially a Roman Catholic tradition experience an instant conversion to 'Eastern' mysticism when they are confronted with the beauty and magic of tantric art. As we have seen, a great part of Tantra, though by no means all of it, seeks the experience of self-realisation through actual or symbolic sexual rites. These are often depicted not in underground pornographic literature, but in explicit erotic sculpture in the temples of religious worship and religious literature.

To portray a goddess naked and in the sexual act is the extreme opposite of Catholic art, where the highest portrayal of women is as a Holy Virgin. By implication, holiness is equated with virginity, and the ascetic denial of sensual pleasure is exalted as a religious virtue.

The Protestant Reformation, however, revolted against this distortion of biblical teaching. It reaffirmed that the Bible taught that Adam and Eve were created as male and female to 'cleave to each other' and be united as 'one flesh' even before they fell into sin. Thus sex was a part of their original blessing in paradise, given not simply for procreation, but also for their enjoyment, for bonding them into oneness, and for personal fulfilment.

The Bible did not exalt Mary because she was a virgin. Her greatness was seen in that she was willing to trust and obey God at great personal cost. She was engaged to be married to Joseph. For her to be willing to get pregnant meant that in order to give birth to the Saviour of the world she was willing to forgo the pleasure and security of marriage. She was not living in a society where being an unmarried mother was acceptable. No one would believe that she had not been sexually immoral and that her conception was the result of the creative work of the Holy Spirit. Mary knew that she would be ridiculed, scorned and punished. The punishment of immorality could extend to being stoned to death.

Mary's greatness lies in the fact that she did not say to the angel, 'It is very kind of God to consider me, but I am already engaged. I am hesitant to risk my marriage, therefore why don't you call someone else to serve you?' Instead, displaying astonishing faith and humility, Mary said, 'I am the Lord's servant. May it be to me as you have said' (Luke 1:38).

This aspect of Protestant revolt did not just result in a Catholic monk like Martin Luther choosing marriage rather than celibacy, it also made it possible for Rembrandt to paint his nude wife waiting for him in bed! But the era of Rembrandt has been history for a long time, even in Protestant circles. Contemporary Protestantism has become too other-worldly to dare to celebrate life. Can anyone deny that Protestant scholars in this century have spent more time explaining away Jesus' first miracle of turning water into wine at a wedding than expounding that miracle as an example of Jesus' teaching that we should enjoy physical life?

Tantra undoubtedly helps liberate those men and women in the West who as a result of unbiblical Christian traditions are unnecessarily bound by guilt and shame about their own sexuality. The most stringent critic will have to admit that there is indeed something liberating about Shirley MacLaine's positive affirmation of her body as a dancer, and of her sexuality as a lover, even if it is agreed that by sharing the beds of married men she is violating the sanctity of their marriages.

The attraction of tantric sex in the East

In the East, too, there are understandable reasons for the attraction of a tantric view of sexuality. Christian religiosity has often been guilty of violating its own doctrine that the physical world was created good; that Adam and Eve were created to live in paradise with God as sexual beings, enjoying one another physically as much as enjoying fellowship with God spiritually and intellectually. Ironically, Hindu-Buddhist thought has rarely affirmed the metaphysical goodness of the physical creation, including our bodies as male and female. On the contrary, it has generally seen physical life as intrinsically evil, bondage and suffering. Therefore the positive contribution of Tantra in a culture such as India's is infinitely greater than what it can ever give to the West. That is why Amaury de Riencourt is one of many who point out that Tantra saved Indian society from itself:

The life-denying vision of the Vedantists would have

destroyed Indian society if the great bulk of the people had not instinctively counteracted it with the help of life-affirming creeds emphasizing the positive side of things . . .

In Tantra we see finally the bankruptcy . . . of the life-denying philosophers . . . The Indian people . . . would have disappeared from the face of the earth if they had all adopted the Vedantic outlook . . . From the 'Apollonian' attitude of the Vedanta, the Tantric devotee travels all the way to the 'Dionysian' acceptance of life with all its joys and sufferings, with its refusal to make a cowardly escape from the coils of a now venerated matter (prakrti) . . . The sensuous and spiritual aspects of the world are now viewed as indivisible, and through full enjoyment of the world (through food, drink and sex), the Tantric disciple (sadhaka) can hope to overcome the world of dualism just as well as those [Vedantins] who frown upon them.[25]

A celebration of life?

We have noted the positive contributions of Tantra in both the East and the West. But does the tantric affirmation of sex equal a celebration of life? 'Even in its affirmations', writes Brooks Alexander, 'Tantra is haunted by paradoxes. The naturalness of human life is affirmed, but only as a means for its ultimate dissolution. Human existence is validated, but only as a platform for leaving humanity behind.'[26]

As Rajneesh says, in sex a tantric does not make love to a woman. He uses her merely as a door, as a means for his own enlightenment. Shirley MacLaine admits that sex in Tantra is not meant to fulfil two people by uniting them into one bond, but rather is used by each partner to discover his or her own completeness as an androgynous being so that each may become complete without their partner.

When a tantric uses a woman to reach maximum arousal for himself, and then withdraws without ejaculation, he may be seeking higher bliss for himself, but he is certainly condemning his partner to frustration.

Tantra does unabashedly embrace human sexuality in its spirituality. But because it uses it for individual gain rather than for binding two people in love, it turns sex into frustration. It does not fulfil men and women as sexual beings, nor does it celebrate life. It seeks to deny or transcend the essence of what we are as male and female. Like Mrs Dinga above, Shirley MacLaine too ends up viewing tantric indulgence as worthless, when she concludes her chapter entitled 'Sex and the Chakras' in this way:

> Many people, in their rapidly blossoming spiritual awakening, are beginning to relate differently to sex than they used to. They describe sexual tension as dissipating because they are becoming more balanced within themselves. They feel as though sex is giving them up – not the other way around. No longer is it so direly necessary to seek and find a partner to fulfill one's physical needs. Self is becoming fulfilled and clarified within. People are feeling more consummated in themselves.[27]

Is it another way of confessing that ultimately tantric sex has become utterly frustrating?

6

DOING ECOLOGY IS BEING HUMAN

The spiritual essence of the ecological vision seems to find its ideal expression in the feminist spirituality advocated by the women's movement, as would be expected from the natural kinship between feminism and ecology, rooted in the age old identification of woman and nature.[1]

The earth, then, is a living system; it functions not just like an organism but actually seems to be an organism – Gaia, living planetary being.[2]

Fritjof Capra

The earth – A danger zone

Many dedicated women and men have struggled hard to generate awareness about the seriousness of today's environmental crisis. To say that our greed, rivalry and short-sightedness have made us the most endangered species today is an understatement. We have risked the very existence of life on this unique planet.

The ozone layer which protects us from the harmful effects of the sun's radiation seems to be thinning in some parts as a consequence of our consumerism and growth-orientated economies. We know that refrigerators, air-conditioners and some packaging materials, when handled improperly, release chloro-fluoro-carbons (CFCs) which destroy the ozone layer. Technological methods of preventing the leaking of CFCs are already available, but many industrialists do not use them because to do so would be to become economically uncompetitive. Our leaders also continue to be so worried about the competitiveness of our national economies that they feel we cannot 'afford' to develop technologies to repair the damage already done. In another decade or so the sunshine may become 'out of bounds' for our children.

Many rivers, lakes and beaches are already out of bounds for them. What was only 'pollution' a decade ago, caused by our industrial wastes, has now become poison. If it was only this, it would be tragic enough. But we are making our waters uninhabitable for marine life as well – and that is catastrophic.

Our planet was a marvellously balanced eco-system in which the plant kingdom inhaled carbon dioxide and released oxygen, while the animal kingdom used that oxygen and exhaled carbon dioxide for the plants. Now in the name of progress we are spewing out massive volumes of carbon dioxide on the one hand, and destroying forests – the 'lungs' of the planet – on the other. The balancing capacity of the eco-system has already reached a critical point. Add to this the fact that the extra carbon dioxide being produced traps the tremendous heat generated by our industry, life-style and modes of transportation, and it is clear that we are already getting a foretaste of what it will be to live in an ecologically imbalanced 'greenhouse'.

Before the military operation 'Desert Storm', President Saddam Hussein of Iraq threatened to blow up the oil and gas fields in Kuwait if a war was thrust upon him. He understood, he said, that fires of such magnitude, even without a nuclear war, may bring about the worst imaginable greenhouse effects around the globe. The ice caps could melt, and some of the most prosperous parts of the world could be submerged under oceans. His retreating army did set hundreds of oil wells on fire, and although his threat proved to be exaggerated it showed what humans are already capable of doing to themselves and their planet.

It would be too alarmist to go on to describe the ecological horrors that await us as nuclear weapons come within the reach of rulers not accountable to anyone but themselves. For those who manage to survive an all out nuclear war, much of the earth will indeed be a danger zone – out of bounds. What are the root causes of our ecological crisis, and what must we do to begin to turn things around?

Bandwagon ecology: Rescuing a goddess in distress?

If there are issues which can unite us in action, in spite of our religio-ideological differences, ecology is undoubtedly one of them. But unfortunately, however respectable, ecology has become a bandwagon to smuggle in a whole variety of belief systems. The following examples will illustrate the point.

Animism

The cabbage worms were causing havoc in Machaelle Wright's garden at Perelandra, Jeffersonton, Virginia, USA. She was against the use of chemical or organic methods of killing any form of life, including pests, so she requested the deva (or nature spirit) of the cabbage worm to be co-operative; it obliged. She soon learned that even the devas of the carrots and rodents are more intelligent than humans – we need therefore to listen to them and obey. Machaelle teaches through demonstration, writing and lectures that our ecological problems will be solved when, to quote the title of her book, we start 'Behaving as if the God in all life mattered'.[3]

What is the deva? In Hinduism the term refers to the celestial beings. In Theosophy it refers to the hierarchy of spirits which help rule the universe. In Zoroastrianism it refers to malevolent spirits, ruled by the god of darkness. In the New Age it seems to refer primarily to spirit beings behind natural phenomena, making the New Age a reincarnation of animism.

This neo-animism, which teaches us to conduct pest control by petitioning the deva of rats instead of using chemicals to kill them, might succeed in taking away our desire to have dominion over nature. But will it leave us with the sense that it is our responsibility carefully to research the causes and cures of imbalances in the eco-system? Are we responsible for caring for and managing nature, or are the devas? When a river is polluted by industrial waste, are we to speak to the deva of the river, or should we address the director of the factory? Machaelle Wright confesses that in the second year, when she again tried to tend her garden merely with the help of 'nature intelligences', the result was an embarrassment. This, she was told, was to teach her some spiritual lessons. What, one wonders, did she do in the third year?

The Findhorn community, situated at Moray Firth, Scotland, where the soil is poor and the weather is unfavourable to agriculture, has had remarkable success in growing forty-pound cabbages and sixty-pound broccoli with the help of devas. However, as David Spangler, an ex-spokesman of Findhorn saw it, the magic of Findhorn was not primarily about ecology, but was about a religious transformation of humankind. 'The myth of Findhorn', he says, is the 'rebirth of man emerging into a totally new consciousness . . . to see the true divine nature of the planet'.[4]

How can one see the divine nature of the planet? It is not a question of a conceptual shift from a materialistic philosophy to a spiritual one. Findhorn advocates our 'identification' with these spirit beings in order to see the 'true nature' of nature.

Robert Ogilvie Crombie, for example, describes his experience of 'identification' with the horned god of pastures, flocks and woods. Called Pan, it has cloven hooves and shaggy legs. Crombie says:

> He stepped behind me and then walked into me so that we became one and I saw the surroundings through his eyes. At the same time, part of me – the recording, observing part – stood aside. The experience was not a form of possession but of identification. The moment he stepped into me, the woods became alive with myriads of beings – elementals, nymphs, dryads, fauns, elves, gnomes, fairies – far too numerous to catalogue.[5]

So, for some, doing ecology means seeking 'nature spirits' – or even being identified with or possessed by them.

Mysticism

In the closing session of the 'Festival for Body, Mind and Spirit' held in the Royal Horticultural Halls of London from 24 to 28 May 1990, England's best known psychic healer, Matthew Manning, led over two thousand people in a healing session. It is not enough, he taught, to heal individuals when our planet itself is sick. It is also impossible to heal the environment in England while the industrial activities on the continent contribute to the pollution in the English Channel and the North Sea and the air over England. The globe itself has to be healed. And that, he said, calls for us to send out the healing vibrations of our united psychic energies to envelope the globe. So we all closed our eyes and 'visualised' harmonious, healthy vibrations going out of the hall, beyond London, beyond England, beyond Europe, to cover the whole earth. If the universe is a process in the divine mind of man, then our psychic energy is certainly enough to restore the eco-balance. Because New Age thought does not make a distinction between consciousness, physical energy and matter, it sees the heart of our environmental problem in terms of a disturbance in the earth's psyche:

> The main problem for the Earth [is] She is feeling unloved ... The dark energy forms that our aggression, anger, fear and resentment have created are the most destructive contribution we have made to the planet's decline ... The Earth is a living being with feelings and emotions ... Strange weather patterns we have experienced in every part of the world are the result of the Earth-Spirit suffering the effects of, particularly, emotional pressures. She is becoming confused. This is making her lose control and the natural order of the planet is failing.[6]

If the ecological problem is a psychic problem, the solution lies in sending positive psychic vibrations to the earth – especially through its leylines and psychic centres. The idea of the earth's leylines corresponds roughly to the Chinese idea behind acupuncture, that the chi or life-energy flows through certain meridians in the human body. The idea of there being psychic points on the earth corresponds to the tantric idea that the human body has certain psychic pulse points.

In the New Age, psychics attempt to find the earth's psychic points and transmit their psychic energy to it. As we saw in the chapter on UFOs, the extra-terrestrials are also said to be working on these leylines and psychic centres.

However, is the present ecological crisis a result of the bad vibrations that we have sent out? Or are they caused by our intentional, and unintentional, foolish actions? If deforestation in India is caused by a nexus of greedy contractors, corrupt officials and unscrupulous politicians, then are we to 'visualise' reforestation – or upright politicians? My intention is not to question the sincerity of a person like Matthew Manning; however, when someone advocates that 'creative visualisation' is the action needed to clean the rivers, to repair the ozone layer, to reforest the Himalayas, etc., is it churlish to wonder whether we are being offered an ecological panacea, or is ecology simply being used as a bandwagon to smuggle in a religious world-view?

Mythical feminism

When James Lovelock, a chemist, and Lynn Margulis, a microbiologist, set forth their hypothesis in Lovelock's book *Gaia*[7] that the earth has to be regarded as a single living organism, they were trying to make sense of the riddles of nature that scientists have known of for a long time.

The earth just does not seem to obey the laws of physics. The second law of thermodynamics states that all systems tend toward increasing entropy, or disorganisation. If so, the calculations indicate that after five thousand million years a cold, lifeless inertia should have overcome the earth. Yet why does it continue to bloom with life? Why are the seas not as salty as the computers calculate they ought to be? Or why is there not as much carbon dioxide in the atmosphere as mathematics says there should be, given the supposed age of the earth and our heroic efforts to generate the greenhouse effect? One plausible explanation, according to Lovelock, is that the laws regulating the planetary system are not those of physics and chemistry, but of biology. This would then imply that the planet – its solid portion, or lithosphere, its biological portion, or biosphere, and its atmosphere – is a single integrated and living system, as capable of renewing itself as are our bodies. Lovelock boldly goes on to the logical conclusion of his line of thinking, to assert that our planet is a living being – the largest living being in our solar system. Recognising that his hypothesis represents a renaissance of an ancient Greek myth, that the earth is a goddess, Gaia, he then goes ahead to name it as such.

Lovelock himself does not seem to go all the way as to look upon the earth as a sentient being, a surrogate God.[8]

But that is exactly how many in the New Age interpret him. Authors such as Fritjof Capra see the answer to our ecological crisis in this hypothesis. Their argument, though sophisticated and backed by great detail, is in fact quite simple: men have exploited the earth because they have considered it to be non-living and therefore inferior to themselves. Capra says: 'Our attitudes will be very different when we realize that the environment is not only alive but also mindful, like ourselves.'[9] His reasoning is that if an attitude of religious awe towards Mother Earth as a goddess replaces the desire to dominate nature, then there is a greater chance we will give better care to the planet.

There is an obvious problem with this view: Is it in fact true that human beings tend not to exploit what they consider to be alive and mindful? We acknowledge forests, foetuses, children, 'lower' castes, women, 'blacks', employees, etc., to be very much alive; but does that, by itself, prevent us from abusing and exploiting them? Do we not exploit our mothers, and even God? It needs no documentation to show that Jews, Christians, Muslims, Hindus, Buddhists, animists, etc., have all been guilty, whether privately or institutionally, of exploiting what they believed to be divinity. Gods and goddesses are in fact much easier to exploit – they have no fundamental rights guaranteed by our constitutions.

The argument of 'feminist spirituality', that people would become more tender towards the earth (as well as towards women) if it was looked upon as a goddess, is unfortunately not backed by history. For example, it was in Calcutta, the heart of the goddess cult in the Indian sub-continent, where two hundred years ago William Carey, the first Protestant missionary in India, started to fight against the evil of *sati* – widow burning – the ultimate denial of individuality to women in a culture which calls woman devi or goddess. Sadly, in his fight for women's rights Carey was pitched against the entire religious establishment of the goddess cult. It is interesting to note that he fought for women's rights because he believed that they were made in the image of our heavenly Father – who is neither male nor female.

Just as Carey believed that we cannot love the Father without respecting women who reflect his image, he was also convinced that we cannot worship the creator without valuing his creation. Therefore, because of his 'patriarchal' world-view, he became the first man to plead for the forests of India, and started a forestry programme in his seminary at Serampore. Worship of the goddess did not result in a concern for the environment in India. But Carey's journal, *Friend of India*, pressurised the government to appoint Dr Brandis of Bonn to care for the forests of Burma and Dr Clegham those of South India.

To be fair to Capra, we have to give him credit for admitting honestly that in presenting feminist spirituality as a basis for ecological reform he is not offering scientific truth, but a myth. In a lengthy interview with Mike McGrath entitled 'Zen and the Art of Changing the World', Capra admits candidly:

> At the beginning, I still thought, well the Old Physics – the Newtonian worldview – has influenced medicine and economics and everything, so now let's build a new set of Sciences patterned after the New Physics. Then I changed my way of thinking, shifting away from physics as the model for other sciences, and as the source of our metaphors about reality . . . The new 'paradigm' or the new vision of reality is an ecological vision.[10]

Simply paraphrased, Capra is saying that in earlier times life and society were built on what was thought to be the truth about the universe. But now the mechanistic worldview has been shown to be untrue. At first Capra thought the New Physics (or his mystical interpretation of it, expounded in his book *The Tao of Physics*[11]) could provide an alternative intellectual basis for building life and society. Upon realising the new physics cannot be such a basis, he has given up attempts to build life on truth, and he now builds life on truth, and he now builds life on what appears ecological to him.

But, what is ecological? Should we become goddess worshippers simply because it is said to be ecological? Are we still grappling with straightforwardly ecological issues, or has ecology been subtly turned into a religious issue? This is not to imply that the ecological crisis should not force us to question our belief systems and seek a spirituality that is ecological. Far from it: our ideas influence our choices. Therefore ideas that have shaped the present anti-ecological culture must be exposed and rejected in favour of true ideas. But this cannot be allowed to mean that any ideology can claim our allegiance simply because it raises the banner of ecology and differs from the previous ones. A belief system which is true to the way the cosmos actually is would be truly ecological. A viewpoint cannot be accepted as true simply because it claims to be ecological. Men might decide to act heroically when they see a damsel in distress. But if the earth is to be revered as a goddess because of its amazing capacity to maintain its life-supporting temperature, water and air, in spite of the odds against it, including the laws of physics and chemistry, it is hard to imagine why we should see her as a goddess in distress in need of rescue. Would it not be more reasonable just to worship her and trust her to take care of both herself and us, who are no more than cells in her body?

Ecology as activism *vs* ecology as being human

The essence of my argument in this chapter is that to be ecological is simply to be human. Human civilisation, or un-civilisation, has become anti-environmental primarily because we have lost a basic understanding of who we are and what the purpose of human work is.

As a family we have struggled to save a few infants who would have become victims of 'female infanticide'. Our fourteen year old daughter Nivedit has helped look after such children. 'When I finish my studies,' Nivedit says, 'I am going to serve and teach children.' Anandit, who is twelve, says, 'I want to be a veterinarian, because grown-ups are so cruel to animals in India.' Quite instinctively both these children have assumed that work is something that enables you to express your love towards people (orphans) or nature (animals). 'Work' is in other words what bonds us to our social and physical environment.

As Nivedit and Anandit grow up they will inevitably face pressures to change their outlook and conform to 'adult' attitudes towards work. For most people today work means 'a job' – a source of earning one's livelihood. When work is understood as making money, then the human self is valued in terms of economic success. You are a successful human being if you make more money than others, and more quickly. As a young graduate put it recently. 'I will remain unemployed rather than accept *that* low-paid job. Working for *that* firm will lower my market value.' For him, his worth was equal to the money he made.

For many other people, especially professionals, work often means 'a career'. The purpose of work for these people is to earn self-esteem through progress in their chosen profession. The measure for this progress includes social standing, prestige and ever-expanding power over others.

These attitudes towards work look upon the external world of other people and material resources as things to be used for one's self. They tend to isolate the self from its physical and social relationships. Ironically, instead of fulfilling us as human beings, they tend to be destructive – both of our self-esteem as well as of our relationships.

It has been observed that by 1981 almost 60 percent of all retirements in the United States were voluntary. For many of these people, work had not become a lifelong interest, so they were trying out full-time leisure as an alternative means of personal fulfilment. Their reasons for quitting work were expressed differently. Some people were just 'sick of working'. Others 'hated' the pressure. Many had 'paid their dues'. Most wanted to 'get out of the rat race'. Still others said that they had retired because they 'never thought their work was socially necessary'.[12]

These attitudes to work lead not only to frustration, despair, high blood pressure or heart disease, but in the long run they also become socially and ecologically destructive, making social or ecological activism a necessity – a safety valve.

Ecological activism, which translates environmental concerns into specific projects such as social forestry or the harnessing of solar power, as well as issue-based agitations such as organised protests against a proposed nuclear reactor or a massive dam that would submerge tropical forests, is good and necessary. However, these are essentially attempts to douse the fire after human foolishness has already struck the match.

There is a third and a much stronger perspective on what work really is – a 'calling'. Historically, this attitude to work grew out of the biblical understanding that God took Adam (man) out of the *adamah* (the earth) to be its caretaker. From this perspective of 'calling' the purpose of work is neither self-aggrandisement nor a search for self-esteem. As the Westminister Catechism puts it, 'The chief end of man is to glorify God.' When I work with a sense of calling, I work not for myself, but for my God. When I understand that 'I', as a son of Adam, was taken by God from the earth and made to care for the earth, then work intrinsically means to take care of the earth. Ecology thus cannot be a matter of specialist interest or projects, but becomes the essence of being human. In this approach, the self is fulfilled not by isolating it from the social and physical environment, but by reaching out to it in a spirit of commitment, and responsibility.

If the origin and destiny of Adam is indeed intertwined with that of *adamah*, how did we manage not to only isolate ourselves from it, but to pitch ourselves against its interests as well? What must we do to set things right?

The returning point

Fritjof Capra's book *The Turning Point*, which has also been made into a film, *Mindwalk*, has become something of a manifesto for the New Age movement and a source of inspiration for the feminist spirituality of theologians such as Matthew Fox. It contains, among other things, Capra's ecological vision. Besides the proposal that feminist spirituality be developed for the sake of ecology, Capra also discusses two other aspects of the ecological problem. The first which receives major attention is our modern, secular outlook, which has been shaped by the teachings of René Descartes and Isaac Newton. This views the universe, man and his society as machines. This world-view, Capra thinks, is at the root of all our problems. Therefore the book issues a call to turn the present culture away from this mechanistic outlook to a holistic world-view based on the General Systems Theory.

The second cause of the ecological crisis which Capra identifies is the 'human' problem. Capra's world-view, how-ever, does not permit him to identify it as a moral problem. It therefore receives no more than a few passing references.

Ecology and General Systems Theory

When physicists such as Einstein were struggling to find a 'Unified Field Theory' which could explain all physical phenomena, an Austrian-born biologist, Ludwig Van Bertalanffy, proposed, in the 1930s, that a true theory which explains everything could not be constructed merely by studying physics. He believed there are a given number of natural laws that determine the functioning of all systems. 'All systems' include physical, organic, psychological and social elements, and even conceptual thought. He argued that a theory that would give a unified explanation of the organising principles common to all phenomena could only emerge on the basis of a mathematically precise interdisciplinary study of all systems. Prior to Bertalanffy, in 1925, Jan Christian Smuts had already advocated a holistic perspective in his treatise *Holism and Evolution*. But it was Bertalanffy's rigorous scientific basis for this approach which triggered the whole gamut of interdisciplinary studies and the holistic movement of the 1950s.

Even though we are still nowhere near formulating an all-encompassing theory, the exercise has already yielded many useful results. Some aspects of the holistic health movement are a good example of this. It is obviously folly to focus all medical effort exclusively on disease after it is already in the body, rather than looking at the psychological, dietary, social and cultural factors which may have contributed to the problem, and developing preventive medicine.

As in medicine, so with the economy. Economists are becoming increasingly aware that they consistently fail to understand, predict and control macro-economic problems because they have artificially isolated the discipline of economics from the rest of life. They have focused on a narrow field which exists as an independent entity only in the textbooks of economics. The economics of quick unlimited growth creates as many problems as it solves. Economists have therefore begun to address the economic issues in the context of larger socio-ecological factors. The economist Ernst Schumacher brought some of these issues to the attention of the international community through his groundbreaking book *Small is Beautiful* (1973), in which he argued for an 'economics as if people mattered'.

Capra feels that the earlier attitude of isolating economics from the rest of life and ecological issues was a result of the Cartesian outlook. By contrast, systemic thinking promotes a more integrated approach. To give up narrow specialisation in favour of a systemic approach is the crucial *conceptual* turning point for Capra. Simultaneously to turn away from a nuclear age to a solar age is his *practical* proposal, argued with considerable conviction and backed up by considerable research.

Reading Capra and other New Age authors, one cannot help but feel that both the 'mechanistic' outlook and 'patriarchal' values have become the favourite whipping boys of many New Age thinkers. Laying on them the major, if not the exclusive, responsibility for our ecological crisis is at best an incomplete analysis. A goddess-worshipping Indian village whose world-view is not mechanistic but organic and animistic is often just as anti-ecological as the mechanistic, patriarchal urban West. A deeper problem is that while 'systemic' metaphysics may account for the harmony and integrity of creation, it cannot explain the obvious disharmony and alienation in creation which is the crux of the problem that ecology seeks to address: Why has humanity turned against nature and itself?

The overlooked dimension
Capra dismisses Darwinian and neo-Darwinian evolutionary theories on several grounds. One is that a central tenet of the doctrine that evolution takes place because of a 'struggle for existence' is untrue, as well as anti-ecological. He berates 'social Darwinists' for seeing life exclusively in terms of competition, struggle and destruction, because they have 'helped create a philosophy that legitimates exploitation and the disastrous impact of our technology on the natural environment'.[13] While species undoubtedly compete with each other, Capra argues that such competition usually takes place within a wider context of co-operation, so that the larger system is kept in balance.

Capra admits that human beings are the only exception to this rule of co-operation in nature: 'Excessive aggression, competition and destructive behaviour are predominant only in the human species and have to be dealt with in terms of cultural values rather than being "explained" pseudo-scientifically as inherently natural phenomena.'[14]

In another (perhaps the only other) mention of this human dimension of the ecological problem, Capra admits that this aberration in man is deep, but still he asks us to gloss over it rather than face it:

> 'New Age' movements have shown clear sign of exploitation, fraud, sexism, and excessive economic expansion, quite similar to those observed in the corporate world, but these aberrations are transitory manifestations of our cultural transformation and should not prevent us from appreciating the genuine nature of the current shift of values [i.e., from the ethos of *competition* of Darwinism to that of *co-operation* in the systemic perspective].[15]

If this exclusively human aberration (which the New Age movements have not been able to eradicate) has already created an ecological crisis which the planet had not hitherto faced in its supposedly billions of years of existence, then can it be glossed over that easily, as merely a transitory phase of cultural values inherited from a neo-Darwinian outlook? Were not human beings the same before Darwin, Newton and Descartes? Do they not behave the same way in matriarchal tribes and goddess-worshipping societies?

In another context Capra himself admits that it may be more than a question of cultural values, when he approvingly refers to Paul MacLean's theory of three brains in man, which has been popularised by Arthur Koestler.[16] Koestler says that one of evolution's 'countless mistakes' is that it has given three brains to man. When our ancestors were reptilians, they evolved poisonous aggressiveness as a necessary means of self-defence. This is the 'archaic' brain in us. Two other brains were added to this aggressive reptilian core during the process of evolution. While this aggressiveness was all right when we were crocodiles, and later on horses, today it has become self-destructive because with the help of nuclear power we will destroy not only our enemies, but ourselves as well.[17]

In spite of this one-off slip into a 'pseudo-scientific' explanation for the 'aberration' in man, Capra's overall position is that there is nothing inherently wrong with human beings, because they are a part of the goddess Gaia, which is itself a part of the process in the universal mind.

Therefore, if there is any problem at all, it stems from the passing cultural values inherent in the mechanistic world-view of Descartes and Newton.

This, I suggest, is too superficial a way to explain the human factor in our crisis. Capra ignores it because his world-view does not permit him to consider the moral dimension of the universe and human nature. Even if it turns out that one day a General Systems Theory gives a unifying explanation to all the phenomena of the cosmos, such a theory will have to explain, not contradict, the obvious fact that it is possible for humans to know what is true and good and yet choose that which is false and harmful to themselves and to their descendants. If our world-view cannot deal with the human capacity to make wrong choices, we cannot hope to cope with the problems that our choices create.

This, I propose, has to be the *returning point* from the road down which Capra and others are taking us. In emphasising the centrality of the moral dimensions of the ecological crisis I am not seeking to minimise the necessity of turning from a mechanistic/reductionistic outlook to a holistic outlook. But since that aspect has already been so well covered by Capra and others, I will here seek to focus primarily on the relationship between morality and ecology.

Has man evolved or fallen into the ecological morass?

If human beings have a capacity to make choices that are wrong and destructive for themselves, others and the 'divine' environment, then it is possible to imagine the likelihood that man has 'fallen' rather than evolved into the present mess. This is the biblical view. According to this view, man is not intrinsically bad in the sense that evolution made him inherently defective. He was created good, in God's own image, but he was given a finite and independent self, with an independent mind and will capable of independent thoughts and choices. Man's choices are significant. They have real consequences – beneficial or harmful. Man is not a zero.

Before we examine the possibility of the 'fallenness' of man, it will be helpful to notice a few other relevant features of this viewpoint.

The nature of moral law

When a mother says to her child, 'We will not take you swimming unless you make your bed,' she is affirming that 'family' is not simply a biological or a social unit, but also a moral one. Breakdown of morals means temporary or permanent disintegration of the family. Moral laws are not mechanical, but personal, i.e., the laws of persons in authority – in this case the mother.

A made-up bed and swimming have no cause and effect relationship in the mechanistic sense of causation. By contrast, the law of gravity is an example of a mechanical law. If you jump from a roof you will come down. The results are predictable. But the consequences of disobeying the mother are unpredictable. She could say, 'You will come swimming, but will not get any ice-cream.' The logical connection between a made-up bed and swimming is a moral and personal one. Children must learn the hierarchic and moral nature of the family through obeying their parents. Disobedience does not result merely in natural cause and effect consequences, as the theory of karma postulates, but also in particular consequences such as no swimming – which reminds the child that parents have to be obeyed. Children are dependent on their parents, but they do not exist as a creation in the minds of their parents. They have an existence of their own. They can choose to go against their parents' will, even though they know that their good and happiness lies in being at one with their parents through obedience, love and trust.

Human beings have a similar relationship to God. They are dependent on God. They can have an interpersonal oneness with him because they are made as independent selves, similar to God's own infinite self. Personal oneness with God means a harmonious relationship of loving obedience. Disobedience is possible, but it has consequences.

The earth and the earthling

As we have seen, in the Hebrew language of the Old Testament the word for the earth is *adamah*. God created *adamah* outside of his own being and saw that it was good. After creating the wonderful variety of life on the *adamah*, God separated Adam not from his own being, but from the *adamah*: 'The Lord God formed the man from the dust of the ground and breathed into his nostrils the breath of life, and the man became a living being ... The Lord God took the man and put him in the garden of Eden to work it and take care of it' (Gen. 2:7,15). Eden means 'delight' or 'bliss', implying that God's intention for man was not the deprivation of slums, but the bounty of paradise. The source of bliss was not inside human consciousness, but outside of Adam in his natural and social environment, as well as in friendship with God.

To minister means to serve
The earthling Adam was taken out of the earth (*adamah*) not so as to live in heaven as God's servant, but on earth as its servant or minister.

All creatures that live off the earth also minister to it, as Capra points out. But the earthling was created as the pre-eminent servant. It is for this reason that we do not ask the lions to save the endangered species in the forest, but we rightly ask human beings to do so. One cannot be held to be pre-eminently responsible without having the authority to govern. God gave to the planet's minister/servant the required authority to manage or govern it: 'Be fruitful and increase in number; fill the earth and subdue it. Rule over the fish of the sea and the birds of the air and over every living creature that moves on the ground' (Gen. 1:28).

Most people will agree that human beings (who are endowed with greater rationality than other creatures) need to be governed by other human beings. If some human beings should have authority over other human beings, why should no human have authority over non-human creatures? True, we have abused our authority over the planet. But human rulers have also abused their authority over the people they govern. No responsible New Age leader argues that a president or a prime minister or a king should not rule over a nation because historically the idea of ruling and governing has been exploited ruthlessly. Why then should we say that the idea of governing the earth must be abandoned because it has been abused?

One tragic consequence of 'the fall' of human beings is that they abuse their ministership – so much so that as biblical influence has declined the word 'minister' or governor has almost lost its original meaning of 'servant'. What in India we call a 'maidservant' was earlier in Christianised cultures called a 'governess'. As Jesus, who washed his disciples' feet, put it:

> You know that the rulers of the Gentiles lord it over them, and their high officials exercise authority over them. Not so with you. Instead, whoever wants to become great among you must be your servant, and whoever wants to be first must be your slave – just as the Son of Man did not come to be served, but to serve, and to give his life as a ransom for many. (Matt. 20:25–8)

Three implications

This view of the relationship between Adam and *adamah* has at least three important implications for us. First, the earthling is taken out of the earth, and therefore is dependent on the earth. If the earth suffers, he suffers too. Second, just as when the prime minister of a nation becomes wicked the whole nation suffers, so also when the planet's minister becomes wicked the whole planet suffers. Adam and *adamah*, though distinct, are nevertheless interrelated. Third, human authority over the planet is delegated authority. In putting man in charge of his garden, God was not abdicating his sovereignty. He knew that man needed a constant reminder that he was the gardener, not the owner of what he surveyed. Therefore God's first act after putting Adam in the garden was to command him, 'You are free to eat from any tree in the garden; but you must not eat from the tree of the knowledge of good and evil, for when you eat of it you will surely die' (Gen. 2:16–17).

Man was not commanded to refrain from eating because the fruit was poisonous, but because he needed a daily reminder that he lived in a hierarchical universe where he had authority over some things and was himself under authority. His relationship with God was to be like a child's relationship with his parents – one of love, trust and obedience. Loving a superior necessarily implies obedience. A child cannot live simultaneously in disobedience and in the warmth of parental love. Nor could a servant disobey his master and claim to love him. In the same way that a family is a moral unit, so the cosmos is a moral unit where human beings have to obey their creator. Disobedience destroys relationships and brings about alienation.

Adam and Eve disobeyed God and fell from harmony into the disharmony we see around us. The visual reminder of the forbidden tree is no longer necessary because the unhappy moral consequences of that disobedience are all around us, hinting that we do not live only in a physical and social world, but also in a moral universe with a given hierarchy and rules, The breakdown of moral law causes alienation and disintegration.

In recent years many thinkers have argued that in order to recover an ecological consciousness we need to realise the integrity of creation. Likewise I feel that without a true understanding of alienation we cannot hope to find a genuine basis for ecology.

Marks of alienation

The early chapters of Genesis give us an explanation of the alienation that we see both in humanity and in the natural world around us.

Alienation from ourselves

Shame
The Bible says that before Adam and Eve ate the forbidden fruit they were at ease with themselves: 'The man and his wife were both naked, and they felt no shame' (Gen. 1:25).

The first consequence of their disobedience was that their consciences were activated. They were no longer at ease with themselves: 'They realised that they were naked; so they sewed fig leaves together and made coverings for themselves' (Gen. 3:7).

Capra is right, man is the only species in which excessive aggression, unnecessary competition and destructive behaviour predominate. But that is not the only way in which man is different. Man alone wears clothing, because he alone is ashamed of his 'nakedness'. Is our sense of shame at our naked bodies caused purely by social conditioning? Some in every generation have tried to throw off clothes – to live naturally and consistently with their belief that man is only an animal. Parents who try to be 'natural' in

front of their children by practising nudism find that their
children feel the parents are unnatural! Nudist communes
don't succeed. Clothes remain daily reminders that man is
no longer 'natural' – no longer as he was created.

Guilt

Adam and Eve hid from the Lord 'among the trees of the
garden' because they were afraid (Gen. 3:8–10). In spite of all
his searching for God, when fallen man actually confronts
the holy God his instinctive response is often, 'Go away
from me, Lord; I am a sinful man!' (Luke 5:8; cf. Isa. 6:5).

One can proclaim the metaphysical oneness of the universe and the intrinsic divinity of man, but it is hard to
deny man's inner alienation – his condemnation of himself.
The best we can do is to try to explain it away as social
conditioning. But when we dispense with notions of 'guilt'
and 'conscience' we turn ourselves not into divinity, but
into beasts, removing the last traces of the beauty of our hu-
manness. Our alienation from ourselves gives us clues about
the ultimate cause of alienation in the natural world.

Alienation from animals

Each time we admire a bird and it flies away from us we are
confronted with the reality that birds do not instinctively
feel at one with us – which they should surely do if the
mystics were right. We have to make efforts to win their
confidence. But why?

Before his disobedience all the animals came to Adam and
he named them and sought their partnership (Gen. 2:19–20).
At that time man did not eat meat, for he was given only
'seed-bearing plants . . . and every tree that has fruit with
seed in it', while the animals were given 'every green plant'
(e.g., grass) for food (Gen. 1:29–30).

The authority to rule over animals had been given to
man even before the fall (Gen. 1:26–8), but it did not include the right to eat them or the food that was given to
animals (i.e., the green plants). Animals did not fear human
authority. Nor was there competition for food between man
and animals. However, after one of the animals tempted
man, *all* animals came under 'the curse'. God said to the
serpent: 'Cursed are you above all the livestock and all
the wild animals!' (Gen. 3:14).

Man remained a vegetarian even after the fall, though his diet now included green plants which had earlier been given exclusively to animals (Gen. 3:18). This started a competition for food between man and animals. Constitutionally we are frugivorous, made to eat seed-bearing plants and fruit. We can generally eat them without having to cook them. But green plants usually have to be cooked or at least seasoned with dressings to be made edible. As our wickedness grew, so did the alienation between animal and human life. The flood came and Noah, a righteous man, was called to build a boat to save the animals. Yet the alienation between human beings and animals became worse after the flood. God said:

> The fear and dread of you will fall upon all the beasts of the earth and all the birds of the air, upon every creature that moves along the ground, and upon all the fish of the sea; they are given into your hands. Everything that lives and moves will be food for you. Just as I gave you the green plants, I now give you everything.
>
> But you must not eat meat that has its lifeblood still in it. (Gen. 9:2–4)

When we eat a non-vegetarian dish, we cannot just glibly thank God for it. As we will see in the next chapter, the permission to eat meat was granted under exceptional circumstances. The flood had destroyed all vegetation. The animals would have starved or turned carnivorous anyway. By eating some of their offspring, all the species, including human beings, could survive. Adam was allowed to eat the fruit of the garden because he tended the garden. Noah was allowed to eat the animals because he served and saved them. When we use someone or something without serving them, or taking care of them, we exploit them.

At that very time when God allowed human beings to eat animals, God himself took care to protect the interest of animals. When he said that the fear and dread of man would fall upon the animals, he meant that they would no longer innocently trust human beings, but would take care to protect themselves. In other words, God did not cease being interested in protecting the lives of animals after the flood. Nor can we assume that the authority given to Noah to eat meat has been passed on to us without also assuming that the responsibility given to Noah to save animals rests upon us too. The later command not to eat blood was intended to be a reminder that we do not own the lives of the animals. Our rights and authority are derived and limited. Non-vegetarianism is thus another reminder, like clothing, that we live after the fall, and that the integrity of the creation has been fractured. There is alienation between animals and us. This alienation ought to remind us of our wickedness and encourage us to a life of repentance and obedience, as it did in Noah's time. The biblical concept of righteousness still implies care for animals: 'A righteous man cares for the needs of his animal, but the kindest acts of the wicked are cruel' (Prov. 12:10).

Womanhood and the alienation of the sexes

An evil that is common both to patriarchal cultures and to matriarchal tribes is the oppression of women both by men and by fellow women. It was mothers, as often as fathers, who sacrificed their infant daughters to the life-giving goddess Ganges, as well as to the life-taking goddess Kali, in the time of William Carey. It was not a change of religious ideas *per se*, but political action which put an end to such religious rituals. Gradually the religious ideas had to be changed too.

Yet even in cultures where women have never been oppressed as they were in goddess-worshipping India, and where they are more liberated now than during any other era of human history known to us, women still 'feel' oppressed. Can this be explained purely as psychological or social conditioning?

Feminism in the West fought for and has largely won the right of women to equal job opportunities and financial independence. Many women have convincingly proved themselves to be as capable as any man in executive leadership and entrepreneurial roles, yet not without a price. Many women experience what Dr June Singer, a Jungian psychoanalyst, calls 'the sadness of successful women'.[18] Dr Singer's long experience of counselling successful women in Palo Alto, California, led her to conclude that in order to achieve success in the economic sphere women often sacrifice a very special aspect of their feminine psyche – relationships as wives, mothers, grandmothers, etc. The glamour of success and the joy of achievement do not adequately compensate for the loss of deep family relationships, however much money some of these successful women spend on psychoanalysts or psycho-technologies. This is not to imply that family life is by itself wholly fulfilling. Ultimately, if women, like men, are made for God, they cannot be fulfilled without a vital, personal relationship with God.

The biblical account of the fall of human beings focuses on two noteworthy features in this regard.

The blessing of children and the curse of labour pain
A woman's ability to give birth is a part of the 'original blessing' of creation. In bearing the child for nine months in her womb, the woman begins to bear the family in her psyche. But labour pain is a reminder that we live after the fall, when 'natural birth' is no longer the norm, because one consequence of the fall was the judgement, 'I will greatly increase your pains in childbearing; with pain you will give birth to children' (Gen. 3:16).

The universal fact of labour pain which unfortunately accompanies such a natural event as childbirth should cause us to consider the story of the fall more seriously. If labour pain is 'natural', in the sense of being a bio-physical necessity, then why do all species not experience it? If it is 'unnatural' in the sense that it can be easily removed, why is it so universal a human experience?

It is right to desire to be delivered from the curse, to push back the consequences of the fall, to minimise labour pain. But harsh as it sounds, the reality of labour pain also acts as a 'reminder' to women – and to men – of the consequences of human disobedience towards God.

Oneness and alienation in marriage
God's intention in marriage was that a man will leave his father and mother and be united to his wife: no separation, no divorce, but 'oneness'. This 'oneness' included equality and freedom, with both man and woman directly and equally under the authority of God – acknowledging the given hierarchy of the moral universe. Before the fall it was man who needed the woman. God said, 'It is not good for the man to be alone' (Gen. 2:18).

Disobedience – that is, the refusal to acknowledge the hierarchy – affected the integrity of marriage. God said to

Eve: 'Your desire will be for your husband, and he will rule over you' (Gen. 3:16). A woman's desire for the exclusive possession of her husband is an essential psychological ingredient which makes the family a natural organism rather than merely another social organisation. Even if a husband is careful not to exploit the desire of his wife for him, but is grateful for it, a feeling of dependence followed by a feeling of oppression, often come as corollaries of that possessiveness. This is true even if women choose not to have husbands but only lovers. The oneness of the sexes is no longer what it was meant to be. Since Eve rejected God as her head, she is now saddled with the husband (or the lover) as her head. Many New Age women have tried to get away from this by having neither husbands nor lovers, but 'soul mates'. The story unfortunately remains the same. The relationship works only if one of the partners – usually the woman – is prepared to accept a subordinate status.

Sondra Ray, a New Age leader and the creator of Loving Relationships Training, abandoned monogamy after her divorce. She enjoys the freedom of loving relationships with many partners. However, she recognises that even those relationships cannot last without submission. Bobby is one of her partners in the training programme and their relationship works. Sondra describes the secret:

> One day I looked at Bobby, knowing we were in this forever together and knowing that we had to get along 24 hours a day in all kinds of tough situations, and knowing that we were both extremely powerful and knowing that I did not want this relationship messed up, and it could blow up with all that energy unless I thought of *something* to handle it. I *finally* said 'Bobby, I think we should play this game. In order to keep it from blowing up. Let's agree to a game where we each surrender to the highest spiritual thought at any moment. If you have it I surrender and *get off* . . . my former position. If I have the highest spiritual thought you surrender' . . . The only time Bobby ever screams at me is when my mind is stuck . . . I try to make sure he never has to scream at me very long and very often. The minute he starts screaming I realize my mind must be stuck . . . He has always been right.[19]

If such surrender was only a game that an actress played in a movie it would not matter. The tragedy is that it is not a 'game' but a curse.

In the biblical account of the origins of man and woman, Eve's sin is that she refuses to acknowledge the hierarchy in which she and Adam are accountable to, and must obey, God. This is the moral form of the universe which gives freedom. She will now have to learn personal freedom and fulfilment through the daily acknowledgement of hierarchy in sexual relationships and the family.

Feminists are right to oppose the tendency to institutionalise this curse. Our goal should be to seek deliverance from it, so that women may enjoy ever-increasing freedom and equality of authority, and thus make their full contribution to life on this planet. For the Christian, redemption from sin includes ever-increasing deliverance from this curse of alienation within marriage. But marriage has fallen and must be redeemed so as to become a partnership of equality. The biblical teaching is that we do not need to live under the curse, because Jesus Christ bore the curse on the cross. However, redemption comes from the obedience of faith. Therefore feminist attempts to redeem the situation by refusing to acknowledge the social consequences of the fall can only produce greater alienation and harsher consequences – separation, divorce, single-parent families, poverty, depression, emotionally handicapped children, homosexuality, prostitution, AIDS, etc. The breakdown of the family is as big a problem as the breakdown of the ozone layer. For some people environmental activism becomes an escape from an unhappy relationship at home. That in itself may be a creative way of transforming a personal tragedy, but if we cannot save our families, our children are likely to be far more destructive to our cultural and natural environment than our own generation has been.

Alienation between Adam and *adamah*
If disobedience turned the pleasures of childbirth into a painful experience for women, then it turned the blessing of work into the pain of daily toil for men. God said to Adam:

> Cursed is the ground because of you;
>   through painful toil you will eat of it

all the days of your life.
It will produce thorns and thistles for you,
    and you will eat the plants of the field.
By the sweat of your brow
    you will eat your food
until you return to the ground. (Gen. 3:17–19)

The whole planet has suffered the consequences of its first governor's refusal to acknowledge the sovereignty of his creator. But man is the only 'animal' that has to endure painful toil in order to eat. While other animals just eat what the earth produces, man has to toil and sweat – a daily reminder that if he wishes to 'govern' he must first be willing to be governed by God.

Work was a part of the original blessing (Gen. 1:28; 2:15). But since the fall work now includes having to deal with 'thorns and thistles', whether we are out in the fields, sitting in an air-conditioned office or in the cool of the Himalayas. There are always thorns by our sides if not below us or above us. The more privileged our work is, the greater the pressure. If your thorns and thistles do not make your feet and fingers bleed, they give you high blood pressure and heart attacks – constant reminders that we have not evolved to our present heights, but have fallen into them!

This curse, more than any other, presupposes the interdependence of Adam and *adamah*. Man is not only a ruler over the earth, but is also dependent on it. If he uses it in a way he is not supposed to – e.g., eating the fruit he is told not to eat – he hurts the earth as well as himself. If you overstep your authority over the earth, it rebounds on you. If you refuse to bow before God's authority over you, you will not get spontaneous obedience from those under you.

This curse, visible to us every day, is another reminder that moral law is not a natural cycle of cause and effect, as the theory of karma postulates. The consequences of disobedience can be devastating and final. The prophet Isaiah echoes this aspect when he laments:

See, the Lord is going to lay waste the earth
    and devastate it;
he will ruin its face
    and scatter its inhabitants . . .
The earth will be completely laid waste

and totally plundered.
The Lord has spoken this word.
The earth dries up and withers,
    the world languishes and withers,
    the exalted of the earth languish.
The earth is defiled by its people;
    they have disobeyed the laws,
violated the statutes
    and broken the everlasting covenant.
Therefore a curse consumes the earth;
    its people must bear their guilt. (Isa. 24:1, 3–6)

The psalmist elucidates this perspective on the relationship between ecology and morality in these words:

He [God] turned rivers into a desert,
    flowing springs into thirsty ground,
and fruitful land into a salt waste,
    because of the wickedness of those who lived there.
                                            (Ps. 107:33–4)

Happily for us, the opposite also happens when we turn away from evil and return to God to follow righteousness. The psalmist continues:

He turned the desert into pools of water
    and the parched ground into flowing springs.
There he brought the hungry to live,
    and they founded a city where they could settle.
They sowed fields and planted vineyards
    that yielded a fruitful harvest;
he blessed them . . . (Ps. 107:35–8)

Death – The final alienation

Are birth and death, creation and destruction the normal rhythms of nature? If death is normal, why do we mourn, build memorials and long for immortality? Death is not normal. If simple one-celled organisms such as bacteria and amoebas are indeed our original ancestors, as the evolutionists claim, then these do not die 'natural' deaths. They reproduce by cell-division, which means they just live on in their progeny. If bacteria have existed on earth for four billion years, as they say, then the bacteria today are the same as those which lived billions of years ago. And if for three billion years there was no other form of life but them,

then that means that for three-quarters of the time that life
has existed on the planet, death did not exist. How can life
evolve into death? It can only degenerate in order to die.

Human beings were not meant to die. God breathed the
spirit of life into them and permitted them to eat fruit from
the tree of life, which was removed from Eden only after
the fall. He warned them that they would lose life if they
did not acknowledge the moral nature of the universe, and
ate from the tree of the knowledge of good and evil. God
said to Adam and Eve: 'You are free to eat from any tree
in the garden; but you must not eat from the tree of the
knowledge of good and evil, for when you eat of it you will
surely die' (Gen. 2:16–17). In rebelling against his creator
man lost his gift of life. God said to Adam: 'Dust you are
and to dust you will return' (Gen. 3:19).

Life is precious. Therefore we must strive to push back
death – the final consequence of the fall.

We must struggle for the protection of a life-sustaining
environment because God still wants us to have life. If
shame, guilt, dread of man in animals, labour pain in childbirth, oppression of women, and pain and sweat in work
are undesirable but real abnormalities, then death is more
cruel than them all. In a moment it snaps the holistic
relationship between human life and its physical environment, between a person and his or her human community.
For the same reason, the cruel fact of death must remain
a constant reminder that we are meant to walk humbly
with our creator moment by moment, seeking forgiveness
for sin and the gift of eternal life.

New Age thinkers, because they do not attach significance to our individuality, glamourise death as a necessary
step in evolution. Yet, paradoxically, they display tremendous anxiety over the ecological crisis which threatens life.
From the Christian point of view, the eco-system should be
cared for because each life is unique and significant. Jesus
cried when he stood before the tomb of Lazarus. He was
angry at death because, as the final consequence of sin,
it negates the most precious creation of God – human life.
Jesus raised Lazarus back to life, reaffirming the precious-
ness of each individual life as God's intended gift, and
providing a foretaste of what he was able to do for all
those who would believe in him (John 11).

Alienation and the environment

The thinning of the ozone layer threatens to cut down the life span of coming generations. The Bible says that before Noah our ancestors used to live for hundreds of years. Then the flood came and the human life span was drastically reduced to 120 years. What happened? We read in the Bible:

> no shrub of the field had yet appeared on the earth and no plant of the field had yet sprung up, for the Lord God had not sent rain on the earth and there was no man to work the ground, but streams [or mist] came up from the earth and watered the whole surface of the ground. (Gen. 2:5–6)

In the light of Genesis 1:6–8, which says that God separated the water below and the water above with the expanse of the sky between them, this suggests that prior to the flood there was no rain; rather, a layer of gaseous water covered the earth which filtered sunrays more effectively than today. It allowed a uniform climate through the year and created an environment which was far more conducive to life than what we now have. A lack of prior experience of rain and/or flood would have made Noah's contemporaries unwilling to heed his prophetic warnings. A different atmosphere then would also have meant that Noah would never have seen a rainbow before, which was given after the flood as a sign of God's protection from future floods. Genesis 9:15 says: 'Never again will the waters become a flood to destroy all life.' There could be no universal floods now, because the atmospheric layer of water is no longer there.

Even if this interpretation of the text is only conjecture, the Bible records that the atmosphere, which earlier was capable of sustaining individual life for centuries, changed drastically for the worse after the flood.

Why did the atmosphere turn against us? The Bible says:

> The Lord saw how great man's wickedness on the earth had become, and that every inclination of the thoughts of his heart was only evil all the time. The Lord was grieved . . . and his heart was filled with pain. So the Lord said, 'I will wipe mankind, whom I have created, from the face of the earth' . . . But Noah found favour in the eyes of the Lord. (Gen. 6:5–8)

In Noah's day the floodgates of the heavens were opened: rain fell on the earth for forty days and forty nights (Gen. 7:11–12). Today our ever-growing wickedness is causing acid rain and showers of ultra-violet rays, further reducing our life span. It is legitimate to seek to understand the physical causes of changes in our environment. But it is not logical to argue that there is no causal relationship between wickedness and the flood. We saw earlier that although there is no mechanical relationship between making a bed and swimming, there is in fact a logical connection, because we live in a personal and moral universe. Likewise, the cause and effect relationship between moral wickedness and life-threatening changes in the environment is consistent with the moral and personal nature of the cosmos.

Alienation in society

Nuclear fission in the sun is a life-giving blessing. Then why is it that nuclear fission in a reactor has become a dreadful threat? New Age writers like Fritjof Capra and Marilyn Ferguson argue forcefully against nuclear power and in favour of solar energy. But solar energy is also nuclear energy! How can one get away from the conclusion that in human hands such power is dangerous precisely because of the depravity of the human heart?

When God asked Adam, 'Have you eaten from the tree from which I commanded you not to eat?' Adam promptly put the blame on Eve – the person he was supposed to be 'one flesh' with: 'The woman you put here with me – she gave me some fruit from the tree, and I ate it' (Gen. 3:11–12). Alienation had certainly crept in between them. Their son Cain killed his brother Abel because he was angry and jealous (Gen. 4:1–17). Now we kill our brothers for other reasons – economic competition, racial prejudice, religious or ideological differences, personal convenience or even for the sheer pleasure of murder.

If the New Age is correct to interpret Jung's notion of the collective unconscious as meaning that there is a single, unbroken consciousness that runs through each one of us, then why is it that human society is characterised by such vast differences? Why, for example, do we not have one common language?

The biblical story of the Tower of Babel offers an explanation. God had said to man, 'Be fruitful and increase in number; fill the earth and subdue it' (Gen. 1:28). In direct disobedience, men said, 'Come, let us build ourselves a city, with a tower that reaches to the heavens, so that we may make a name for ourselves and not be scattered over the face of the whole earth' (Gen. 11:4).

God therefore confused human language so that people could not understand each other and were scattered over the earth, thus fulfilling the purpose of their existence – to take care of the whole planet. Experts who had assumed that different races originated at different times in different parts of the globe are amazed to discover that human brains and human language have a common structure. That is why one language can be translated into any other language. This points to our common ancestry and an original, single language.

From the Christian viewpoint, the differences between the races, and the alienation they cause, though real, are later and abnormal, and are caused by sin (at the fall). Redemption therefore includes uniting people from all nations and languages back into 'one body'.

The New Testament says that fifty days after the resurrection of Jesus, when the Holy Spirit came upon his disciples' on the day of the Jewish Festival of Pentecost, 120 of them started speaking in 'tongues' they had not learned. The people who had come to Jerusalem from dozens of different nations were amazed and perplexed when they heard them declaring 'the wonders of God'.

'How is it,' they asked, 'that each of us hears . . . in his own native language?' (Acts 2:8). At that great moment in the history of redemption, the reality of the Tower of Babel was being reversed. It was a foretaste of things that are yet to come.

God desires that the results of sin be pushed back; that the alienation of man from man be replaced by understanding and respect, harmony and love.

Man is alienated from himself, from other men, from animals, and from the planet because he chose not to stand in a right relationship with his creator – a relationship of trust and loving obedience. That is sin. Ecological salvation must therefore entail repentance from sin and a return to God.

Environmental problems are not caused by bad vibrations we have sent out, nor because we have failed to worship the nature spirits or Mother Earth herself, but by our sins of omission and commission with regard to God's commands to us about our ministry to the planet.

God said to Solomon, the wisest king of Israel:

> When I shut up the heavens so that there is no rain, or command locusts to devour the land or send a plague among my people, if my people . . . will humble themselves and pray and seek my face and turn from their wicked ways, then will I hear from heaven and will forgive their sin and *will heal their land*. (2 Chron. 7:13–14)

The prophet Hosea based his call to repentance on the same understanding of ecology:

> Hear the word of the Lord . . . because the Lord has a charge to bring against you who live in the land: 'There is no faithfulness, no love, no acknowledgment of God in the land. There is only cursing, lying and murder, stealing and adultery; they break all bounds, and bloodshed follows bloodshed. *Because of this the land mourns*, and all who live in it waste away; the beasts of the field and the birds of the air and the fish of the sea are dying . . .
>
> Their deeds do not permit them to return to their God. A spirit of prostitution [idolatry] is in their heart; they do not acknowledge the Lord.
>
> . . . Let us acknowledge the Lord; let us press on to acknowledge him. As surely as the sun rises, he will appear; he will come to us like the winter rains, like the spring rains that water the earth.' (Hos. 4:1–3; 5:4; 6:3)

7

VEGETARIANISM – SELF AND SELFISHNESS

We are the living graves of murdered beasts,
Slaughtered to satisfy our appetites,
We never pause to wonder at our feasts
If animals, like man, can possibly have rights.
                                        George Bernard Shaw

The first step in the pursuit of righteousness, said the great
Russian idealist Leo Tolstoy, is abstinence from animal
food. In butchering animals to eat their corpses, man in-
flicts suffering and death on innocent creatures. He also
'unnecessarily suppresses in himself that highest capacity
of sympathy and pity towards creatures like himself.'[1]
    It is possible to choose a vegetarian diet for purely nu-
tritional reasons. However, as the ex-president of the Vegetarian Society of France, Dr J. de Marquette, points out:

> Almost invariably after five or six years of a blood-
> less diet, newcomers to Vegetarianism in France de-
> velop a new interest in the higher aspects of the inner
> life in Theosophy, Rosicrucianism, Anthroposophy, Free
> Masonry ... Vegetarianism ... has proven itself to be
> a sort of royal road to God.[2]

Vegetarianism and non-vegetarianism represent two different views of the human self and its relationship to God
and the world. This chapter seeks to clarify the opposing
conceptions.
    Tolstoy's reasoning, as outlined in his essay 'The Morals

of Diet or the First Step', was that God's grace is not
sufficient for righteous living. Man needs to exert his own
effort to be righteous. The primary step in such an effort is
what Socrates called 'abstinence'.

Abstinence, Tolstoy said, implies a rejection of the desire
for all luxuries such as fats, sweets, drinks, music, parties,
and comforts such as a soft bed and hot water for which
servants had to labour. Abstaining from meat, however, is
more important. For if a man seriously aspires to a righteous
life, the first abstinence he will cultivate is

> abstinence in food – i.e. fasting. And in fasting . . . his
> first act . . . will be abstinence from animal food, because
> not to mention the excitement of the passions produced
> by such food, its use is plainly immoral, as it requires an
> act contrary to moral feeling – i.e. killing, and is called
> forth only by greed, daintiness.[3]

Tolstoy's idealism, together with Howard Williams' book
The Ethics of Diet, in which Tolstoy's essay appeared as a
preface, were seminal influences on Mahatma Gandhi. A
substantial portion of Gandhi's autobiography *The Story of
My Experiments With Truth*[4] is an apology for vegetarianism.

Vegetarianism as a religious phenomenon began in India
when Jainism and Buddhism revolted against the cruelty
of animal and human sacrifice in Hinduism over six hundred years before Christ. By 1908, when the International
Vegetarian Union was founded at Dresden, Germany, vegetarianism had become an organised global movement.
Now it is no longer a fringe phenomenon, indulged in
by some cranks. It has usurped the moral high ground
and effectively put non-vegetarianism on the defensive.
Its attack on the non-vegetarian tradition is multifaceted,
covering nutritional, health, economic, ecological, ethical,
metaphysical and spiritual dimensions. Its greatest contribution is that it has raised our sensitivity towards
man's inhumanity to animals.

Unfortunately, some vegetarians undermine their cause
by employing dishonest or misleading arguments. It seems
they are compensating for their lack of reason with highly
emotive language, such as 'murdering animals', 'eating
corpses', or the 'tragedy of eating meat'. Such emotive
language precludes the possibility of cool-headed analysis.

Nevertheless the central issue – cruelty to animals – merits honest discussion.

Before we come to that, it would be helpful to deal with those issues which appear peripheral to the critics, but are of crucial importance to many vegetarians.

Secular arguments in favour of vegetarianism

Nutrition and health

For centuries non-vegetarians condemned the vegetarian diet for its inadequate nutrition and resulting poor health. Mahatma Gandhi says that he too was swayed by the then prevalent argument that 'We [Indians] are weak people because we do not eat meat. The English are able to rule over us, because they are meat eaters.'[5] Gandhi recalled it as a great 'tragedy' that even he began secretly to eat animal flesh in his student days in India.

The fact is that a balanced vegetarian diet is as capable of giving complete nutrition and good physical health as a non-vegetarian diet. As Swami Satyananda Saraswati of Bihar School of Yoga says:

> Not everyone wants to have the stamina of an ox, although many people would like to have the proverbial memory of an elephant and possess his strength. Many would like to have the grace and swiftness of a deer, or the agility of a mountain goat who leaps with incredible ease and dexterity of foot over gaping chasms and lands with perfect precision on a one foot square piece of rock. These special attributes of the creatures of nature – or animals as we call them – are the envy of many humans . . .
>
> These vastly different creatures have one factor in common. They are non-carnivorous and derive their sustenance and strength from plant life only and yet possess their special abilities of strength, speed, stamina and grace.[6]

The great English poet Shelley claimed in his essay 'A Vindication of Natural Diet', published in 1813:

> There is no disease, bodily or mental, which adoption of vegetable diet and pure water has not infallibly mitigated, wherever the experiment has been fairly tried. Debility

is gradually converted into strength, disease into health-fulness ... even the unaccountable irrationality of ill-temper, that makes a hell of domestic life, into a calm and considerable evenness of temper ... [7]

However, Shelley had tried vegetarianism for only eight months when he wrote the above!

The irony is that vegetarians have adopted the earlier folly of the non-vegetarians in condemning the non-vegetarian diet for resulting in poor nutrition and disease. Unbiased research must examine questions such as: Does a meat diet cause some forms of cancer? Or is meat protein the main reason why successive generations of Americans have been taller than their previous generations – suggesting that at least some kinds of vegetarian diets may result in stunted growth? The often-heard assertion that vegetarians live longer, stronger and healthier lives is clearly too sweeping a generalisation, and unproven.

Dr J. M. Jussawalla, in his paper 'All Life is Sacred', pres-ented to the twenty-fourth World Vegetarian Congress in 1977, restored moderation to this controversy when he said: 'The health argument is a spurious one. Some vegetarians are strong, some weak, as are meat eaters. Some live long, some die prematurely. It is the reverence for life of ... [the vegetarian] way which distinguishes it from the other.'[8]

Ecology and economy
Mrs Maneka Gandhi,[9] India's minister of state for the en-vironment during 1989–91, often says: 'If we care for the green cover in India, the first thing we must do is to become vegetarians.' She argues that in eating 1 kg. of chicken we are effectively consuming 35 kg. of grain.

Vegetarians in America lament that 85% of all the corn that is grown there is fed to cattle. If people did not eat animal corpses, they argue, there would be enough food for the poor of the whole world.

British vegetarians, too, have protested the uneconomic use of land for the non-vegetarian diet, which requires six to seven times more land per person than the vegetarian diet. If British farmers were growing only for vegetarian diets, with the amount of land and effort being used at present, they could, it is claimed, grow enough food for 800 million people.

While this concern for the poor must be respected, it unfortunately weakens the moral case for vegetarianism itself.

Firstly, the argument implies that human beings should not grow food for animals, and that land and forests should be used only (or mainly) for human consumption.

Vegetarians are obviously concerned for the welfare of animals. By using the above argument, however, they open themselves to the criticism that they are selfish. Most vegetarians will no doubt agree that the land belongs to animals as much as it does to human beings. Therefore it is right that enough of it should be used to grow food for animals. To criticise the killing of animals is one thing, to criticise growing food for animals is throwing the baby out with the bath water.

The second problem with the above 'economic' argument is that its proponents do not seem to understand basic economics.

Most farmers in America would gladly grow corn for the starving human population of Africa and Asia instead of growing it to fatten calves for their own tables. But someone has to buy it for the poor. Surely we cannot demand that the farmers grow and ship food to the poor at their own expense.

If the cattle breeder did not buy the corn, 85% of American corn-growing farms would have to grow something else or become, say, commercial complexes or golf courses. The farmers cannot produce what no one is buying.

Likewise, if a poultry farm did not buy 35 kg. of grain for a chicken, the farmer would simply not grow that grain. India would then have even less green cover than it does at present. To produce greenery in India requires extra effort at irrigation, etc. The farmer makes that effort because the poultry farm provides him the market. If the market goes, so does the green cover.

The poor do not lack food because cattle and chicken are eating their rightful share. They starve because they are enslaved by social evils such as casteism or racism, oppressive political, economic or religious systems, debilitating beliefs and moral codes – in short, they are enslaved by the 'powers and principalities' of this dark age (cf. Col. 2:20). Our turning vegetarian would in no way alter these conditions. Nor would it increase green cover. If it could, a country such as India, where vegetarianism has been held in such high esteem, would know neither hunger nor deforestation on the massive scale it does – especially since there are still 900 million hectares of land which, according to the Government of India, could be cultivated or turned into forests.

To help the poor, we have to emancipate them from their moral, mental, social, religious or political enslavement – or just buy food for them. For reasons that will become apparent, the traditional 'vegetarian' preoccupation with self in Jain, Buddhist and Hindu societies has never worked towards empowering the poor, or organising charity for them. It has usually demanded that the poor should give charity to the religious people, such as monks and ascetics. These traditions do not have a track record of conducting research to find out what kind of food is most conducive for human health, leave alone a record of championing the cause of green cover in India.

It took a nineteenth-century Baptist missionary – William Carey – to raise the Indian consciousness about forestry. Vegetarians like Mahatma Gandhi, who did take up the cause of the poor, were educated in England, not India. Some of their basic ideas and motivations were derived from non-Hindu sources. It would be digressing too much from our subject if we discussed the fact that contemporary research into the nutritional, economic and ecological aspects of diet is the product of a culture with a high view of physical reality. This interest is neither produced, nor can it be sustained, by the metaphysical assumptions behind vegetarianism.

We must be grateful that Mrs Maneka Gandhi has emerged as India's first 'Green' politician. Her uniqueness, however, also proves that 2600 years of vegetarianism did not bring about ecological consciousness in India.

Metaphysical arguments in favour of vegetarianism

'Natural' food

One basic argument used by vegetarians has been that non-vegetarian food is unnatural to man.

Richard Wagner said to the twenty-fourth World Vegetarian Congress in 1977: 'I start with the religious conviction that the degeneration of the human race has been brought about by its departure from its natural food; the only basis of a possible regeneration [is] a return to it.'[10]

Dr Gordon Lotto, a naturopath in England and an ex-president of the International Vegetarian Union, says that mammals are divided into four groups. The first group consists of *predatory carnivorous* mammals such as lions and tigers. Their teeth and jaws are admirably constructed for tearing flesh and eating meat. The second group comprises *ruminant herbivorous* mammals such as cows and horses. Their jaws and teeth are perfect for grinding and chewing food. The third group are the *omnivorous* mammals such as bears. Their jaws and dental structures are designed for eating both plants and animals. Finally, there are *frugivorous* mammals, such as chimpanzees and humans, whose teeth, jaws and stomachs are designed for fruit.[11]

Dr M. M. Bhamgara adds many more details to Dr Lotto's argument. He points out, for example, that our hands are, like those of apes, meant for plucking fruit and vegetables, but are not equipped with claws for tearing flesh. Our saliva is alkaline, containing ptyalin to digest carbohydrates, whereas the saliva of carnivorous animals is acidic. Unlike carnivorous animals, we do not have fangs to bite into flesh. The gastric secretions of carnivorous animals are four times more acidic than ours. The size of their intestines and the volume of their intestinal secretions are larger than ours. This enables them to digest the excessive nitrogenous waste and broken-down fat of a meat diet.

From these observations Dr Bhamgara concludes that 'Structurally and functionally, we are vegetarian animals in the same class as the primates, the higher apes such as gorillas, chimpanzees or orangutans.'[12]

Vegetarians reinforce this argument by quoting the biblical teaching that when God created Adam and Eve, he said to them:

> I give you every seed-bearing plant on the face of the whole earth and every tree that has fruit with seed in it. They will be yours for food. And to all the beasts of the earth and all the birds of the air and all the creatures that move on the ground – everything that has the breath of life in it – I give every green plant for food. (Gen. 1:29–30)

The problem with the literal application of this text is that if we should eat only that food which we are 'naturally' made to eat, then we should logically be 'fruitarians', not 'vegetarians', since man is not made to eat herbs or green plants but only fruit and seed-bearing plants. In fact all cooked food is 'unnatural'.

A greater problem with the argument is that it fails to grasp an essential aspect of human nature. Human beings are naturally creative. They are not made like birds to fly in the air. But they do. Nor are they 'naturally' made to go to the depths of the sea like fish, but they do. A non-vegetarian may reason, 'Since I am creative enough to compensate for my lack of claws and sharp teeth with knives, and lack of acidity with cooking, therefore I can also enjoy what Mother Nature gives her children to enjoy. If she did not want me to use my creativity, why did she give it to me in the first place?' Indeed, Mother Nature is not against non-vegetarian food *per se*, since she made lions and bears to eat such food!

Human creativity results in culture. To dismiss culture as 'unnatural' is to violate the essence of human nature. The argument is as absurd as saying, 'We should not wear clothes, because if Mother Nature had wanted us to wear clothes she would have given us hair or fur or feathers.'

The greatness of men like Tolstoy and Gandhi need not be denied. But for them to demand that women and men should not seek to satisfy the desires of their palates by using spices and condiments is inconsistent. For they do want us to satisfy the 'lusts' of our intellects by reading their stimulating books. Is it not also 'unnatural' to turn wood into the paper on which their books are printed? To single out creativity with regard to food for condemnation as 'unnatural' smacks of arbitrary moral authoritarianism.

Whenever a person (or a sect) decides that righteousness is obtained not by faith and obedience but by our own efforts, he invariably proceeds towards some form of asceticism. There are limits to what you can deny yourself. The options are mainly in the area of food, clothes, sex, health and cultural participation and enjoyment. A person can deny all of these to himself and decide that spirituality means living naked, celibate, without food and in silence. He will then live only for a short while, though he will have the satisfaction of being considered 'holy' by those who share his ascetic perceptive but lack his capacity to put it into practice. If the ascetic chooses to permit himself the right to 'indulge' in some of the normal 'vices' of life, he necessarily has to be arbitrary in deciding what is acceptable and what is not. For example, a vegetarian may abstain from meat but indulge in eggs and milk-products, even though they are not derived from vegetables. Or he may take unfertilised eggs, but reject the fertilised eggs. Or he may reject cow's milk, but accept goat's milk, as Gandhi did. He will always have his reasons, and he will judge those who do not draw the line where he draws it as 'less holy' or 'less enlightened'. To the 'unenlightened' outsiders these lines will necessarily seem to be drawn arbitrarily.

'Your food forms your character'

Many vegetarians contend that you are what you eat, and that meat-eaters become cruel, aggressive and 'passionate'. For a time Mahatma Gandhi also believed this to be a metaphysical truth. He believed it in spite of the fact that he was well aware that his own, vegetarian, caste of Banias was hated all over the country for usury, extortion and oppression. The belief became untenable, however, when Adolf Hitler – a fanatic vegetarian – became an embarrassment to vegetarians worldwide. Gandhi therefore cautioned his followers:

> A man eating meat but living in the fear of God is nearer his salvation than a man religiously abstaining from meat and many other things but blaspheming God in every one of his acts . . . It is wrong to overestimate the importance of food in the formation of character or in subjugating the flesh . . . To sum up all religions in terms of diets, as is often done in India, is . . . wrong.[13]

The Lord Jesus put this issue in perspective when he taught:

> [The food that] goes into a man's mouth does not make him 'unclean', but what comes out of his mouth, that is what makes him 'unclean' . . . Don't you see that whatever enters the mouth goes into the stomach and then out of the body? But the things that come out of the mouth come from the heart, and these make a man 'unclean'.

For out of the heart come evil thoughts, murder, adultery, sexual immorality, theft, false testimony, slander. These are what make a man 'unclean'. (Matt. 15:11, 17–20)

Why, then, does Mahatma Gandhi assert that 'vegetarians are made of sterner stuff'? It is obvious that the vegetarian diet of itself cannot strengthen the human spirit. However, to refuse meat dishes in a non-vegetarian society, such as English society, would require enormous inner strength. Each time the vegetarian is tempted and pressurised to conform, he has to assert his will power to say 'No, thank you'. Such resolve will undoubtedly strengthen the soul.

What we must remember, however, is that the opposite could also be equally true. For a person growing up in a vegetarian home to defy his society's norms and choose a meat dish could be equally strengthening of his will power and inner resolve. Conversely, to eat meat secretly, with guilt feelings, would weaken the spirit. The practice of choosing what appears to be better, and sticking to it, in spite of opposition, adds to our inner strength only during the initial stage of self-discipline. It is like giving up smoking: at first it takes and gives strength, but once non-smoking becomes the habit, it neither requires strength nor adds to our inner strength to refrain from cigarettes.

The occultic basis of vegetarianism

Shirley MacLaine says that it was her spirit guide that directed her to adopt a vegetarian diet. It said: 'You need to keep your channel to me clear. Therefore, I would recommend eating moderately; vegetables, fruit and water. No dairy products!'[14]

Dr Annie Besant, the most famous of all Theosophists, taught in her lecture entitled 'Vegetarianism in the Light of Theosophy' that our physical world is interpenetrated and surrounded by a world of subtler matter, called the 'astral' world. This subtler world is inhabited by 'forces' or souls of living creatures. When animals are butchered, they persist in the astral plane over the slaughter-house for a considerable period of time. A clairvoyant person, claims C. W. Leadbeater, another prominent occultist, can see the souls of the butchered animals hovering over the city. They pour out their feelings of indignation and horror at all the injustices and torment inflicted upon them. That is why, for example, the atmosphere in a city like Chicago is so dark and frightening: 'The nauseating stench which rises from those Chicago slaughter houses . . . settles like a fatal miasma over the city.'[15]

One difficulty with this teaching is that many of those who claim to be gifted with occult vision tell us that everything in nature, including the vegetable world, is inhabited by intelligent spirits. The Findhorn community in Scotland is one well-known exponent of this view (see chapter 6, 'Doing Ecology is Being Human'). Since the devas (nature spirits or intelligences) of carrots and cabbages must also feel the torment of being 'butchered' and boiled, how can we justify eating vegetables?

'All life is equally sacred'

A fundamental metaphysical assumption of modern vegetarianism is that all life is equally sacred. Kavi Yogi Maharishi Shudhananda Bharat declared to the World Vegetarian Congress:

> From grass to Godmen all are equal souls, sensitive to joy and grief. A plant fades in the hot sun and smiles in the cool breezy evening. It cheers up when watered well. It weeps when the bud is violently plucked . . . The intelligent mental man must treat plants and animals with tender love and compassion . . . Unrefined man cuts the throat of crying animals and gluts his stomach.[16]

Speaking in the same vein, India's ex-prime minister Sri Morarji Desai said: 'We have as much right to live as all the living organisms in creation.'[17]

There are only two possible theological foundations upon which a belief in the sacredness of all life can be based. The first is the belief that all life is sacred because all life is created by God and declared good by him. The second is the belief that all life is sacred because all life is God. This second view is called monism or pantheism. The secular viewpoint which rules God out of the picture completely cannot permit us to view anything as sacred.

If you accept the first position, that all life is sacred because it is all created by God, then you cannot deny God the right to give to his children good and sacred gifts. Those who believe that God owns all life reject vegetarianism as an absolute moral principle because it denies God the right and the authority to give to us what he owns.

If you accept the second, monistic viewpoint – that all life is sacred because it is all God – you run into several problems:

a) If a cow and grass are equally sacred because they are equally God, then should we not deny the cow the right to eat grass? How does one arrive at the absolute principle that one form of life should not merge into another? Especially when in essence the two things are really one thing – God! When a cow eats grass, in a sense the grass continues to live in the cow. If one follows the logic that all life is sacred and that what is sacred must not be eaten, then there is no intellectually honest way to eat vegetarian food either.

b) A deeper problem is that if all reality is ultimately 'one', then we cannot say that anything is right or wrong. Shirley MacLaine must be given the credit for being a consistent monist at this point. She recognises that her belief system does not allow her to say that non-vegetarianism is wrong, or that vegetarianism is right. All that she can say is that her spirit guide recommends a vegetarian diet.

c) Monism or pantheism, which says that all life is one and equally divine, reduces the status of the human individual to the level of grass or bacteria. Ultimately it has to reject all individual forms as maya or illusion because if reality is one, then what appears to be different cannot be real. And how can you respect animal life if it is maya?

Karma and reincarnation

'The saints' insistence on a vegetarian diet', writes Shri V. K. Sethi,

> is based on the law of Karma . . . those who kill will in turn be killed; who make the living their food, will one day become food for others. Such is the process of cause and effect that every debt has to be paid, the account of every debt has to be cleared. In the court of retribution there is neither mercy nor appeal.[18]

Sethi is right. Vegetarianism in India did not base its appeal on the superficial arguments of ecologists, economists or nutritionists. It has been based on metaphysical concepts such as karma and reincarnation. It is therefore inevitable that these ideas will travel to the West along with vegetarianism.

Fred C. Whittle, the Founder of the Vegan Society of Victoria, Australia, wrote:

> The exploitation [by] man of his lesser brethren, all animated by the same life force, is to be regretted, and no doubt the Law of Karma, i.e. the Law of Cause and Effect, will eventually be the teacher and lead him to a better understanding of his role in life, his purpose which is to live in harmony with all life.[19]

Believers in karma and reincarnation hold that you should not kill and eat an animal because it could be your grandfather, reborn to experience the suffering he inflicted on animals.

Since these concepts will be discussed at length in the following chapter, here it is enough to point out that by using this argument vegetarians open themselves to the charge of being inconsistent. Eating vegetables also results in karma, and the vegetable you are eating today could be your grandmother. To think that the karma of eating vegetables is negligible and could be compensated for by meditation is folly. For as V. K. Sethi says above, 'In the court of retribution [karma] there is neither mercy nor appeal.' Karma, being an impersonal law, cannot forgive.

The irony is that a non-vegetarian can also legitimately use the belief in karma to support his practice. What if he is sincerely convinced that he was a chicken, fish, turkey, rabbit, sheep, deer, goat, pig, cow and buffalo in his previous lives? Each time he was killed and eaten by men. These men have been reborn as animals now, and he has been reborn to repay them the due consequences of their karma! Would it not be logical, therefore, to assume that animals which are being eaten today are suffering the due consequences of their karma from a previous life?

If taking life and eating food adds to our karma, then the only logical thing is to deny oneself food and starve to death. Jain saints understood this to be the true implication of their faith. Therefore the greatest of them still commit

suicide by starvation. One may concede to them the right
to espouse and practise their philosophy. For their part,
they have to permit their opponents to believe that their
life-negating religion does not come from God, who is the
giver of life and all good gifts. What then is the real source
of their teaching? The Bible has this to say:

> Some will abandon the faith and follow deceiving spir-
> its and things taught by demons. Such teachings come
> through hypocritical liars, whose consciences have been
> seared as with a hot iron. They forbid people to marry
> and order them to abstain from certain foods, which God
> created to be received with thanksgiving by those who
> believe and who know the truth. For everything God
> created is good, and nothing is to be rejected if it is
> received with thanksgiving, because it is consecrated by
> the word of God and prayer. (1 Tim. 4:1–5)

The central issue – Cruelty to animals

Non-vegetarians may legitimately reject all the foregoing
arguments in defence of vegetarianism as groundless. One
fact they cannot deny, however, is that non-vegetarianism
involves killing animals. And killing is cruel. To that issue,
therefore, we must now turn.

Is it possible that vegetarianism may be more cruel to
animals than non-vegetarianism? Before answering the question, take a ride with me through the bazaar in Allahabad,
the holy city of the Hindus where I grew up. Our car is
suddenly stopped by a crowd. We both get down to see
what the matter is. A young man is mercilessly beating a
cow on her head with a big stick, in the middle of the road.
The crowd, including the police, watch with indifference or
amusement. No one tries to restrain the young man. You are
shocked and confused, tempted to conclude that the Hindus
are cruel to their animals. I suggest that your inference is
unwarranted. What you have witnessed is a minor glimpse
of the cruelty inherent in vegetarianism.

Let me explain. The cow is old, beyond the age of fertility.
It gives neither calves nor milk. The owner was having a
hard time feeding the family. To carry on feeding the old
cow was impossible. Cow slaughter is banned. He cannot

sell the cow for meat, leather or bones. So he just lets the cow loose, to fend for herself.

The young man you saw hitting the cow normally worships her. He would gladly drink her urine as an act of piety. Today he is mad at the cow because she again helped herself to his mother's basket of vegetables. He has repeatedly tried to teach her (sometimes even harshly) that those vegetables are not for her. They are for sale. The cow keeps ignoring the lesson, driven by hunger pangs.

This, as I said, is only a small incident. Come to my childhood home in Allahabad. My father was a philosopher, not a farmer. But he loved animals. Therefore we grew up with dogs, cats, rabbits, chickens, ducks, goats, pigeons, parrots and guinea fowls, besides of course his home-grown fruits, flowers and vegetables, round the year. Sometimes I envied my older brother who inherited my father's green fingers, while I had to remain content with his analytical mind. Love for animals, however, runs through the family, now championed by Anandit, who has sometimes felt that she should grow up to be a veterinarian or a politician to raise a special police force in India to prevent cruelties such as those described above.

I am not sure whether it was love for animals or human beings, or both, that motivated me to start a poultry and dairy farm near Khajuraho (M.P.) in 1980. All eggs were then imported into our district from outside. The state of milch animals was such that a man who owned a hundred cattle would consider himself lucky if he got 10 kg. of milk in a whole day. Therefore, as a part of our rural development effort, our community decided to teach local people how to start and manage small-scale poultry and dairy farming.

Our efforts came to an abrupt end when our community was burned down in 1984, during the government-sponsored anti-Sikh riots, following the assassination of the then Prime Minister Mrs Indira Gandhi. Happily, however, the experiment had taught me some basic lessons in economics.

One of these lessons was that a poultry farm did not make a profit on eggs. Egg sales barely covered the daily costs, not even the overheads. The profits came only when the hens which had stopped laying eggs were sold for meat.

If we did not want to sell our birds for meat, then we had three options. We could let them loose to find food from neighbours' homes and farms. They would then be eaten by the neighbours, stray dogs or wild cats or foxes. This would be no less cruel than selling them for meat. Our second option was to keep them in a room and let them starve to death. Did we have the heart for this? The final option was to keep feeding them till they died a natural death. This sounds humane. But who would pay for the feed? The cost could not be covered by doubling or tripling the price of eggs. The income from one egg could not feed a chicken for more than three days. If a chicken lived for 150 days without laying eggs, we would need to raise the price of eggs at least forty times, perhaps more. Eggs cannot be sold at that price. Similar facts apply to dairy farming. A dairy cannot be run on the price of milk alone.

Vegetarians would no doubt say at this point that the answer to our dilemma is in fact quite simple – stop using or selling eggs and milk. Do not keep dairy animals or poultry, and you will then not have the problem.

I wish the solution was that simple, but unfortunately it is not.

Domestic animals are vulnerable creatures. Most chickens, sheep, goats and cows will not survive if human beings do not take care of them. They cannot fly, climb trees, dig underground, run fast, or fight back with claws, horns, jaws or poisonous fangs. They cannot dig wells or draw water for themselves in the summer months. Someone has to plan for their food during the years of drought and famine. If shepherds did not look after the sheep, they would soon be an extinct species. Taking care of a sheep is a full-time job. If a person loved the sheep and therefore took up the responsibility for their care full time, he would have to live off the sheep.

Committed vegetarians could respond in two ways at this point. Some could argue that man has domesticated and made these creatures dependent and vulnerable. If they were let loose, the 'evolutionary process' would enable them to develop adequate mechanisms for self-defence.

Such faith in the evolutionary process is possible only if one chooses to be blind to the facts of natural history. Any number of animal species have in fact become extinct, without receiving any help from merciful evolution. Did God make man or evolution to take care of these animals?

When brought to this point, most committed vegetarians have replied that it is better for these species to become extinct than for them to be butchered by us. At least we would not incur the karma of murdering them and eating their corpses.

What? Are you a vegetarian in your own self-interest or for the sake of the animals?

If for your own spiritual progress you are prepared to have the entire species of these animals wiped out, then how is vegetarianism less selfish or less cruel than non-vegetarianism?

The case for non-vegetarianism

Many in the secular world are calling non-vegetarianism an indefensible cruelty. That is because they have forgotten that the moral basis for eating animals is rooted in the biblical story of Noah, found in Genesis 6–9.

Non-vegetarianism started with Noah, whom God judged to be the most righteous man of his time. Noah demonstrated his righteousness by, among other things, building a boat to save some of all the species of animals from a flood that God sent to punish the ever-growing wickedness of man.

The animals stayed with Noah's family for over ten months in the boat, living and multiplying off the food that Noah had saved for them.

When the animals finally came out of the boat, they found that all the vegetation had been destroyed by the flood. There was nothing to eat. Men and the animals would either have to starve or turn carnivorous to survive.

Until that time, according to the Bible, human beings were indeed vegetarians. It is interesting to note that after he came out of the boat, the first act of Noah – the vegetarian – was to build an altar to the Lord and sacrifice some animals to express his gratitude. In this act of offering a living being to the creator and saviour, Noah acknowledged that God was the giver and owner of all lives. Life belongs to God. We, as sinners, deserve only death. The Bible records that this attitude of worship pleased God. Therefore, since Noah acknowledged that God, not man, was the owner of all life, including animal life, he was given permission to eat animals. The Bible records:

> Then God blessed Noah and his sons, saying to them, 'Be
> fruitful and increase in number and fill the earth. The
> fear and dread of you will fall upon all the beasts of the
> earth and all the birds of the air, upon every creature
> that moves along the ground, and upon all the fish of
> the sea; they are given into your hands. Everything that
> lives and moves will be food for you. Just as I gave you
> the green plants, I now give you everything.
>
> 'But you must not eat meat that has its lifeblood still
> in it.' (Gen. 9:1–4)

We need to notice a number of facts about the above
blessing.

*1. Noah was given the right to eat animals because he
served and saved them.* Adam earned the right to eat the
fruit of the garden because he ministered to it (Gen. 2:15).
We exploit when we use someone or something without
serving him, her or it. No one should presume that the right
given to Noah to eat animals belongs to his descendants,
without assuming that Noah's responsibility to care for the
animals also rests upon his descendants.

*2. God did not cease being interested in the protection of
animals when he permitted Noah to eat them.* God himself
had asked Noah to build a boat to save his family and the
animals from the flood. Later, when God permitted Noah to
eat animals, he took care to protect their interest as well.
God said that he would cause 'The fear and dread of you to
fall upon all the beasts of the earth and all the birds of the
air . . . ' In other words, God said that he would ensure that
these creatures no longer trusted human beings with their
earlier innocence. God gave them an instinctive fear of man
so that they would take precautions to protect themselves.

3. God drew limits to human authority over animals. Noah
had already acknowledged the fact that human beings did
not own animal life. It belonged to God. Notwithstanding
how some of us may feel, God does have a right to give for
our enjoyment what belongs to him. However, in granting
man the permission to eat animals, God did not cease being
their owner. The command not to eat animal blood was
intended to be a constant reminder to human beings that
animal life belongs to God, not man. We are not free to
do with them as we please. Later, when man began to

forget to treat animals with respect, God gave many more commandments to ensure that non-vegetarianism did not degenerate into heartless cruelty to animals. For example, in Exodus 23 we read the following two commandments:

'If you see the donkey of someone who hates you fallen down under its load, do not leave it there; be sure you help him with it' (v.5); 'Do not cook a young goat in its mother's milk' (v.19).

4. God made a sacrifice to save animals. In India vegetarianism began in the sixth century BC, when Jainism and Buddhism revolted against cruelty to animals, which had become a part of the Vedic tradition of animal and human sacrifice. Animal sacrifice was a part of the Jewish religious tradition too. There is, however, a significant difference between the two religious traditions. In rejecting animal sacrifice, Jainism and Buddhism rejected the idea that all life is precious and belongs to God. Quite contrary to what many writers claim today, in preferring vegetarianism Jainism or Buddhism did not affirm the sacredness of all life. These systems did not even believe in the sacredness of human life. No, it was because they both sought escape from the 'samsara' – the wheel of life. As mentioned earlier, Jainism even promoted suicide through starvation as the highest spiritual austerity.

In rejecting the significance of human life, these systems also denied that human beings were morally responsible creatures; accountable, and therefore guilty. By contrast, Judaism accepted a human being as a significant creature who was capable of sin. Sin called for punishment, or repentance and propitiation. This deep consciousness of sin was the basis for animal sacrifice in the Jewish tradition.

Any family that has owned pets knows that in only a short time a great emotional bond is established between a family and its pet. It is not easy to kill your own animal; it is hard. That is why animal sacrifice was neither pleasure nor cruelty, but a deep and painful acknowledgement by those who practised it that as sinners they deserved death. Sacrifice is a prayer. In Noah's case it was also an expression of deep gratitude for life.

In time, the Bible records, the ritual of animal sacrifice degenerated into cruelty to animals. The priests began to have a vested interest in the business of selling, killing and eating animals. Some even began to think that God desired the blood of animals. The Jewish prophets, long before Jainism or Buddhism, condemned this perversion of truth. King David, after he had committed adultery with Bathsheba and plotted her husband's murder, said with an attitude of deep penitence:

> You do not delight in sacrifice, or I would bring it;
>   you do not take pleasure in burnt offerings.
> The sacrifices of God are a broken spirit;
>   a broken and contrite heart,
>   O God, you will not despise. (Ps. 51:16–17)

The prophet Isaiah, who lived two hundred years before Gautama Buddha, rebuked the Jewish nation for its cruelty to animals. He said:

> Hear the word of the Lord,
>   you rulers of Sodom;
> listen to the law of our God,
>   you people of Gomorrah!
> 'The multitude of your sacrifices –
>   what are they to me?' says the Lord.
> 'I have more than enough of burnt offerings,
>   of rams and the fat of fattened animals;
> I have no pleasure
>   in the blood of bulls and lambs and goats.' (Isa. 1:10–11)

Again according to the prophet Isaiah, the Lord said:

> 'This is the one I esteem:
>   he who is humble and contrite in spirit,
>   and trembles at my word.
> But whoever sacrifices a bull
>   is like one who kills a man,
> and whoever offers a lamb,
>   like one who breaks a dog's neck' (Isa. 66:2–3)

Isaiah declared that the arrangement according to which human beings were allowed to sacrifice and eat an animal was a temporary one. It was a result of man's sin and its effect on nature. The world will not remain like this for ever. God will renew the earth. The desert, the parched land, the wilderness will become pools of water and bubbling springs, as green as the mountains of Lebanon and as productive as Carmel and Sharon (Isa. 35).

When the curse has been fully removed and the original productivity of the earth restored, Isaiah says, the cruelty of non-vegetarianism will completely cease. At that time:

> The wolf will live with the lamb,
>   the leopard will lie down with the goat,
> the calf and the lion and the yearling together;
>   and a little child will lead them.
> The cow will feed with the bear,
>   their young will lie down together,
>   and the lion will eat straw like the ox.
> The infant will play near the hole of the cobra,
>   and the young child put his hand into the viper's
>   nest.
> They will neither harm nor destroy
>   on all my holy mountain,
> for the earth will be full of the knowledge of the
>   Lord
>   as the waters cover the sea. (Isa. 11:6–9)

According to the New Testament, the Lord Jesus sacrificed himself on the cross not for human souls alone, but for the whole world. A curse was laid upon the environment because of human sin. When Jesus took upon himself the sin of the world, the curse of sin was transferred to him. Because the Lord Jesus has suffered the consequences of human sin, the whole planet, including the animals, will share in the salvation he has made possible. One immediate benefit to the animal world of Jesus' death was that animals were spared from being sacrificed for our sins; Jesus, who was a Jew, brought this religious practice to an end.

The New Testament describes the significance of Jesus' sacrifice for the animals in this respect in the following words:

> 'Animal sacrifices and offerings you did not desire,
>   but a body you prepared for me;
> with burnt offerings and sin offerings
>   you were not pleased.
> Then I said, "Here I am – it is written about me in
>   the scroll –

I have come to do your will, O God." '
. . . We have been made holy through the sacrifice of the
body of Jesus Christ once for all. (Heb. 10:5–7, 10)

The New Testament portrays Jesus both as 'the Lamb of
God' and 'the Good Shepherd'. In contrast to the Jewish
priests, who saw their job as sacrificing lambs, Jesus was
the Lamb of God who sacrificed his life for the remission
of our sins. As the Good Shepherd, Jesus laid down his life
for his sheep. He commanded his disciples, who were going
to be priests in his church, 'Feed my lambs . . . Take care
of my sheep' (John 21:15–19). Jesus upheld the nobility of
a shepherd's ministry by using it as a symbol of his own
work as well as his disciples'.

We are not asked to attempt to establish our own righteousness, whether by sacrificing animals or by various forms
of abstinence and austerity. Like Noah, we are to trust and
obey, accepting God's own sacrifice on our behalf on the
cross.

5. Non-vegetarian food is to be accepted with gratitude. It
is important to note that in the story of Noah animal food
was given to Noah as a blessing. For Noah this blessing
literally meant life. He had shared his food with the animals
in order to save them. Now his family faced death through
starvation. God, who owns the animals, saved Noah's family
by allowing some of the animals to be eaten.

We have already hinted that from a wider perspective the
non-vegetarian tradition became a blessing to the animals
themselves. Man is today protecting strong and independent species such as lions and tigers by keeping them in the
unnatural environment of a zoo. Domestic animals had not
an iota of a chance of survival unless some of their species
were sacrificed as human food for the rest to survive and
grow in number until the end of the present age. The Bible
suggests that the non-vegetarian man is helping the animal
species to survive until the time when the Lord Jesus comes
back a second time to judge the earth by fire, and then to
regenerate it. The curse will then be removed. The earth
will be a paradise, producing abundance. Then we will be
able to enjoy taking care of animals without having to live
off them.

We should give thanks for animal food, too, because in

many parts of the world it has been a necessity for the eco-system. For example, in some desert areas of the Middle East, for thousands of years it was impossible to grow vegetables and fruit. Transporting food there from other parts of the world was also not possible earlier. Therefore human beings could not have lived there at all. Some of these areas did, however, grow grass and herbs. It was therefore possible for some domestic animals to survive, provided human beings were there to provide water and protection. Man could not live on grass and herbs, but he could survive by eating animals, which he served and saved. As the animal food enabled human beings to live in those inhospitable parts of the world, they were able to store meagre rainwater, tap underground or distant river waters, and develop irrigation systems. This has increased the greenery for animals and human beings and aided the overall eco-system of the world. Animal food thus laid the foundation of other forms of human culture and civilisation. That is another reason why we are asked to receive all food that God has given with thanksgiving, not guilt.

The intellectual case for non-vegetarianism rests on the view that bliss, paradise or Eden is to be found not inside the human consciousness, nor in the astral world, but outside, in our relationship with the physical world, with animals, with fellow human beings, and with God. In this perspective, man is made in God's image. Therefore in a limited way he shares God's authority and responsibility over nature. He has to grow food for animals, because the earth's productivity has declined due to his sin. He has to use his creativity in the interests of creation. This is how man fulfils God's purposes on earth.

8

THE REINCARNATION OF THE SOUL

The case for reincarnation

A liberating belief?

Millions of people all over the world are getting excited about the doctrine of the transmigration or the reincarnation of the soul. This doctrine teaches that human souls do not die at physical death, but are reborn into different bodies many more times.

It is indeed a relief to know that the experts were wrong after all. For the last two hundred years they have told us that we are nothing but a complex of molecules and that our consciousness ceases to exist at death. To know that we will outlive our death and that our loves and labours will go with us into many more lives can be enormously comforting, at first glance.

Imagine a young woman, Anita, who has fallen madly in love with her husband Dev. He is sent for advanced training by his company a few months after their marriage. Anita is pregnant. With great expectations she prepares herself and her home for the arrivals of her baby and her husband. Each day she waits for Dev's letter and reads each one over and over again. Dev is to arrive three weeks before her delivery. She goes to the airport to receive him. There she is informed that his plane has crashed. What a shock! Is there any point in love? Any sense in our labours of love when death so cruelly puts an end to our dreams and reduces everything to meaninglessness? Is life truly 'poor, nasty, brutish and short', as Thomas Hobbes (1588–1679), one of the fathers of the Enlightenment, said? What a comfort it can be for Anita to know that death is not the end, and that she will live again with Dev in another life where her dreams will be fulfilled.

The old rationalist view
The common scientific view that grew out of the eighteenth-century European 'Age of Reason' states that man is, in effect, a complex machine. Our mind is only a function of our brain, and even our loves and deeds of compassion and self-sacrifice are products of impersonal forces such as enzymes, hormones, social conditioning and sexual urges.

It is true that scientists never did disprove the existence of the soul, and their efforts to reduce the mind and consciousness to the mere biological functioning of the brain never did succeed. As the neurologist Wilder Penfield said in his paper on brain research in 1966: 'If we are good scientists we cannot claim that science has already explained the mind.' Man has a solid core to his personality from which his decisions emanate; a core which, Penfield says elsewhere, 'controls his thinking and directs the searchlight of his attention'.

Yet it is equally true that the scientists who assumed that the material world was the only reality succeeded in persuading several generations to accept their belief that the soul and the supernatural were non-existent. Matter, body and brain were all there was to reality.

Mind over body
However, decades of research in parapsychology strongly indicate that the mind is more than the brain and the senses. The results of these researches have been discussed by eminent thinkers such as Arthur Koestler[1] and Sir Alister Hardy.[2]

Most of us know of patients who have defied the diagnosis of their doctors, surviving illnesses that cannot be treated by present-day medicine solely through the exercise of their 'will to live', indicating the power of the mind over the body. This suggests that the mind is not just a function of the body, but has an existence of its own. If a woman sitting in New York 'knows' – whether through telepathy or through a dream or through a spirit – that her son in New Delhi has had an accident, and this is later confirmed by a fax message, then that would suggest that the mind may be more than a machine that is totally dependent on the physical senses.

The simple fact is that millions of people have attested to direct experience of the 'spirit' world – faith-healing, mediums (or channels), spirit-possession, exorcism, etc. Their faith in the reality of the soul is strengthened by research in parapsychology, but it does not rest on it. They know from their own first-hand experience that the soul and the supernatural are real, and they are simply not willing to accept a view that reduces them to the level of monkeys or machines.

Dr Raymond A. Moody, whose book *Life After Life* sold over three million copies, studied three hundred cases of people who had either had close encounters with death or who were actually pronounced clinically dead by doctors but revived. These people claimed that during their experience of death they left their bodies, saw and heard the doctors who were trying to revive them, and met dead relatives, other spirits and a 'being of light'. Similarly, Shirley MacLaine has described her experiences in Peru, where her soul left her body lying by the Mantaro riverside and flew around for a while.[3] Dr Moody admits: 'Not one of the cases I have looked into is in any way indicative to me that reincarnation occurs.' But he adds: 'However, it is important to bear in mind that not one of them rules out reincarnation either.'[4]

Dr Moody's research, reinforced by such independent researchers as psychiatrist Elisabeth Kübler-Ross, supports the claim of those who say that they have had out-of-body experiences. If these claims are true, then, not withstanding the difficulty of understanding what the soul is, they imply that there has to be something more than merely the material body.

The empirical evidence for reincarnation

Even if one accepts the existence of the soul as a fact, that does not automatically prove that souls reincarnate. The evidence for reincarnation comes from two sources.

Past-life recall under hypnosis

A. de Rochas in France and J. Bjorkhem in Sweden published some of the early reports (in 1924 and 1943 respectively) of the experiments using hypnosis to take or 'regress' the memories of their subjects back in time to before their present lives. The results of these experiments did not carry much weight with psychologists and the general public. It was soon discovered that the 'personality' evoked in a hypnotically induced regression to a 'previous life' was, in fact, a mixture of the subject's current personality, his expectations of what he thought the hypnotist wanted, his fantasies of what he thought his previous life should have been, and perhaps some information which could be considered to have been obtained paranormally or from 'spirit-sources'.

In our day past-life recall, induced by hypnosis, acupuncture, meditation or other psycho-physiological techniques, has become popular again.

In her book *Dancing in the Light*, for example, Shirley MacLaine describes her experience in Galisteo, New Mexico. There Chris Griscom assisted her with the help of acupuncture needles to recall her past lives, lived thousands of years ago.

The Californian hypnotherapist Helen Wambach, in her book *Reliving Past Lives: The Evidence Under Hypnosis*, has tried to revive the argument that hypnotically induced past-life recall is in fact a proof of reincarnation. Literally tens of thousands of people have gone through such past-life recall sessions now. But the problem with this argument is that, as we saw in the chapter on UFOs, it has been clinically demonstrated that what is 'remembered' under hypnosis is not necessarily a memory of something that has actually happened. For example, one hypnologist, Dr John Kappas, was able to help the Hollywood actor Robert Cummings to 'remember' his next life. Speaking in a hoarse mutter under hypnosis, Cummings claimed that he was born in 1988 in Canton, China, where he became a doctor. The average life span in the year 2097, he said, was 150 years.

Dr Bruce Goldberg, a comedian and dentist in Baltimore, USA, specialises in 'progressing' memories to future lives. In his book *Past Lives, Future Lives*, he presents many cases of 'progression'. Unfortunately, however, all of these are for coming centuries, and no one 'remembers' the next few years which could be verified.

In 1962 the *International Journal of Parapsychology* published the reports of Dr E. Zolik's experiments entitled
'Reincarnation: Phenomena in Hypnotic States'. Dr Zolik
first hypnotised his subjects, regressed them, and then in-
structed them to remember and recount their previous lives.
Details reported were noted.

In later sessions he hypnotised the subjects again, but
instead of regressing them to a 'previous life' he 'scanned'
their memories of their present life to trace the origin of
some of the information and personality traits they had
described in the earlier session as their 'previous life'. Zolik
discovered that most of the 'memories' of the 'previous
life' were in fact fantasies derived from people, books or
theatrical productions which his subjects had known.

Dr Zolik's discovery was independently verified by Dr Ian
Stevenson, who, as we shall soon see, has done more than
anyone else to give academic respectability to the belief in
reincarnation. In his well-researched book *Twenty Cases
Suggestive of Reincarnation* he says:

> During one of my own experiments with hypnotic regres-
> sion, the subject first experienced a 'previous personality'
> evoked with the images of a small boy whom she watched
> playing and in other activities. Initially the images of
> the boy were separate from the narrating self. Later, the
> subject identified herself with the boy and continued
> the narration of her 'previous life', talking in the first
> person about what was happening to this boy, suppos-
> edly herself in a previous life.[5]

Spontaneous past-life recall among children
Many journalists and researchers have investigated the
testimonies of children who seem spontaneously to 'remember', as part of their normal memory, their previous lives
in another family. Some children even attempted to run
away from the present family to the previous one. The
researchers found that the details narrated and the people
'remembered' by these children could be checked out and
found to be true. In many cases the testimonies could not
be explained away as frauds or publicity stunts perpetrated
by the families concerned. In some cases the families either
did not know each other or had not heard of each other's
village or town.

At present in India the most celebrated case of reincarnation is that of Sri Satya Sai Baba, a guru from Andhra Pradesh who has perhaps the largest personal following of all the gurus. The original Sai Baba lived at Shirdi in Maharashtra State and died on 15 October 1918, eight years before the birth of the present Baba. On 9 March 1940 Satya Narayan Raju had an experience after which he began to claim that he was the reincarnation of the original Sai Baba. His claim was authenticated by the miracles he began to perform. The catalogue of his reported miracles now matches the miracles of Jesus recorded in the New Testament. In the eyes of his followers these miracles give validity to his claim that he is the reincarnation of Sai Baba of Shirdi, who also performed miracles.

The meticulous and painstaking research into such cases by Dr Ian Stevenson, a professor of psychiatry and neurology at the University of Virginia Medical School in Charlottesville, has compelled the otherwise sceptical academic world to consider the hypothesis of human survival after death, and its subsequent reincarnation, as a distinct possibility. Dr Stevenson's files now contain some two thousand reports of such cases from around the world.

His conclusion is that these cases are not fraudulent, but 'are memories of some kind, and the question is whether they are memories of what he [the subject] has heard or learned normally, of what he has experienced para-normally, or of what he has experienced in a previous life'.[6]

Spirit-possession rather than reincarnation?

In one of the twenty cases that Dr Stevenson reports, a child called Ravi Shankar was born six months after his 'previous personality', six year old Munna, was murdered. This means that he had been conceived three months prior to Munna's death. In another case a child called Jasbir was at least three and a half years old when his previous personality, Shobha Ram, was allegedly poisoned and died. Jasbir, who metamorphosed into the 'reincarnation' of Shobha Ram, reported that while he (as Shobha Ram) died, he met the spirit of a sadhu (a wandering ascetic) who advised him to 'take cover' in the body of Jasbir, which (the spirit of) Shobha Ram did.

Jasbir (who now calls himself Shobha Ram) said that he

had continued to meet the sadhu occasionally in his dreams. Throughout his book Stevenson maintains that these cases, whether one explains them as mental aberrations or as a supernatural reality implying human survival beyond death, are an established, well-documented fact. He repeatedly admits the possibility that the alleged cases of reincarnation may in fact be instances of spirit-possession. His primary reason for preferring to view them as instances of reincarnation rather than spirit-possession is that children under investigation normally interpret their own experiences as reincarnation. But could that not be due to cultural conditioning? It is not without significance that of the twenty cases Stevenson reports, the first seven are from India, where the doctrine of reincarnation is most highly developed. There are also three cases from Ceylon (present-day Sri Lanka), two from Brazil, seven from the Tilingit Indians of South Eastern Alaska, and one from Lebanon.

Stevenson offers some arguments as to why these cases are better understood as instances of reincarnation rather than spirit-possession, but eventually he admits:

> I do not consider any of the foregoing arguments decisive as between reincarnation and possession in explaining the usual case of the reincarnation type. Two hundred years ago Swedenborg [the Swedish scientist turned mystic] stated that apparent cases of reincarnation were in fact instances of influence on the living by discarnate personalities . . .
>
> Swedenborg's argument still has much cogency today and gains support from the case of Jasbir, in which we can feel confident that the deceased personality influencing the behaviour of Jasbir (or his body at least) died several years *after* the birth of Jasbir's body. Other cases of the present group of 20 cases may be instances of similar 'possessing influences' in which the previous personality just happened to die well before the birth of the present personality's body.[7]

Stevenson says he personally favours reincarnation rather than possession as a hypothesis because if these were cases of possession, then the spirit ought to know everything about the previous life, as well as what happened to the personality after its physical death. But what if, just like an embodied soul, a disembodied soul may also pay attention to and remember only those things that interest it? If embodied souls do not know everything, or are often mistaken or tell lies, then how can we assume that once they become disembodied they have perfect memories, and all the answers to scientific and philosophical questions? After all, much of the influence of the discarnate spirits on living people has often been seen to be undesirable. That is why most people do not like living in houses allegedly occupied or 'haunted' by the spirits of the dead – let alone having these spirits live in their own bodies!

Nevertheless, for those who believe in reincarnation there are pragmatic advantages to their belief which may compensate for the weakness of empirical evidence. It is worthwhile to summarise some of them.

Benefits of belief in reincarnation

It gives a plausible explanation of otherwise inexplicable suffering, injustice and inequalities
Why is a child born lame, poor, blind or unwanted? When the disciples of Jesus saw a beggar who was born blind, they asked, 'Rabbi, who sinned, this man or his parents, that he was born blind?' (John 9:2). If the blindness was a result of the man's own sin, then he must have sinned either in the womb or in a previous life.[8]

The belief that the good or bad actions (karma) of one life determine its future incarnations suggests that the undeserved suffering of this life may be caused by the deeds done in a previous life.

In his monumental work of 1860, *A Critical History of the Doctrine of a Future Life*, the Unitarian clergyman Rev. W. R. Alger wrote that the 'theory of the transmigration of the soul is marvellously adapted to explain the seeming chaos of moral inequality, injustice, and manifold evil present in the world of human life'. The biggest philosophical advantage of this belief is that it seems to allow one to believe in a just universe. If suffering and inequalities are a product of pure chance, then we have to concur that the universe is fundamentally amoral and unjust. If these sufferings are ordained by God, then how can a God who is 'loving' and 'just' allow new-born babes to be crippled for life for no fault of their own?

It gives a basis for hope to imperfect human beings
One short life of sixty to eighty years is simply not enough for anyone to become perfect, to realise their ambitions and achieve their goals, including the desire to know the truth. If a man has to find the truth and become perfect, he will need more than one life! If a single life is all that one has in which to find the truth, there is no hope. But faith in reincarnation gives one the hope that through experience and information received in millions of lives one can get to know the truth and eventually become perfect.

It seems to result in respect for all life
If animals and plants also have souls, and if there is a possibility that I may one day be reborn as an animal or a plant, then I ought to treat all life with respect and develop ecologically responsible behaviour.

It puts one in the company of great sages
Even though belief in reincarnation as a central doctrine has been confined mainly to Hinduism, Buddhism and Jainism for the past three millennia, it is indeed a very ancient idea that has existed in many creeds throughout the world. The ancient Egyptians used to embalm the dead so as to prevent or delay reincarnation; the Greek philosopher Plato accepted the Orphico-Pythagorean views that the soul is immortal, the number of souls is fixed, and that reincarnation occurs regularly; and the Tibetan Book of the Dead has exerted much influence in our day to inspire belief in reincarnation.

In their book *Reincarnation: An East-West Anthology*, Joseph Head and S. L. Cranston give a long list of prominent men and women who believe in reincarnation. They conclude:

> Reincarnation is frequently regarded as an oriental concept incompatible with western thinking and traditional belief. The present encyclopedic compilation of quotations from eminent philosophers, theologians, poets, scientists, etc., of every period of western culture, and the thoroughly documented survey of reincarnation in the world religions will serve to correct this error in thinking.[9]

It helps those who are dying
In the earlier part of her career the psychiatrist Elisabeth
Kübler-Ross effectively promoted the use of belief in reincarnation to comfort terminally ill patients; death is not
the end, but is the gateway to a new beginning in another
body. In a recent book that she has edited, *Death – The
Final Stage of Growth*,[10] she does not seem to be promoting
that practice any more. Perhaps this is due to a recognition
that the doctrine is at best a double-edged sword. If it
comforts some dying patients, it can add to the fear of
others about the unknowable karma of their previous lives.
It can also create anxiety regarding what the karma of this
life will produce in the next.

*It seems easier to believe in a 'new body' than in a 'resurrected
body'*
For many believers in an afterlife who grow up in cultures
shaped by Judaeo-Christian beliefs, it is sometimes hard to
conceive how bodies burned to ashes or eaten by worms in
the earth or by sharks in the seas can be 'resurrected'. It
seems easier to believe that a soul just enters a brand new
body after the death of the earlier one, than to believe that
the same body will be resurrected.

Its notion of the soul is superior
Some philosophers, such as Arthur Schopenhauer and
David Hume, have argued that the doctrine of the soul
presupposed by belief in reincarnation is logically superior
to that implied in the Judaeo-Christian doctrine of resurrection. While the latter assumes that the soul has a beginning
but no end, the former has greater 'symmetry' in that it
teaches that what is endless is also beginningless.

*It seems to offer an explanation for otherwise inexplicable
facts*
How could the Irish mathematician Sir William Hamilton
(1805–65) perform remarkable mathematical feats at a very
early age or master no fewer than thirteen languages, including Persian, Sanskrit and Malay, before he was an
adult? What made Mozart a child prodigy?

In *The Christian Agnostic* Leslie Weatherhead asks: 'Is it
an accidental group of genes that makes a little girl of eight
a musician far in advance of grown men and women, who

have slaved for many years in that field?'[11] To Weatherhead it appeared self-evident that child prodigies must have acquired their skills and knowledge in a previous life. Louisa M. Alcott, the author of *Little Women*, said: 'I must have been masculine [in my previous life] because my love is all for girls.'

Many Indians explain 'Love at first sight' as a result of the relationships continuing from previous lives. The so-called *déjà vu* experiences, in which we have a feeling of having met someone before actually meeting them, or having seen a place when we have in fact never been there, could also be explained as the results of memories from previous lives.[12]

The case against reincarnation

It does not satisfactorily explain the problem of suffering

If a child is born blind or crippled through no fault of his or her own, or is killed as an infant in a war, a flood or an earthquake, it is natural to wonder why this child had to suffer like this. Such 'inexplicable' suffering causes some naturalistic thinkers to conclude that the universe is fundamentally unjust, ruled by blind chance, not by a loving, just and all-powerful God.

This 'logical' conclusion fails to explain a simple phenomenon, and it creates some bigger problems. It fails to explain why human beings who are themselves products of amoral 'blind chance' ask moral questions such as, 'What was this child's fault?' If as a part of a 'chance universe' we are amoral creatures, why do we expect the universe to be moral in the first place? Does not the core of our own being demand that the suffering should have a moral rationale behind it? The problem that the naturalistic view creates is that it implies that the universe is amoral; thus all morality is subjective and arbitrary, and we just create our moral laws and impose them on each other. If this is so, then there is no intrinsic reason for me to do what you tell me is right. If the universe itself gives you undeserved suffering, why should it not make you suffer through me?

The reincarnationists hope to avoid such conclusions by extending the natural law of cause and effect to previous lives. They argue that our present suffering is just, because it is caused by our karma in previous lives.

There are, however, some serious problems with their argument.

Even if our present experiences are caused by our actions in a previous life, how does that prove that the cosmos is just? Because an effect (e.g., the suffering of a child) has a cause, does it mean that the effect is just? If a husband is beating up his wife because he is drunk, the effect of beating is caused by the drunkenness. Just because there is a cause, it does not follow that the effect is just. If the wife is pregnant and the foetus is hurt due to the violence or the accompanying emotional trauma, then we would still know the cause of the child's later suffering, but we could not call it just. Cause and effect does not equal justice.

The reincarnationists' view of justice has no practical corrective value. The punishment received in one life can have value for the next only if we know for which karma we are being punished. Because of the absence of this memory, reincarnation has no value so far as the soul's development or 'evolution' is concerned.

The view of justice implied in karma and reincarnation also has no exemplary value for others. If you do not know what I am being punished for, there is nothing you can learn from my experience. Perhaps the enlightened beings know my past, but if they are already enlightened they will gain nothing.

If karma and reincarnation do not imply that the cosmos is a just system, then do we have to accept the naturalistic view that it is an unjust system? At this point the Judaeo-Christian belief deserves reconsideration. The biblical view is that when God originally created the cosmos it was a just system, good and perfect. We have innate moral feelings which demand that a child should not have to suffer unjustly, precisely because the universe is a moral system. But man's free will means that he can break both natural laws as well as moral laws. When, instead of choosing to love God, man and woman chose to disobey, their sin brought about an alienation between man and God, man and woman, man and nature, as well as self-alienation. After the fall we came to live not in a normal universe, but an abnormal universe. It is still a moral cosmos, but the earth now grows 'thorns and thistles'. There is sorrow, sickness and death. The 'inexplicable sufferings' are part of the present and temporary abnormality of the cosmos which God will set right after the final judgement. This view implies that we have to accept neither the nihilist's view that we live in an amoral universe of chance, nor the determinist's view that there is, despite all the evidence, a 'just system' of strict cause and effect.

It does not promote justice

In the previous section we saw that the explanation for evil and suffering offered by the doctrine of karma and reincarnation is very inadequate. A still bigger problem is that these beliefs actually hinder our commitment to alleviate suffering.

Reincarnationists say that we have the free will to help those who suffer. But the problem is that their belief system can give no guidelines about the point at which we can or should interfere with cosmic justice.

If a man is starving in this life because of his evil in a previous life, why should we interfere with cosmic justice? It is like breaking into a jail to free a criminal who has been awarded a judicial life imprisonment for a gruesome murder.

When Christ's disciples wondered if the congenital blindness of the beggar was due to sins he committed prior to his birth (John 9:2), Jesus rejected their speculative theory. He considered it his privilege and duty to care for the blind beggar. So he healed the man. When the beggar became a victim of social ostracism Jesus must have welcomed him into his community, as he did the other blind beggars whose eyes he opened and who stopped begging (Mark 10:46–52).

By contrast, a professor of Hindi at Delhi University said that acts of compassion on behalf of the suffering were foolish: if we did succeed in cutting short someone's suffering, he would still have to be reborn to complete his due term of suffering, so what is the benefit of interfering with the law of karma?

It is interesting that historically reincarnation has justified racism and sexism. Shirley MacLaine finds it a comfort to know that a soul is reborn sometimes as a male and at other times as a female. Reincarnation to her therefore implies the equality of the sexes. Sadly, in India the doctrine of the transmigration of souls has failed to produce an egalitarian society. In fact, its logic perpetuates racism and sexism. It says 'you are born an untouchable or a woman to serve me because of your past karma'. As Romila Thaper says in *A History of India*: 'The doctrine of karma also provided a philosophical justification for caste. One's birth into a lower or higher caste was also dependent on one's action in a previous life.'[13]

It undermines the foundations of morality and individual significance

The theory of karma which lies behind the belief in reincarnation undercuts the foundations of morality because it views morality as a mechanical system of cause and effect.

In Hindu thought human individuality is without significance. Buddha went so far as to postulate that humans have no soul – it is only karma which is incarnated. There is nothing comparable in Indian thought to the Western idea of unrepeatable events, unique historical avatars or messiahs, an exclusive God, and exclusive and true religion or a standard of constant value. Because the doctrine of reincarnation negates the significance and uniqueness of individuality, it trivialises death and inevitably opens the door to murder. Historically, in India the tragic implications of this were to justify the widespread practice of widow-, leper- and bride-burning, as well as infanticide and human sacrifice. Even in the Western world, where the doctrine of reincarnation is gaining ground, the practice of human sacrifice is also sneaking in through some cults.[14]

Sri Krishna teaches in the Bhagavad Gita that death is like changing clothes. Just as you discard worn-out clothes, so the soul discards one body to adopt a new one: 'As a man leaves an old garment and puts on one that is new, the spirit leaves his mortal body and then puts on one that is new' (Bhagavad Gita II.22). The soul is never really born and never dies. Krishna says to Arjuna:

> Thou dost feel pity where pity has no place. Wise men feel no pity either for what dies or what lives. There never was a time when I and thou were not in existence, and

all these princes too, nor will the day come hereafter, when all of us shall cease to be . . . (Bhagavad Gita II. 12–13)

That is why in *Out on a Limb* Shirley MacLaine says that 'Perhaps our belief in death was the gravest unreality of all.'[15] At one point she even suggests, albeit guardedly, that the six million Jews killed in the Holocaust were simply working out their collective karma from previous lives: 'In *Dancing in the Light* Ms MacLaine narrates many of her previous incarnations which involved gory murders. Through these she learned that even murder was not evil. 'There is no such thing as evil.'[16] Such blatant justification of immorality becomes possible because the law of karma is ultimately viewed as an amoral, unknowable law – 'a cosmic joke'.[17]

Ms MacLaine uses reincarnation to explain and justify not just murder, but sexual immorality. For her, homosexuality arises where a soul which was female in its previous life and is male now is working out the residual karma in this life with the soul which was its husband then.[18] The spirit-channellers assure her that her adulterous relationships are all right: she and her politician boyfriend Gerry are working out the karmas of a previous life, so his wife should not look upon their relationship as unfaithfulness to her.[19]

It is hopelessly cyclical

Many modern reincarnationists assume that a belief in reincarnation is a logical extension of the theory of evolution. If organisms have already evolved from a microscopic level of unconscious life to the higher level of human consciousness, then the next logical step would be to evolve to even higher planes, perhaps eventually culminating in the attainment of cosmic or God-consciousness.

There are, however, some difficulties with this belief. If the state of the next life is determined by the karma of this life, then bad karma must necessarily mean devolution in the next life. Hindu scriptures such as the Manusmriti go into great detail specifying which deed will lead to what kind of animal birth. Logically, it is just not possible simultaneously to believe in karma and reincarnation and in the inevitable evolution of the soul towards divinity.

Indeed within the Hindu scriptures it has been understood that very few souls do in fact attain divinity or 'salvation'. As Lannoy summarises:

> There is no kingdom of heaven on earth in Hinduism: unity is either atemporal, mystical and private or temporal, cyclical and collective. Overarching the entire system is the Cycle of Brahman, the inexorable law of eternal renewal within which the cosmos and man are successively born, degenerate and die. At the most a few rare souls dissolve into the inexhaustible plentitude of the divine enlightenment on the wheel of rebirth until another year of Brahama ends, a cosmic holocaust ensures that the whole process begins again.[20]

It is a fundamental negation of life
Many modern Hindu scholars have lamented that

> Two sentiments that are more often associated with the idea of salvation in India are disgust for the world and fear of rebirth . . .[our] religious books are heavy with these two sentiments. And our people in general have sought in religion only one blessing, a cessation from rebirth. This fear of life, this hope of salvation, this intense desire to escape from rebirth, have gone so far as to throw into the shade the problems and prospects of the brief spell of human life on earth. This helped to develop a negative attitude which in its extreme form is illustrated in the sentiments of a German poet:
> Sweet is sleep, death is better
> But it is best never to have been born.
> This negative attitude has been digging deep into the Indian mind during the last thousand years.[21]

Even Mahatama Gandhi concluded that 'reincarnation is a burden too great to bear'.

During his research in India, Ian Stevenson noted this pessimism about life, but seems to have remained uninterested in perceiving its logical connection with the doctrine of reincarnation:

> I asked Prakash where, if he had the chance and choice, he would like to be reborn. He said he would not like to be

reborn. (In the west such a remark might be interpreted as indicative of a clinical depression accompanied by a wish to die, but in India the wish not to be reborn is almost universal and indeed a positive aspiration of devout Hindus.)[22]

The biblical teaching about resurrection

As we have already seen, Jesus firmly repudiated his disciples' view that the beggar may have been born blind because of his sin prior to this birth (John 9:3). He taught that after death there is judgement, and then the wicked 'will go away to eternal punishment, but the righteous to eternal life' (Matt. 25:46). The claim made by many New Age writers, that Jesus taught reincarnation and that it was later removed from the doctrines of the church, is totally unsubstantiated. Admittedly, during the first few centuries some isolated gnostic sects within the church believed in reincarnation, but orthodox theologians invariably repudiated it.

Belief in reincarnation was rejected by the church as heresy first of all because after his death Jesus was not reincarnated in another body, but resurrected in the same. His tomb was empty and his disciples saw his nail-pierced hands. Jesus did not lose his previous memory. He knew his disciples and, more importantly for our purpose, the disciples recognised him. The church rejected reincarnation because it conflicts with biblical teaching in several respects. According to the Bible, this world, even though under a curse, is essentially good and is not a place of punishment where souls are sent to be in bondage to the body, to take the consequences of their karma. Likewise, the human body, though subject to decay and death due to original sin, is essentially good and to be enjoyed. It is redeemable and will be saved by the sacrificial death of Jesus Christ (1 Cor. 15:42-4, 51-7). Our individuality, though finite, is good and eternal. We are meant to live for ever as God's children, not lose our individuality by merging into an impersonal, universal consciousness.

According to the Bible the earth was to be the paradise in which Adam and Eve and their children would live for ever and ever in fellowship with God, each other and nature. They were not meant to die, but their eternal life was contingent on their loving obedience to God. Death came as a consequence of the sin of disobedience (Gen. 3:17–19). Sin disturbed the integrity of creation, including the oneness of body and soul in man.

Christianity does not trivialise or glorify death. Death is a tragic abnormality because it was not a part of God's original intention for mankind. Because it fractures our personal unity, disrupts the loving relationships we are meant to have with one another, and interrupts our care for the earth, death is seen in the Bible as an enemy, something to be resisted and overcome.

Death came because of Adam's disobedience. It was defeated by Christ's obedience at the cross. Salvation, which includes the forgiveness of sin, means setting right the harmful consequences of sin, including restoring the unity of body and soul, which is fractured at death. Therefore, according to the Bible, salvation is completed only when the unity of the human person is restored in a resurrected body. Those who identify with Christ's death and resurrection through repentance and the baptism of faith will share in his victory over death. They will receive a new imperishable or 'glorified' body which is not subject to death and decay.

Resurrection affirms the basic goodness of the material world and our individuality. It affirms that man is more than a material body, but it does not minimise the body. The material universe, being God's creation, is good – very good (Gen. 1:31). Resurrection does not mean my becoming something or someone else in the next life, but the same me, in the same body, being raised to life and being glorified – just as the crucified body of Christ was raised and glorified. Resurrection offers hope and meaning not simply for my life and for my body, but for my world as well.

9

MY COURSE IN MIRACLES

We must remove the word 'impossible' from our vocabulary ... Anyone who does not believe in miracles is not a realist ... terms like 'spontaneous remission' or 'miracle' mislead and confuse us ... these healings occur through [the patient's own] hard work. They are not acts of God.

Bernie S. Siegel[1]

The search for self becomes a search for health, for wholeness ...

Marilyn Ferguson[2]

We disregarded the spirit in our efforts to cure the body. Now in finding health, we find ourselves.

Marilyn Ferguson[3]

This chapter, the most personal in this book, has two objectives. It seeks to help those who may be looking for a cure for themselves or their loved ones after frequent frustrating visits to specialists. It also attempts to understand and evaluate the New Age movement's approach to what is often called 'alternative medicine'.

It is not a study of 'alternative therapies' such as homeopathy, ayurveda, acupuncture, bio-feedback or psychic healing *per se*. My aim is to examine the claim that the human self is the only healer and that the success of these therapies points to the unlimited potential of the self.

Some of these therapies are called 'traditional' medicines because of their ancient origins. They are sometimes portrayed as 'alternatives' and at other times as 'complementary' to the mainstream medical system called 'allopathy'. At times these medicines are also described as part of the 'holistic health movement', implying that they treat the whole person, including the mind and spirit, and not just the biochemical body.

I would like to begin by narrating one of my own experiences with homeopathy. Experiences like these demand an explanation — that is, a world-view which makes sense of them.

Healing experiences requiring an explanation

The wonder of homeopathy

One often hears of tumours, even malignant tumours, disappearing through faith-healing, psychic healing or creative visualisation. My own experience is simpler, but I think still worth recounting, in order to illustrate an important aspect of the New Age view of sickness.

I think it was in 1986 when I experienced what I thought was the astounding effectiveness of homeopathy.

A small boil appeared under my right shoulder towards the back. I had never been one to be bothered with these little ailments. I took no notice of it, assuming it would disappear just as quickly as it had appeared. As a matter of fact I would not have even noticed its existence, if it had not been irritating, forcing me to scratch it. Before I knew it, the boil had become an abscess. The pain and pus ensured that it could no longer be ignored.

My doctor, a good family friend, made a tiny incision, drained out the pus, applied some ointment, bandaged the spot and gave me some tablets. The pain and itching had increased by the following morning. The doctor removed the bandage to discover that the abscess had become a wound. The entire bandaged area was red with rash and several more small boils had appeared. There was more pus than before. She cleaned it all up again, drained out the pus, applied a different ointment, bandaged a larger area, and sent me off with some stronger capsules. She said it should be okay.

The next day I was forced to abandon work again and return to the hospital. The itching and pain were now intolerable. The red skin had turned yellow, oozing with pus. The surrounding area was also red and soft, and covered in a rash.

The cleaning and dressing were repeated, and I was put on strong antibiotics. Yet the wound grew worse. The doctor finally guessed that I was allergic to the plastic tape they were using for bandaging the wound. She therefore concluded that my trouble could not be called 'iatrogenic'. At the time I was in too much pain to find out that 'iatrogenic' meant 'caused by the doctor'!

My doctor friend loved surgery, but I have no doubt that she prescribed it only because she believed that nothing else could cure me faster. The cut she had to make was so deep and so large that it took almost two months to heal fully. I began to believe that at the old age of thirty-seven my body was beginning to lose its capacity to heal itself.

A few months later I was in Bhopal, the capital of Madhya Pradesh. My mission was to persuade the National Bank of Agriculture and Rural Development (NABARD) to finance small-scale, rural-based potato-dehydration projects we were starting. Less than an hour before I was scheduled to meet the bank officials, I noticed a small boil on my chest, exactly like the earlier one. The memories of my previous experience horrified me. The pain and the expenses were bad enough – but worse, I could not afford the time to be sick. I asked for directions to the nearest clinic, hired a three-wheel auto-rickshaw, and dashed off to see the doctor, hoping I would not be too late for my appointment with the bank.

The 'clinic' turned out to be the residence of a retired civil servant who practised homeopathy in his living room, 'as a hobby'. Under normal circumstances I would have certainly turned around and gone in search of a doctor practising allopathic medicine. I had never been able to trust those systems of medicine in which the practitioner was not willing to write down what treatment he was prescribing and why. If he knows what he is doing, he should make himself accountable. If he is reluctant to state and explain his diagnosis and the prescribed treatment, how could I be sure that he knew what he was doing? How could I trust myself in his care? I was in a cleft stick. If a highly trained professional had messed up my previous boil, how could I trust myself to an amateur practitioner now?

The meeting scheduled for that morning with the bank

officials was crucial. I was certain that the officer dealing with my proposal would be sympathetic towards my presentation, but would not make any decision. He would simply send me to the 'higher' authorities, and I would spend the whole day repeating, explaining and defending my plan, until the time I had to rush to the station to catch the train. The next opportunity to see a physician would not be for the next thirty hours. I did not have the courage to see this boil turn into an abscess.

The homeopath – a kind, confident old man – asked his ten year old grandson to prepare my medicine. He poured a strong smelling liquid on to tiny white sugary balls, put them in a glass bottle, and gave it to his grandfather. The 'doctor' shook the bottle for a while as he explained the dosage to me. It was much later that I learned that this shaking is called 'succussion' in homeopathy. The purpose of shaking is not to mix the chemicals. It is a technique to 'potentise' the medicine. There are virtually no 'active' or therapeutic chemicals in homeopathic medicine.

Samuel Hahnemann (1755–1843), the founder of homeopathy, believed that a disease is cured by the same substance which causes the ailment in the first place. In his book *Organon of the Art of Healing* published in Torgaou, Germany, in 1810, he called it 'the law of similars' – like cures like. 'A substance which produces symptoms in a healthy person, cures those symptoms in a sick person.'[4]

Hahnemann arrived at the above 'law of nature' through the scientific method of experiment, observation and deduction on the basis of observed data. He experimented on his patients with toxic substances such as mercury and arsenic. Not surprisingly, their symptoms were aggravated. That alarmed both the patients and his fellow physicians. Therefore Hahnemann decided to dilute his medicines to one-tenth their previous amount. That, he found, was not good enough. Therefore he diluted them further, to one-hundredth, then one-ten thousandth and up to one-millionth of the original amount. Obviously, by then not even a single molecule of the original active, 'therapeutic' ingredient remained in his medicine. However, Hahnemann discovered that while this dilution made his medicines completely safe – i.e., without any side effects – their healing power could be retained, even

increased, if he submitted his diluted medicines to vigorous
shakes. Homeopaths have not sought a scientific explanation of why shaking 'potentises' their otherwise ineffective
medicines. They just know from their experiences that
it does. They venerate Hahnemann for this miraculous
discovery.

For example, David Icke, former chief spokesman of the
Green Party in England, says:

> Few people can understand why diluting a plant extract
> again and again can possibly have any power over dis-
> ease, but in fact the vibration of the plant is still present
> in the water and it is the vibration, not the substance
> of the homeopathic preparation, that has the effect on
> illness.[5]

We will return to a discussion of this later in the chapter.
For the moment, let us continue with my story.

The homeopath charged me only three rupees, which
equals about eight pence. 'The boil will dry up in two
days,' he said coolly. Needless to say, it did dry up within
twenty-four hours, to my great relief, astonishment and
joy.

A few months later I had to return to Bhopal to clinch a
deal with the bank. In the train I discovered another boil
on my thigh. This time I did not even think of going to
the allopath. I went straight to the homeopath and told
him how grateful I was for his wonder drug. He did not
bother to look at my thigh. He handed me another bottle.
'This is a stronger dose. If you complete the course your
blood will be thoroughly cleansed, and these boils will not
recur,' he said. The boil did dry up in a day or two. I was
not interested in checking if my blood had anything to
do with these boils. I do not remember how long after
this course I had my first boil again. Since then I have
had the occasional boil, but I seem to have gone back to
my old habit of not bothering with them at all, to no ill
effect.

Homeopathy 'worked' for me in that situation. The question is, how does it work when there are no active ingredients in the medicine? Since the pills themselves have
neither the power to do any good or harm, does shaking
really 'potentise' the pill? Since no mechanistic explanation

seems possible, are we to conclude that the realities of sickness and healing are beyond rational laws? If so, then why bother with expensive scientific medicine, which so often compounds our problems? Is the optimism, strong in some New Age circles, justified, that 'Surgery with a knife [will] be outmoded. Only the use of hands, colour, crystals and waters [will] be necessary [for healing] before the century's end'?[6]

Self – the deadliest virus or the only healer?

Most computer-users know that they use only a fraction of their machine's capabilities. Many do not even know what their computer is capable of. A human being is more complex and powerful than a computer, yet, similarly, most of us go through life without even becoming aware of our own physical and mental abilities.

I know a young man whose mother died in tragic circumstances. She had a minor accident. She fell off a scooter, got up and went home. There she fell unconscious. She did not regain consciousness, and died after many weeks in the hospital. Her death had a devastating impact on her son. He would spend hours in the cemetery. He cut himself off from all his relatives and friends, and stopped communicating. He would not bathe or change his clothes. After all attempts to restore him to normality failed, his uncle decided to take him to a psychiatric centre. They found that even half a dozen men had difficulty pinning down this very ordinary young man. They had to use an extraordinary amount of tranquillisers to knock him out.

Some people wondered if his new 'superhuman' strength had a spiritistic source. He was spending far too much time in the graveyard. His great-grandfather had been one of India's foremost spiritists at the beginning of this century. The family was now living in the same house where he used to conduct seances. The New Testament records that a man possessed by a legion of demons also proved physically stronger than many men. He broke iron chains when tied hand and foot with them (Mark 5:1–20).

Was the boy's strength demonic? Maybe, but not necessarily. People sometimes demonstrate apparently 'superhuman' strength in emergencies. It is certain that all human beings have natural untapped physical and mental potential which surfaces under special circumstances. The influence of another spirit could be one factor which releases this potential. The practitioners of martial arts try to make conscious efforts to harness this untapped resource within themselves. Their success demonstrates that just as a computer-whiz can exploit a much greater part of his computer's potential, so human beings can discover and use their inner strength in dealing with stress and disease. Medical scientists are now admitting that, contrary to what we usually think, as many as seventy per cent of our diseases may in fact be cured by our own inner strength, and not by a doctor's prescription.

My friend Dr Raju Abraham, a neurologist in London, often quotes a formula he calls '70:15:15.' 'Seventy per cent of patients,' he says, 'get better no matter what therapy you give them. Fifteen per cent don't get better no matter what you do. A physician makes a real difference to only fifteen per cent of the diseases he encounters.'

Doctors now know that even minor changes in one's life can cause major stress, shock and considerable feelings of helplessness and hopelessness, resulting in sickness. Such changes could be just about anything, such as a husband giving away a family puppy to a stranger, or a child getting a minor electric shock. The child could be playing again after only a few minutes, but the mother might need to be put on tranquillisers in a hospital.

Life changes such as the following are common causes of many a stress-related sickness: the death of a spouse, divorce, marital separation, the death of a close family member, imprisonment or confinement in a mental hospital, major injury, marriage, retirement, being made redundant, an addition to the family through birth or adoption, relatives moving in, a change at work, debt, a son or daughter leaving home, a wife beginning to or ceasing to work outside the home, a drastic change in working or sleeping hours, a change of boss or school, a minor violation of the law, a minor accident, or even a holiday.

Involuntary change, even where that change later proves to have been for the better, may cause sickness, even death. Obviously it is not the change itself, but our fears about it and our inability to cope with real or imaginary hardships, stress and dangers that cause disease.

Some physicians refuse to acknowledge and learn how to use the inner capacities of their patients to heal themselves. Some are committed to a philosophy that a self beyond and above the physical body does not exist. Others have always believed that a human being is more than a body. They are simply put off by those colleagues who have recently discovered that materialism is wrong and that the mind is more than matter. These physicians who have reinvented the wheel get so excited about their discovery that the human self has power over the physical body that they begin to downplay matter, medicine and surgery. They begin to insist that the self is the only healer; that all healing is self-healing. Indeed from the fact that we can cure many – maybe even seventy per cent – of our diseases, it is logically impossible to conclude that we can cure all our illnesses; that the human self is infinite.

The plain fact is that the young man who displayed enormous strength could eventually be knocked out, that someone who in an emergency lifts a car is not able to lift a truck. Even the greatest healers become sick and die, proving that they too cannot heal all diseases.

We do make ourselves sick, but others can also make us sick. An 'impossible' husband can make his wife sick by his insensitivity, meanness and cruelty. I know that when I am hard-hearted and foolish I can make my children sick. A rude and arrogant boss can make his otherwise excellent secretary sick. I know a son who because of his moral wickedness and stubborn selfishness caused his father to have a near-fatal heart attack.

A sick wife, a father, a child or a secretary need not always blame themselves for their sickness. We reach the limits of our tolerance and break down emotionally and/or physically for the same reason we enter into human relationships in the first place – because we are finite. If we were infinite, our emotional and physical capacities would be unlimited. But then we may not need to relate to finite, irritable and mean spouses, parents, children and employers. It is true that all of us can stretch more by being more loving, bend more by being humbler, and be stronger by being more trusting, and thus save ourselves from many sicknesses. Nevertheless, being finite, we all must reach a breaking point. When we do reach our limits and become sick, before trying to change others it is sensible to see where *we* can change, to heal ourselves.

Alternative therapies and the New Age movement

The New Age movement is a social phenomenon which has originated in our generation. Some of the 'alternative therapies' are hundreds, even thousands of years old. These therapies are based on mutually contradictory assumptions about human beings, illness and healing. An Indian witch doctor may assume that a girl's 'convulsions' are caused by a demon. A traditional therapist from China may believe that the flow of chi (i.e., the 'vital energy') to that same girl's spleen has been blocked in one of the twelve 'meridians' – the invisible channels in our body through which the chi flows. An Indian ayurvad may diagnose her problem as having its cause in an excess of 'fire' or 'earth'.

One assumption which is common to all these therapies is that a sick person needs a therapist. This assumption is fundamentally opposed to New Age thought. If my self is the fundamental principle of my universe, then how can a healer be more powerful than my sick self?

However, most practitioners of alternative therapies are very happy to belong to the New Age. For too long they have been treated as quacks by the mainstream medical elite. Now a social-intellectual movement has appeared in the form of the New Age movement which challenges medical science on its own turf. It gives a sympathetic hearing to the 'traditional' therapists. It mobilises funding, publicity, and research into their art, thereby adding respectability to their profession.

What the practitioners of 'alternative medicine' often do not seem to realise is that the New Age movement is simply and temporarily using them as evidence against the secular, materialistic, mechanistic world-view. In reality New Age thought is as much opposed to the alternative therapies as it is to mainstream medicine.

We have already seen that when a homeopath cures a person with chemically neutral medicines, that healing raises the question whether the essence of a human being, his sickness and health, lies beyond the boundaries of biochemistry. If an allopath abandons a little girl who is visibly suffering convulsions, with a statement that there is nothing wrong with her, while an illiterate witch doctor can help her recover in an instant, then the girl and her parents are more likely to trust the witch doctor. An individual who has experienced the effectiveness of 'colour therapy' or 'psychic surgery' is likely to have no difficulty in rejecting the arrogance of materialism and mechanistic science, which are the chief enemies of the New Age movement. Herein lies the usefulness of 'alternative medicine' to the New Agers who neither respect nor fear the metaphysical assumptions behind these therapies. The immediate enemy of the New Age is the secular world-view, and it wants to enlist the support of these therapies in weakening the iron grip of this enemy over the Western mind-set.

Most thoughtful New Age authors are quite clear that many alternative therapists cannot be called New Agers, because their practices flatly contradict the essence of the New Age belief that self is the only reality and is therefore the only healer. They admit that although many of these therapists are quacks, exploiting the gullible public,[7] for the moment, however, they are useful to their cause. The 'miraculous' cures they perform force people to ask: Is a human being only a biochemical machine? Is the mind, spirit or self an entity separate from and more powerful than the body? Is there a 'life-force', a 'chi' or a 'prana' that connects a sufferer with a healer and with everything else in the universe? If a psychic surgeon can put his hand through my body and take out the 'negativity', in the form of blood clots; if the psychic vibrations emanating from a healer's brain can make a tumour disappear, then could it be that the body, including that tumour, is nothing more than a materialised thought? If the meaningless words of a mantra, a flower's smell, a crystal stone, an inactive pill, a touch, or a word can cure an illness in an instant, then might that not suggest that reality may ultimately be irrational, even an illusion?

Marilyn Ferguson is one of those New Age authors who states explicitly that alternative medicine is not an intrinsic part of the New Age movement. It only serves as an 'intermediate step' by undermining faith in rationalism. She writes:

While psychic healing may prove a useful adjunct to medicine in the future, it is unlikely to become a primary mode of treatment [in the Aquarian Age] – for a simple reason. A 'healer' is ministering in much the same way as a doctor, doing something to the patient. Shamanic healers – the curanderos of South America for instance – tell those they treat that they can affect the symptoms but they cannot change the inner process that produces disease. The symptoms may disappear for a time but too often the deeper matrix of disease has not been changed. Only the individual can effect a healing from within.[8]

Ferguson's chapter on health is entitled 'Healing ourselves'. Her central thesis is that the human self is the only real healer; the body is a 'responsive field of energy'. The placebo effect 'offers dramatic proof that all healing is essentially self-healing'.[9] Therefore

Bio-feedback is the ultimate placebo, an intermediate step for those clinicians and patients, reassured by 'hard' science, who have not yet noticed that all action is in a soft brain and vanishes into whirling particles on closer inspection. [Sickness and health are] all in the imagination . . . we can have it as we imagine and as we will.[10]

Ferguson looks at alternative medicine only as an intermediate step, rather than reality, because of her a priori commitment to the view that the physical universe, including the human body, is only a hologram, a process in our mind.

Matthew Manning is a good example of the impact of New Age thought on alternative therapists. Twenty years ago he was a 'psychic healer'. Now he is a promoter of self-healing. From the proven fact that 'through mental imagery and suggestion [people] could rid themselves of pain' he concludes, in his *Guide to Self-Healing*, that they can also 'change their perception and illusion of illness. That, in fact, there [is] nothing the mind [cannot] do.'[11]

While in theory Manning has become a doctrinally 'pure' New Ager, in his practice realism prevails. He keeps emphasising that a patient usually needs the supplementary support of family, friends, healers and physicians – including drugs and surgery.

'When illness hits one member of the family,' Manning writes,

> each other member of that unit needs time to stop and evaluate what this will mean . . . time is needed to work through fears and plan ways of coping . . . close friends are essential to provide additional emotional support and comfort outside of the family unit.[12]

Manning also considers whether the 'healer' plays a significant part in healing, or whether his presence has only a 'psychological' benefit to the patient:

> In 1980 I participated in a pilot study at a well-known hospital, the objective being 'to discover what effects, if any, Matthew Manning's healing technique has'. I was asked to treat a number of patients, all of whom were suffering from chronic pain which was not responding to conventional medical treatment. Although I appeared to treat all the patients, I was in reality only properly attempting to heal half of them because, whilst I placed my hands on all of them, with half I was only pretending to heal and was not going through any mental process as I would normally. The object of this deception was to assess whether any benefit that was derived could be accounted for in terms of psychological factors or placebo. If healing were explicable in such terms one would expect all patients to have benefited, or for those who were helped to be randomly distributed throughout both groups of patients in the study. In fact those patients who had benefited came from the group who had been properly treated.[13]

In Manning's own judgement he possesses some real healing powers, even though, somewhat paradoxically, he calls his healing method 'self-healing' by his patients. What is the source of his healing power? His own mind, or another spirit?

Before answering these questions it is necessary to point out that, as Manning implies in the first quotation above, the only consistent New Age view of sickness and healing is that all sickness is illusion. This view is best exemplified in *A Course in Miracles*. The Course is not an abstract metaphysical statement. It prescribes a step-by-step method to enable the readers to begin to see disease as illusion and thereby find self-healing. The 'Teacher's Manual' of the Course states:

> There can be no order of difficulty in healing . . . because all sickness is illusion . . .
> Healing involves an understanding of what the illusion of sickness is for . . .
> Sickness is but a faulty problem-solving approach, it is a decision . . . The acceptance of sickness as a decision of the mind . . . is the basis for healing. And this is so for healing in all forms. A patient decides that this is so, and he recovers. If he decides against recovery, he will not be healed. Who is the physician? Only the mind of the patient himself . . . Special agents [therapists] seem to be ministering to him, yet they but give form to his own choice. He chooses them in order to bring tangible form to his desires. And it is this they do, and nothing else. They are not actually needed at all. The patient could merely rise up without their aid and say, 'I have no use for this'. There is no form of sickness that would not be cured at once.
> What is the single requisite for this shift in perception? It is simply this; the recognition that sickness is of the mind, and has nothing to do with the body. What does this recognition 'cost'? It costs the whole world you see.[14]

It is not difficult to see the power of this teaching. On this view, the inactive sugar pills of the homeopath healed me not because he had potentised them, but because my disease was in fact an illusion.

I have had such boils occasionally, ever since I was a child. I have had them since the homeopathic course. A boil would come and go on its own. It became an abscess on that occasion because I exposed my skin to infection by scratching it. The problem was aggravated by the tape to which my skin was allergic. My suspicion that my body was losing its power to heal itself was also an illusion, as proved by later experiences. The illusion bred fears and anxieties at Bhopal when I saw the boil on my chest. My excitement at the effect of the homeopath's tablets was directly proportional to the fears and anxieties I had had. The boil would have disappeared without the tablets, as usual, if I had been careful not to scratch it. The tablets had no active ingredients. The dear old homeopath did not even know that those boils had nothing to do with bad blood. If my body had lost the power to clean my blood, I would be heading for something more serious than those occasional boils.

When Samuel Hahnemann discovered the 'law of similars' it was as a scientist attempting to use empirical methods, basing his system of medicine on what he thought to be a law of nature. Even allopathic medicine uses the same law to make vaccines and to treat allergies. But genuine science has to remain self-critical. For a scientific theory is never really 'true'. It can only be 'probably true', because it is seeking to discover universal laws from a small number of observed facts. Scientific laws have to be rejected and new laws formulated when facts are observed which do not fit within the framework of previously accepted laws. If a law cannot be revised simply because a great man – whether Newton or Hahnemann – articulated it in another century, then that law has ceased to be a law of science, it has become a dogma of a man-made cult.

What was true of homeopathy in my case applies equally to remedies such as 'Bach Flower Therapy'. During the economic depression of the 1930s many people lost jobs and securities. Their fears and emotional traumas resulted in all kinds of sicknesses. An English doctor, Edward Bach, then developed thirty-nine colourful remedies, derived from flowers, trees and plants. These too were distilled past the level of chemical potency. Their healing power lay in the effectiveness of colour and aroma to affect a patient's emotions.

The above is not of course to imply that all homeopathic medicines always work in the same way as in my case. If homeopaths continue to seek more information about sickness and healing, and have the courage to reject laws and medicines that are not tenable in the light of new discoveries, then their research could be considered properly scientific. Allopaths too must remain open to observe data to see if genuine physical sickness is sometimes caused by non-physical, even demonic influences. And New Agers must also remain intellectually open to consider if other spiritual forces are also active in a healing besides the patient's own self.

Before discussing this last point, let us examine one 'empirical proof' which is often put forward to support the view that the body and its diseases are an illusion.

Psychic surgery: Evidence for illusion?
In her book *Going Within* Shirley MacLaine argues that not only disease, but the body (along with the rest of the physical universe) is an illusion, a hologram, a materialised thought. Therefore, she writes:

> Totally self-realized people rarely become diseased . . . Disease in the body, as I have learned from experience, begins first with a blockage of energy in the spirit. For me, all of my physical problems begin in my consciousness . . . [sickness] relates to some fear, rejection or feeling of 'nonworthiness'. I try to reconnect with spiritual harmony and God. If I'm successful, I get well. This particular aspect of New Age thinking – self-healing – is a highly developed stage, obviously a long way down the road to full-awareness.[15]

In spite of her commitment to this idea of self-healing (perhaps because, even though her self is God, it sometimes fails to heal), Ms Maclaine devotes an entire chapter entitled 'My Body as Ultimate Atoms of Awareness' to the subject of psychic surgery. She narrates many experiences when Alex Orbito of Manila performed surgical operations inside the bodies of her friends and herself with bare hands. The following is the first description involving her friend Chris Griscom, a spiritual acupuncturist from Galisteo. Chris had not complained of any trouble in her heart, still:

> 'Take off blouse,' Alex said, 'I must work on heart.' Chris lifted her blouse off over her head. I was glad she was wearing a bra. I remembered I wasn't.
> Alex's wife and assistant sat beside him. As though by command Alex's arms went up in the air, found a direction of some kind, then gently plunged into Chris' mid-section, whereupon he deftly began to knead the skin of her torso above the waist . . . until his hands seem to separate the skin and suddenly both hands were inside her chest. There was blood, and there was a sloshing sound as his hands searched for something near her

heart . . . His hands were actually in there! Both of them.
And no, I wasn't dreaming.[16]

Ms MacLaine is convinced that the entire world is
a dream. Yet she wants us to believe that these 'sixty
second' operations, in which the psychic surgeon put his
bare hands into her body and removed negativity in the
form of blood clots, were real, that these were not instances
where a magician's hands proved to be swifter than her
eyes. Her higher self told her that these experiences were
given to her as a 'proof that the body is nothing but "dream
thought".' Or, as Chris put it to her, 'That is what a physical
body is – a dream that we have dreamed into believing
is real so we can have the adventure of physical life.'[17]
Whether a psychic surgeon actually inserts his hands
inside a patient's body to remove a diseased tissue or or-
gan can easily be proven if an X-ray of a diseased lung
is taken before and after the surgery. To be convincing,
the surgeon would need to remove the diseased lung, not
simply negativity in the form of some blood clots. This is
because surgeons such as W. Nolen, the author of *Healing: A Doctor in Search of a Miracle*,[18] have so vividly
exposed the tricks many psychic surgeons use. The tis-
sues they allegedly remove from patients have been shown
to be the entrails of chickens, dogs, rats and pigs. The
Forensic Institute of the University of Zurich found that
the blood on one patient's cotton swab came from a pig!

The consequences of viewing sickness as an illusion
New Age therapy is based on the presupposition that reality
is only what I visualise it to be. There is no objective reality
independent of my self. Therefore there is nothing which
cannot be affected by my visualisation. But consider the
consequences of this belief. When visualisation is confused
with reality, we are not left with a wonderful world of
hope, but with a nihilistic universe whose meaning changes
with my moods. For example, the first lesson a student on
a course of self-healing learns is that 'Nothing I see in
this room (on this street, from this window, in this place)
means anything.'[19] The exercise for the second day is to tell
oneself: 'I have given everything I see in this room all the
meaning that it has for me.'[20]

The New Age seems to tolerate all the alternative systems of medicine. But that is indeed only an illusion. The only consistent New Age therapy is the belief that there is no therapy, because self, the only thing that is real, cannot be sick. The *Course in Miracles* sums it up in this way: 'Nothing real can be threatened. Nothing unreal exists.'[21] My child whose body can be threatened by a fall, a snake, a germ or a virus cannot be real. A healer whose therapy is threatened by an incurable disease is not real. That is why, according to Ferguson, alternative therapies such as psychic healing and bio-feedback cannot be important therapies in the New Age – the age of perfection, when man will be God.

We are now ready to question the fundamental assumption of the New Age healers.

Is self the only healer?

We can ignore the fact that Ms MacLaine's faith in psychic surgery weakens the New Age case for self-healing. But we must notice that these surgeons themselves claim that their healing powers are not their own but are derived from other spirits. Ms MacLaine writes this herself about Alex Orbito:

> Orbito was not aware of his healing power until he was fourteen, when he began to have dreams about a mysterious old man who said he was the boy's spirit guide and gave him a personal mantra that enabled Alex to place himself in an altered state of consciousness at will. In these dreams the old man told Alex he was a great healer.[22]

Alex himself told Ms MacLaine that it was the energy (spirit) of another doctor who worked through him.[23]

During the 1990 Festival of Mind, Body and Spirit I was able to hear and talk to two better-known psychic healers. Allegra Taylor is the author of *I Fly Out With Bright Feathers*.[24] She calls herself a 'novice healer'. In her lecture she described how one day she put one hand on her sick child and raised the other to the universe. In her desperation for the child she asked for help. Suddenly she felt as if an electric current had passed through her raised hand, through her body, through the other hand to the sick child, who was instantly healed. She could not honestly call it self-healing. She believed that she had become a channel of another spirit's power.

Matthew Manning, in contrast to Mrs Taylor, argued forcefully that all human beings possessed 'psychic energy' within them to heal.

I had already read that Manning's journey as a psychic healer started on 18 February 1967, when some poltergeist phenomena first began around him. By 1970 the phenomena got focused on him and followed him to boarding school in 1971. He began to hear spirit voices and finally saw a full-blown apparition. Soon he was demonstrating psychic abilities such as bending metals by means of concentration. After meditating for some time in the Indian Himalayas (where I now live), Manning started using this spirit's power to heal the sick. Therefore in my interview I asked him: 'This morning Mrs Taylor said that she was only a channel for another spirit's power. You seemed to be saying that your power comes from a natural source within you, the human spirit. What is the truth? Are you the healer, or are you only a conduit for another power?' Without a moment's hesitation Manning replied, 'No, I am only a conduit for another spirit's power.'

Dr Bernie Siegel also confesses that his work of 'self-healing' began when, during a meditation session, he met a spirit, George – a bearded, long-haired young man, wearing an immaculate flowing white gown and a skull cap. We saw in chapter 3 that at the beginning of his book *Love, Medicine and Miracles* Dr Siegel defines George as a 'meditatively released insight from my unconscious',[25] but towards the end of the book it is clear that he believes that spirits exist as metaphysical entities, outside our consciousness. They can penetrate us and communicate with us.[26]

As we saw earlier in this chapter, not all cases of psychic healing are spirit-healing, or 'self'-healing. One significant factor makes a homeopath's inactive tablets and a faith-healer's touch and a witch doctor's spells as effective as a doctor's placebo. That is, their faith in their treatment and the doctor's lack of faith in his placebo. Facts such as this point towards the conclusion that the mental/spiritual aspects of our being may have a certain authority over the physical aspect of our being. All of us are getting infections and viruses all the time. They are usually fought off by the immune system. That system is like a car that normally works with a self-starter. Sometimes, however, the immune system seems to get stuck like a car's when the battery is low. The car then needs a push. Visualisation can act as a push to start off the engine of our immune system.

The confidence of a therapist or the influence of another spirit could also help start the system. But from the fact that our self or psyche has a certain amount of authority over our own or our patient's physical bodies, we cannot logically conclude that therefore our self is almighty or the only healer.

If the healer is at least as important in healing as the patient, then why do Manning and other New Age healers hide this fact behind elaborate theories of self-healing? Is it only to remain within the theological orthodoxy of the New Age? Or is it because they realise that to admit that healers and disembodied spirits could heal would cause people to seek our creator, God himself, whose power to heal is greater than the power of other spirits? Those who get to know the Almighty Spirit would not have much use for the healing powers of finite spirits.

A guide to divine healing

It must have been late 1982 when ACRA, our rural community, set apart three days for a spiritual retreat. At about 9 p.m. on the last day we were enjoying supper and conversation after a day of prayer and Bible study. The sound of a scooter outside our front door interrupted us. It was the chief of a village about three miles from our farm. He looked sombre and asked, 'Do any of you know "Jhara Phoonki"?'

Jhara Phoonki literally means to sweep and blow a thing (or place) clean. It is a term used to describe what witch doctors or occult healers do through their spells, vibrations, incantations, herbs or magic stones.

'No,' I replied, 'but we pray. What is the matter?'

'A brahmin [high-caste] woman was bitten by a cobra at about 3 p.m., she became unconscious at 6 p.m., now she is dying. She is young and has two little children. We've called all the "knowledgeable people" from the area, they have done all they could, but she is sinking. I had come to call your neighbour Nath [a tribal snake-charmer] but he is away. So I thought it wouldn't hurt asking if any in your community could "sweep" the snake poison. But since you only pray, why don't you come and at least pray?'

The woman was lying on a string cot in a long room of a mud house. There were about fifty women and men sitting in the silence of despair, waiting for her to die. Some of these men were sorcerers who also doubled as witch doctors. One was a medical doctor – an allopath, in charge of the state health centre. He had given the woman glucose intravenously, just in case she had fainted because of low blood sugar. By the time we got there, he too had given up all hope. He explained that they could not keep antivenin because the health centre had no refrigeration.

I had brought some ice with me because our community health manual said that ice was good for snake bites.

The witch doctors had given up casting spells and using their miraculous herbs and magic stones. They knew that if these didn't prove useful soon enough, their spells were generally not effective during the later stages of a snake bite. The witch doctors were called because the local people had witnessed 'miracles' performed by these men. You can be sure that if no one had ever seen a witch doctor perform a miracle, they would not be feared, trusted or invited. Some of their spells do indeed heal, whereas others cause disease and even death. The village folk may be simple, illiterate and superstitious, but they are not fools. They do not believe everything you say. They are suspicious, but willing to try. They remember what works and what does not.

A snake bite has three distinct effects: it gives pain, shock and sometimes lethal poison. The shock and pain generate fears, both in the victim and in his family and friends. The atmosphere of fear and hysteria in turn aggravates pain and shock, affecting pulse rate, breathing, blood pressure, etc. The snake-charmers and witch doctors appear to have no fear. They retain their cool. Snake-charmers seem to have an authority over the snake. Therefore people find it easy to believe that they also have authority over its poison. The first impact of a witch doctor's presence is to contain the fear and hysteria. His presence has a calming effect, for people believe that now they have someone in control of the situation who is more powerful than the snake.

A second factor in a witch doctor's effectiveness is the patient's faith in his spell. Their faith triggers off what medical science calls the 'placebo effect'. We now know that the human brain produces substances known as peptides. One such peptide is called Endrophine, which has effects similar to a morphine injection. The spell cast by a witch doctor, a foot massage by a reflexologist, the acupuncture needles of a traditional Chinese therapist, the ointment of a herbalist, or the 'vibrations' of a psychic healer might act like a placebo. They could start chemical reactions in a patient's brain which remove the symptoms of sickness. Once the shock, fear and pain are gone, there is only the snake poison left to take care of.

Most snakes do not have deadly poison, some have only a little. Even a deadly cobra (which abound in our district) may not have injected its full poison into a victim. It may have fought with a mongoose first and used up most of its poison. The thought of being bitten by a cobra may be deadlier than the poison itself.

Our bodies take care of a certain amount of poison on their own. When a witch doctor's power has healed a snake-victim, it is not necessary to assume that he has taken care of the poison as such. The symptoms that have vanished may have been those of fear and shock, not of the poison. When the spells have not worked, it could mean either that the poison was really there in a deadly amount or that the victim's mental state had reached a point beyond which a placebo could not be effective. Unfortunately many victims do die of snake bites in our villages every year, in spite of the witch doctors' spells.

In this case the power of the spells had not succeeded in countering the viper's venom. The woman was unconscious and motionless. Her hands did not move even when pricked. For me that was an overwhelming experience. I had never seen an unconscious person. Nor had I ever been put on the spot like that to heal a person who, even in a doctor's opinion, was virtually dead. It was impossible to give her a lesson in self-healing, even if I had wanted to. What helped me remain cool and confident was my knowledge that the Lord Jesus had conquered death and given his disciples his own authority. To have spent that whole day in prayer and Bible study became a very valuable source of spiritual strength.

Someone removed the bandage from the woman's swollen foot to show me the blood-red fang marks. I tied the ice cubes back with the same bandage. Then I spoke to those present: 'I am neither a doctor nor a faith-healer. I have no power and I have never healed a person of a snake bite.'

Had I known then that there was a phenomenon called the 'placebo effect', I probably would not have begun in this disastrous way, undermining their faith in myself. I continued speaking simply and in a straightforward manner: 'I know from the Bible and from my previous experiences that God hears our prayers when we make our petitions in Jesus' name. Because then we stand before God not with our sinfulness, but with repentance and in Jesus' righteousness. The Lord Jesus gives his disciples the right to use his name when we ask God for a favour. Jesus is God's beloved son, therefore we are going to pray in his name. I know God keeps the promises he has made to us in his Word. One of his promises is that he will honour our prayers of faith.'

Three of my friends and I knelt down on the mud floor around the woman's cot. We prayed out loud. My prayer was something like this: 'Father, I know you love this woman. She is precious to you, because you have made her. I know you care for the young children you have given to her. I know you have made our bodies. When they go wrong, you can fix them. Lord, I know you are greater than the snake and its poison, for you made it. Therefore, Lord, please heal this woman. Please demonstrate your love for her and your power to heal. I would not presume to ask you for this favour, except that you have yourself said, "Ask and it shall be given unto you." You have said in the Bible: "You have not because you ask not." Therefore I ask for her healing. Please honour your word and show that you are a reliable God. I ask this not because I am righteous, but because Jesus died for my sins. I come before you with this petition in Jesus' righteousness, for I pray in his name. Amen.'

Our prayers could not have lasted for more than ten minutes. I felt no tingling sensation, no electric current passing through my body, though at other times when I have prayed with a certain amount of intensity I have felt God's Spirit filling my body. On that occasion there were no sensations, except for a deep certainty that God was hearing our prayers. As I opened my eyes, the woman also opened her eyes. Needless to say, the first effect in the room was a stunned silence. Seconds later there were whispers of excitement.

I guess by then I had become bold enough to do an unconventional thing. To find out what her mental state was, and also to establish a human relationship with her, I asked, 'What is your name?'

Village women in our district do not use their names. Their normal response is to identify themselves as belonging to their father's village. Therefore I was pleasantly surprised that with a total disregard for the local conventions and the presence of her elders, she told me her name: 'Ramkali.'

'How many children do you have?'

'Two,' she replied.

'How is your pain?'

'There is no pain now.'

I turned to the chief and said: 'She is healed now, but the poison could still be there. I believe in prayer, but I also believe in medicine. We pray because God who made the human body can also heal it. But he also made man to manage the physical world, which includes our bodies, therefore doctors can also heal. Just as a mechanic can learn to fix a broken-down car, even though he did not make the car, so can a doctor learn to fix a broken-down body, at least up to a point. Snake poison is certainly something doctors can handle. So if you would like us to drive her to the hospital in town, our vehicle is at your disposal.'

'Why?' the chief asked in response, with a cool and confident attitude which seemed greater than my own faith. 'She is healed, why do we need to take her to the hospital?'

I realised much later that the government doctor may have already told him that the hospital in town would not be able to do anything without antivenin. Besides, it had to be given soon after the snake bite for it to be effective. At that time, however, I replied, 'I respect your faith, but if the poison becomes active again at night, you can pray to the Lord Jesus. You must also feel free to send for us at any time. We will be glad to come and pray and if necessary take her to the hospital.'

Two days later Ramkali walked three miles to our farm to

say 'Thank you'. In her judgement, as in ours, it was God who had healed her in response to prayers. The glucose, the ice, the sorcerers and the doctor need not have been there, as far as she was concerned. Yet let us assume for a minute that it was not a case of divine healing, but a natural instance of self-healing, the mechanism of which is mysterious at the moment, but may be discovered one day. In that case the question arises: Did our prayers act as positive, healing vibrations?

Ramkali did not know who I was. She had been unconscious. She would not have responded to me, a stranger, as warmly as she did unless she had heard my prayers. As a matter of fact, had I known that an unconscious young woman could hear, I would have been too bashful to pray as tenderly as I did. Obviously my words touched her as a person. My support may therefore have strengthened her will to live for her children. Perhaps her will proved stronger than the poison. Maybe. If so, then the incident, while it weakens the materialist's philosophy, would support the New Age belief in self-healing. However, to rule out the possibility that God healed her in response to our prayers is possible only if one assumes that God does not exist outside of the human self. The New Age healers can insist on self-healing without divine healing only because of their metaphysical presuppositions, not because incidents such as the above prove self-healing. The circumstantial evidence would tend to disprove self-healing.

However, let us assume for a moment that this was indeed a case of self-healing which I took to be a case of divine healing because of my ignorance and prior theological orientation.

One implication, then, is that it was the content (i.e., the meaning) of my words that appealed to her, not the contentless psychic 'energy' or 'vibrations' that emanated from my brain. Let me elaborate this point by discussing another miracle.

In 1990 we went through a personal tragedy. Ritu, my wife's cousin, who was then closer to our family than any other relative, fell on the concrete floor of her school, from a height of over fifteen feet. One of the first people to pick her up was a very competent and experienced nurse who is loved and respected by us both for her professional competence as well as for being a very sensitive and helpful friend. The nurse had a great deal of experience with accident victims. She was convinced that Ritu had no chance to survive.

The classes had just ended for the day when this accident occurred. Many of the students and teachers were still there. Several began to cry, some also prayed as they cried. Fortunately the local hospital had some excellent surgeons. With my wife's formal permission they drilled holes in Ritu's head to make sure there were no blood clots, and to assess her chances of survival. During the surgery many of us kept praying, and some cried as they prayed. Afterwards the doctors confirmed the nurse's assessment that Ritu had little chance of survival. One of them said that if she did, she would be unlikely to be anything more than a vegetable for the rest of her life.

The relevant part of the story is that the nurse took strong exception to our crying. She tried to prevent as many people as she could from crying. Her reasoning was that what had happened had unfortunately happened. We should forget about the body and concern ourselves with Ritu's soul. Our crying, she said, was sending negative energies to Ritu's soul. It could only add to her agony. We needed to send positive, loving vibrations to her soul. That perspective appealed to several in the community, especially because the nurse had Ritu's best interests at heart.

I must confess that I was so irritated by her stance that I found it necessary to speak against it. I believed in miracles. I believed that although self-healing seemed impossible in this situation, and we were not competent to do anything, and the doctors had already done what they said could be done anywhere in the world, God could still save and heal Ritu and make her a blessing. The nurse's prior commitment to self-healing had the effect of limiting her faith. She had ruled out God's power. God's desire for human beings is not that they should exist as disembodied spirits, but as whole persons – body, mind and spirit – in social relationships. So I insisted that it was right to cry and to pray. If my self was the only relevant reality, then crying would be foolish. But if my self was the almighty centre of my universe then I ought to be able to send out my positive psychic vibrations and heal a loved one facing death.

If our psychic vibrations are that creative and powerful, why use them only for Ritu's soul, why not also for her body? If there is a God outside of my mind, and if he has the power to heal, then crying is legitimate. For I cry as God's child. Crying is an acknowledgement that I am helpless and powerless. I am asking God, my Father, to act and to display his love and power.

The nurse was mature enough to remain my friend even though our disagreement had necessarily become public. The happy part of the story is that Ritu not only survived, but has recovered with her memory intact. At the time of writing, she only requires physiotherapy for the results of the fall itself. There are natural emotional disruptions arising from a major accident such as hers: the loss of her job, the frustration of her marriage being indefinitely postponed, her dependence on her family for a long time. These changes could produce secondary illnesses. To triumph over them is another battle, which could require both self-healing and/or divine healing.

Prayer is not a transfer of psychic vibrations from my mind to the patient's. It is a casting of myself upon God, my Father. Prayer is an expression of my faith in his power and an acknowledgement of my powerlessness. It is urging him to act, just as a child would urge his parent to help. New Age thinkers are right in rejecting materialistic medicine as reductionistic because it leaves out the personal dimensions of illness and healing. But do they not also become reductionists when they rule out divine healing and reduce everything to self-healing?

Who is responsible for healing?

Physicians and surgeons such as Bernie Siegel, and psychic healers such as Matthew Manning, report remarkable cures through their techniques of self-healing. Dr Siegel, however, admits that these patients are exceptional. In fact his whole work is with ECaP – Exceptional Cancer Patients who are able to fight disease using their will-power and the power of other spirits. Manning reports that forty per cent of all the patients that come to his centre for healing do not return when they are told that they have to heal themselves. This is not so with divine healing. We can turn to God when neither we, nor doctors, nor any psychic healer is able to help. That does not mean that human beings make no difference to disease. We do, because we are created by God to have authority over the physical realm. But if our spirits and other disembodied spirits can cause sickness or healing, so can God.

In the life of Jesus Christ as recorded in the four Gospels an important aspect of his ministry was to heal the sick. The following seem to me to be the true lessons for our healing.

Human responsibility
Jesus healed many patients who could do absolutely nothing for themselves. Some had even died. Yet we are not insignificant creatures. What we can do we must do. It does not always matter if we are not able to fulfil all the conditions listed below.

Motivation
The apostle John records the healing of a man who had been an invalid for thirty-eight years. Jesus met him when he was lying near a pool called Bethesda, in Jerusalem. The first question Jesus asked him was, 'Do you want to get well?' (John 5:6).

Some patients do not want to get well. Unfortunately, being sick may be the only way they get the care and attention that they deserve and need. For others getting sick may be as a form of registering their protest. Still others may use their sickness as a valid excuse for self-pity. They can now talk about their aches and pains for ever. When their families get irritated, they become more sick, which is their body's way of saying, 'Please love me.' A wise family would respond with love and tenderness. A person who has been sick for thirty-eight years may not want to get well, because health would bring drastic changes – responsibility to work, to provide for one's family. Sickness may indeed seem an easier way to escape the demands of a difficult life.

In order to get well we may need to answer honestly the question, 'Do I really want to get well? Am I willing to accept the challenge of a healthy life?' A strong motivation is also a prerequisite for self-healing. But it does not equal self-healing. For God to heal us against our will would be a violation of the free will that he has given us. There is no disease which is incurable for God, though there are patients who do not want to be cured.

Hope

Some people once brought to Jesus a man suffering from paralysis. The house he was in was so crowded that they had to open up the roof to lower the sick man lying on his stretcher. In order to heal him Jesus said, 'Take heart, son; your sins are forgiven' (Matt. 9:2).

Before losing health we often lose hope. During August 1991 the hardline communists attempted an abortive coup in Russia. Mr and Mrs Gorbachev were under house arrest for nearly sixty hours. The trauma resulted in paralysis of Raisa Gorbachev's right hand. All that she needed to prevent paralysis was to remain steadfast in her hope that evil will not triumph.

Sometimes hope is gone after one has already become sick. Life's problems seem insurmountable. Jesus says to his disciples, 'In this world you will have trouble. But take heart! I have overcome the world' (John 16:33).

Repentance

Sickness is not necessarily a result of our despair due to the evil deeds of others. Our own immorality could become a burden too great to bear. Jesus knew that the man suffering from paralysis needed to be delivered from his own guilt. He needed to experience God's forgiveness and acceptance. Therefore in order to rekindle his hope, his sense of self-worth, Jesus said, 'Your sins are forgiven.'

Sickness is sometimes a result not of germs, nor of our minds, nor even of our finiteness. It is caused by our sin, by our original choice as humans to break God's moral law. King David knew from his own unfortunate experience of adultery and murder that unconfessed sin is a potential source of sickness. He said in one of his psalms:

> When I kept silent,
>   my bones wasted away
>   through groaning all day long.
> For day and night
>   your hand was heavy upon me;
> my strength was sapped

as in the heat of summer.
Then I acknowledged my sin to you
    and did not cover up my iniquity.
I said, 'I will confess
    my transgressions to the Lord' –
and you forgave
    the guilt of my sin.

Therefore let everyone who is godly pray to you
    while you may be found;
surely when the mighty waters rise,
    they will not reach him.
You are my hiding-place;
    you will protect me from trouble
    and surround me with songs of deliverance.
                                          (Ps. 32:3–8)

Repentance brings about our reconciliation with God and with our fellow men and women. That is the true secret of peace, resolving the roots of our conflict.

Faith
A woman had been suffering from bleeding for twelve years. She knew that Jesus had the power to heal her. So she said to herself, 'If I just touch his clothes, I will be healed.' She came up behind him in the crowd and touched his cloak. St Mark records:

> Immediately her bleeding stopped and she felt in her body that she was freed from her suffering.
> At once Jesus realised that power had gone out from him. He turned around in the crowd and asked, 'Who touched my clothes?' . . . [the woman] fell at his feet and, trembling with fear, told him the whole truth. He said to her, 'Daughter, your faith has healed you. Go in peace and be freed from your suffering.' (Mark 5:28–34)

Scientists now know that faith starts chemical reactions in our brain that have healing effects. Faith also honours God and moves him to act. It is not wrong to have faith in yourself, but because you are finite it is wrong to have faith only in yourself. When you trust only yourself, you will soon reach your limits.
When Jesus stood before the tomb of Lazarus he asked the

people standing there to remove the stone which covered the tomb. Martha, the dead man's sister, sought to prevent Jesus.

'But, Lord,' she said, 'by this time there is a bad odour, for he has been there four days.' Jesus rebuked her gently, 'Did I not tell you that if you believed, you would see the glory of God?' After a public prayer of thanks to God, Jesus called in a loud voice: 'Lazarus, come out!' Lazarus came out, 'his hands and feet wrapped with strips of linen, and a cloth around his face' (John 11:38–44).

Those who wish to see a miracle must believe not in themselves, nor in their own faith – Lazarus could not trust, Martha did not trust – but in God, as Jesus did.

Obedience

Dead men do not have enough hidden potential to bring themselves to life. Nor does a psychic healer have that kind of power. But we can and must move the stones we are told to. Obedience is faith in action.

To both the men suffering from paralysis mentioned above, Jesus said, 'Get up! Pick up your mat and walk.' Healing accompanied obedience. The paralysed men got up, picked up their mats and walked.

When Naaman, a commander in the army of the king of Aram, came to the prophet Elisha for healing from leprosy, he was told: 'Go, wash yourself seven times in the Jordan [river], and your flesh will be restored and you will be cleansed.' Naaman took it as an insult and became furious. He had expected the prophet to respect his status, to call on the name of his God, and to wave his hand over Naaman's body and cure him. His servants counselled him to be humble, to trust and obey. He did, and was completely healed (2 Kings 5:1–14).

To open the eyes of a man born blind, Jesus spat on the ground, made some mud with the saliva, put that on the eyes of the blind man, and said to him, 'Go, wash in the Pool of Siloam' (John 9:1–7). Rationalists may ask: 'What is the connection between mud, water and healing?' There is indeed no chemical connection. But chemistry does not open the eyes of a man born blind. God does. Obedience, not visualisation, was the necessary proof in these cases that these men had humility towards God and were willing

to put their faith into action. It was also a proof that the
patients had the motivation and hope of getting well.

Prayer
After delivering his famous Sermon on the Mount, during
which, among other things, he taught, 'Ask and it will
be given to you' (Matt. 7:7), Jesus came down from the
mountainside. He was met by a person with leprosy. He
knelt before Jesus and prayed, 'Lord, if you are willing, you
can make me clean.' Jesus reached out his hand and touched
the man. 'I am willing,' he said. 'Be clean!' Immediately the
man was cured (Matt. 8:1–3).

An important aspect of prayer is to seek God's will and
abide in it. Jesus said, 'If you remain in me and my words
remain in you, ask whatever you wish, and it will be given
you' (John 15:7). St John says, 'This is the confidence we
have in approaching God: that if we ask anything according
to his will, he hears us' (1 John 5:14). Because God is a person, his will is not something static. When King Hezekiah
was ill, 'at the point of death', the prophet Isaiah was sent
to him with this message: 'This is what the Lord says: Put
your house in order, because you are going to die; you will
not recover.' Hezekiah prayed and wept bitterly. The Lord
changed his mind. He said to the prophet, 'Go back and tell
Hezekiah . . . "I have heard your prayer and seen your tears;
I will heal you" ' (2 Kings 20:1–7).

The experience of St Paul, who had himself healed many,
was different to King Hezekiah's. Paul suffered from a
chronic ailment. He says he prayed three times for his
own healing, but God said to him, 'My grace is sufficient
for you, for my power is made perfect in weakness' (2 Cor.
12:9). Paul, who had learned to rejoice in God's will, did
not respond to God's purpose in his continuing illness with
passive acceptance. No, once he knew what God's will was,
he was grateful for it. He said: 'Therefore I will boast all
the more gladly about my [physical] weaknesses, so that
Christ's power may rest on me. That is why, for Christ's
sake, I delight in weaknesses, in insults, in hardships, in
persecutions, in difficulties. For when I am weak, then I
am strong' (2 Cor. 12:9–10).

Needless to say, Paul was only following in the footsteps
of his master. Before his arrest Jesus prayed that the cup

of suffering and death that awaited him might be removed, but he added, 'Yet not as I will, but as you will' (Matt. 26:39). Instead of removing his suffering immediately, God sent an angel to strengthen Jesus so that he might face the cross with courage and dignity. Nevertheless the fact that God did hear Jesus' prayer was demonstrated mightily when God raised him from the dead, demonstrating that death's power is not final.

Prayer is neither visualisation nor psychic vibration. It is conversation. St James talks about its importance in healing:

> Is any one of you sick? He should call the elders of the church to pray over him and anoint him with oil in the name of the Lord. And the prayer offered in faith will make the sick person well; the Lord will raise him up. If he has sinned, he will be forgiven. Therefore confess your sins to each other and pray for each other so that you may be healed. The prayer of a righteous man is powerful and effective. (Jas. 5:14–16)

Fellowship

In the preceding passage St James does not ask us to go in search of faith-healers when we are sick. Rather he expects us to belong to a church of trusting, caring people – with whom we can be vulnerable enough to confess our sins, certain of love, understanding and forgiveness.

There is no doubt that an important factor behind many of our sicknesses today is the breakdown of social relationships of community. Medical science has developed effective antidotes to earlier epidemics such as malaria and smallpox. We have become clever enough to purify our water and sanitise our environment. We know what food is healthy. But alas we have lost the art of health-giving relationships built on respect, trust, forbearance, forgiveness and humility.

One tragedy of the Western world is that what started as an ethic of self-reliance gradually turned into selfishness, destroying relationships. Self-healing can be no antidote to sicknesses that are a result of our selfishness, our inability to live with others. The responsibility of seeking and cultivating the fellowship of faith rests on us before we succumb to sickness.

The church's role in divine healing

The following are the main responsibilities of the church in making healing possible.

Love

St James says in the passage quoted above that the elders of the church must go to the patient. Jesus called us to be good Samaritans to each other. To notice the one who is suffering, to allow our agenda, priorities and budgets to be interrupted for his healing. The good Samaritan in Jesus' parable cared for the injured man across the boundaries of the racial divide at his own expense. He organised the care when it was not possible for him to care personally (Luke 10:25–37).

The church elders are not asked to invite an outside healer for their sick. They are asked to lay their own hands of forgiving acceptance and fellowship upon the patients. They are to seek the fullness of God's Holy Spirit, and his gift of healing (cf. 1 Cor. 12:27–31). There is no doubt that those outside the church are seeking unknown spirits, even demons, because the church is not seeking the fullness of God's Spirit.

The prayer of faith and repentance

The Bible asks the church elders to offer prayers of faith for the sick, while confessing their own sins, because 'the prayer of a righteous man is powerful and effective' (Jas. 5:16).

When we pray for others we are like those caring friends who took the paralytic to Jesus. For divine healing, it is not always necessary for a patient to have faith or be able to pray. The faith of others can also move God to heal a sick person. It is important not to trust in our righteousness, but to come to God with the humility of repentance.

Once a centurion came to Jesus and said, 'Lord, my servant lies at home paralysed and in terrible suffering.' Jesus replied, 'I will go and heal him.' The centurion was ashamed. He said, 'Lord, I do not deserve to have you come under my roof. But just say the word, and my servant will be healed. For I myself am a man under authority, with soldiers under me. I tell this one, "Go," and he goes; and that one, "Come," and he comes. I say to my servant, "Do this," and he does it.'

St Matthew records that when the Lord Jesus heard this reply he was astonished. He said to his Jewish followers who boasted of their knowledge of God, 'I tell you the truth, I have not found anyone in Israel with such great faith.' Then the Lord said to the centurion, 'Go! It will be done just as you believed it would.' His servant 'was healed that very hour' (Matt. 8:5–13).

The centurion understood authority. Soldiers were one hundred, he was one. Many of his soldiers may have been stronger than him. Yet they obeyed him because his authority was greater than them, for it was backed by the power of the state. God, the centurion knew, was almighty and he had given Jesus the authority over diseases, demons and death. Therefore Jesus could just command the sickness to go. It would have to obey.

The centurion also knew that as a 'Gentile' officer of the occupying army in Israel he represented oppression. He knew that although Jesus would respect the fact that he was so concerned for the welfare of his servant (most probably a Jew), that was not enough to establish him as a righteous person. So instead of trusting his own act of kindness towards his servant, he relied on God's grace and therefore confessed his total unworthiness to be a host to Jesus. In healing his servant Jesus also forgave him for perpetuating and defending Roman colonialism.

If faith was the magic required for healing, confession and repentance would not be needed. But faith is acknowledging who God is in practice. He is almighty, but he is also holy, morally perfect. The magic of a sorcerer works even when he is abusive and his intention is to frighten, harm or even kill. Faith in God does not work unless we come to him with repentance. The psalmist says: 'If I had cherished sin in my heart, the Lord would not have listened' (Ps. 66:18).

God's role in our healing

Compassion
When the leper knelt before Jesus and pleaded, 'Lord, if you are willing, you can make me clean,' St Matthew says that 'Jesus reached out his hand and touched the man. "I am willing," he said. "Be clean!" ' (Matt. 8:1–3).

In Israel a 'leper' was ceremonially 'unclean'. It was
against the law to touch him. Social ostracism added to a
person's illness. Today a woman suffering from cancer may
find that her friends dread her disease and that therefore,
when she needs them most, they politely shy away from
her, compensating for a lack of the personal touch with
safe long-distance calls. Her friends obviously feel that
her distress is stronger than they are. Jesus had no such
problems. He touched the leper because he knew that he
was greater than the disease.

We cannot always change our friends and family. But we
can come to Jesus and find acceptance. The woman who had
been bleeding for twelve years was also considered ceremonially 'unclean' for that long, and was therefore unable to
participate normally in Jewish social life. When she touched
Jesus, he said to her, 'Take heart, daughter, your faith has
healed you' (Matt. 9:22). To the man suffering from paralysis
Jesus said, 'Take heart, son; your sins are forgiven' (Matt.
9:2). That the Lord is compassionate means that he accepts
us as his sons and daughters when we turn to him. Which
parent would not want to see his or her child well?

Forgiveness
What separates us from God is not some capriciously divine
power of maya, but our sin – both our sin of unbelief and our
sins of disobedience. In order to heal us Jesus forgives us.

The New Age talks a great deal about forgiveness, but
little about repentance. That is because it does not acknowledge the fact that we live in a moral universe where
real moral laws exist, and that we are guilty of having
broken real laws. Repentance is our part. Forgiveness is
God's part, because we have broken his laws. We could
have self-healing without repentance, but we cannot have
divine healing without forgiveness.

God forgives us because Jesus has already taken the punishment of our sins on the cross. It is not some theological
mumbo-jumbo that Jesus became our sin on the cross. It
is a historical fact. Two thousand years ago, when Jesus
hung upon the cross, everyone who saw Jesus could see
that it was not the justice of man that was hanging upon
the cross, but our injustice, cruelty and rebellion. The jealousy, resentment and hatred of the Jewish establishment

which plotted to eliminate Jesus; the greed of Judas, who betrayed his master for thirty pieces of silver; the lies of false witnesses; the corruption of judicial authorities and the brutality of a wicked state were all there upon the cross for everyone to see. Before his death, during the last supper, Jesus said he was shedding his blood for the remission of our sins (Matt. 26:28). As he hung upon the cross, he prayed, 'Father, forgive them, for they do not know what they are doing' (Luke 23:34). This is why the prophet Isaiah predicted, 'The punishment that brought us peace was upon him, and by his wounds we are healed' (Isa. 53:5).

Our tumours, malignancies and other sicknesses can be remitted because Jesus' blood was shed for the remission of our sins.

Power and authority
God is the almighty creator. He created the universe out of nothing. He gave us life when we did not exist. He can raise us to life when we are dead and can neither pray nor exercise faith.

The Lord Jesus said, 'All authority in heaven and on earth has been given to me' (Matt. 28:18). Jesus' authority extends not only over sickness-causing germs, viruses and poisons, but also over winds, waves or storms, whether they be in the ocean outside of us or within our own emotions. Jesus also has all authority over demons and angels. That is why the Bible asks, 'Is anything too hard for the Lord?' (Gen. 18:14).

Once a man brought to Jesus' disciples his son, who suffered physically because of a demonic influence. The disciples were not able to help the boy. When Jesus came on the scene, the father pleaded, 'If you can do anything, take pity on us and help us.'

'If you can?' asked Jesus. 'Everything is possible for him who believes.' The father exclaimed, 'I do believe; help me overcome my unbelief!' Jesus cast out the demon and the boy was healed (Mark 9:14–29).

Healers who have rediscovered the power of the human mind over our bodies are understandably excited by their discovery. What we must realise, however, is that while our imagination can influence reality in a limited way, imagination itself is not reality. To confuse reality with visualisation has long-term consequences for any culture. For one thing, it means not only that my visualisation has consequences for my body, whether for healing or for sickness, but that the visualisation or the 'Evil Eye' of the sorcerer has power over me. This belief (or superstition) puts us into a bondage of fear.

The limited power of our minds over our bodies is only an indication that the Divine Spirit has all power and authority over physical reality. Normally God works through natural laws. But because God is not bound by nature, miracles are possible. Divine miracles of healing happen because God's eye watches over his children.

Staying well

We are not asked to exercise faith only when we are sick and in need of healing. The scriptures say that 'the righteous will live by faith' (Heb. 2:4; Rom. 1:17).

To live by faith, day by day and moment by moment, is to live above worries and anxieties. Jesus says:

> Do not worry about your life, what you will eat or drink; or about your body, what you will wear . . . Look at the birds of the air; they do not sow or reap or store away in barns, and yet your heavenly Father feeds them. Are you not much more valuable than they? Who of you by worrying can add a single hour to his life? (Matt. 6:25–7)

We cannot increase our lifespan by worrying, but we can definitely reduce it. The most effective antidote to worry is faith.

To live by faith means to live in obedience to God's law. Jesus said to many of the people he had healed, 'Sin no more.'

It also means to replace our covetousness with contentment and gratitude. When we are grateful we affirm our faith in God's goodness:

> Rejoice in the Lord always. I will say it again: Rejoice! Let your gentleness be evident to all. The Lord is near. Do not be anxious about anything, but in everything, by prayer and petition, with thanksgiving, present your requests to God. And the peace of God, which transcends all understanding, will guard your hearts and minds [and thereby your bodies] in Christ Jesus. (Phil. 4:4–7)

EPILOGUE: FINDING OURSELVES

The decisive question for man is: Is he related to something
infinite or not? That is the telling question of his life . . . The
greatest limitation for man is the 'self', it is manifested in
the experience: 'I am only *that!'*
Carl G. Jung[1]

Alexander Pope (1688–1744), the great humanist prophet of
the Enlightenment, summed up a goal of Western civilisation when he wrote:

> Know then thyself,
> Presume not God to scan,
> The proper study of mankind is man.

The idea was that human beings can know themselves without reference to the infinite; that is, that they can be autonomous and 'the measure of all things'. But the attempt ended
in total despair. It is this despair of Western humanism
which has given birth to the New Age.

The first salvo against the significance of the 'autonomous'
man had already been fired before Pope wrote his couplet
by the sixteenth-century astronomers such as Galileo and
Kepler. They proved that the earth was not the centre of
the solar system, much less the universe. After telescopes
reduced the earth to a speck of cosmic dust, what then
could be said of human beings?

The next assault on the specialness of human beings was
carried out by the biologists, led by Charles Darwin. They
reduced human beings to the image of apes. Qualitatively,
we were no more special than animals.

This reduction of human beings was completed by economists and psychologists, who argued that humans were not even monkeys, but machines, completely determined by economics (Karl Marx) or biochemistry and psychological environment (B. F. Skinner). Thinkers such as these therefore argued that we had to go beyond the conventional notions of human dignity and freedom. Where Marxism succeeded, human dignity and freedom were certainly lost. It did not take long for the non-Marxist secular cultures also to begin to treat human beings as machines to be used and exploited. A revolt against such a culture and its underlying beliefs was inevitable.

When Pope said that we ought to know ourselves without reference to God, he was consciously rebelling against the biblical idea that human beings could know themselves only with reference to God, in whose image they were made. John Calvin, the great Reformation theologian, had summed up this teaching in his classic work *Institutes of the Christian Religion*, which begins with the chapter entitled, 'The Knowledge of God and That of Ourselves are Connected'. He said: 'It is certain that man never achieves a clear knowledge of himself unless he has first looked upon God's face.'[2]

We can understand something of what Calvin meant, with the help of the following illustration.

Imagine a child who interrupts his reading to ask, 'Mum, what's a guava?'

The mother replies, 'It's a fruit.'

The child sighs with relief. 'Oh, I thought it was some kind of an animal that lives on trees and was wondering why John [in this story] ate it straight off a tree!'

In philosophical terms, a 'guava' is a *particular*, while an 'animal' or a 'fruit' is a *universal*. The child understands what a particular (guava) thing is only by reference to the universal (a fruit or an animal).

All knowledge is like that. If the mother were to ask him, 'What is John [a particular]?', the child would have to reply with a universal, 'a boy'.

No particular can be understood without reference to a universal. A particular is a specific thing – e.g., a guava or John. A universal is a broader category – e.g., a fruit or a boy. A universal, if it is finite, itself becomes a relative particular. In the above example, John is a particular and 'boy' is a universal. But 'boy' being finite, is only relatively a universal. It too needs a higher universal if it is to make any sense. For example, if someone whose English vocabulary is very limited asks, 'What is a boy?', we can only answer that with a still higher universal – 'a human being' – which makes sense of (relative) particulars like boy, girl, man or woman.

If our question is, 'What is a human being?', then we have to find a universal higher than ourselves to understand ourselves. The 'Old Age' tried to define man (a particular) by reference to himself, but it found that that is impossible. So it ended up defining man by reference to an animal (a universal), or a machine (another universal).

Jean-Paul Sartre (1905–80), the French existentialist philosopher, agonised over this problem and concluded that human life was absurd or meaningless, because no finite point can possibly have any meaning without reference to an infinite point.

Carl Jung tried to find universals that can help us understand ourselves as extra-terrestrials, spirits and/or the collective unconscious. The New Age continues that search and attempts to make the human self itself the infinite universal Self – 'I am the All', or, 'I am one in being with the universe.' Shirley MacLaine says that her quest culminated only when she saw her higher self, with the help of acupuncture needles:

> I saw the form of a very tall, overpoweringly confident, almost androgynous being ... 'I am your higher unlimited self,' it said ... 'I have been with you since the beginning of time. I am never away from you. I am you ... I am the unlimited you that guides and teaches you through each incarnation ... I am God ... God is us and we are God ... What is really important to your growth is that you have finally "seen" me ... Nothing can compare to knowing the unlimitedness of yourself.'[3]

What exactly has Ms MacLaine found? She has simply found that acupuncture needles (or drugs, psychotechnologies or physical and sexual exercises) can so manipulate our nervous system that we can have visions of our own greatness, inside our own heads, and talk to ourselves.

A tragic result of finding God (universal) within our

own heads is that we then have to dismiss ourselves as an illusion – individuals are neither monkeys, nor even machines, but, worse still, are sheer illusions, born of divine ignorance!

We are indeed lost. That is why we search. Like Sue we search for meaning, for relationships that give us dignity and freedom, for we know that we are neither illusions nor machines nor animals.

Do we have to remain lost and attempt to create our own God within our own heads?

No, we are not meaningless, because an infinite reference point, the living God, already exists, whose image we bear. We are able to say, 'I am' because we are made in the image of the one who revealed himself to Moses as 'I am who I am' (Exod. 3:14). That is, he, as the infinite, personal God, is the ultimate reference point for everything in the universe, including himself. We are his image because we share his creativity when we create something new, something that shows that we are free agents. We reflect God's personhood when we love and communicate. We reflect his holiness when we make moral judgements. It is this divine image in us that sets us apart from the rest of the creation; that gives us human dignity.

We are lost because we are separated from him by our sin and moral rebellion; God's image in us has been marred by our sinful choices. Yet we can be restored into being his children. We can find forgiveness for sin and reconciliation with God by repentance and acceptance of the salvation that he offers in Jesus Christ.

The Lord Jesus said that he came to seek and to save that which is lost (Luke 19:10). By knowing him, one can know oneself as a child of God: 'Now this is eternal life: that they may know you, the only true God, and Jesus Christ, whom you have sent' (John 17:3).

APPENDIX:
FROM THE NEW PHYSICS TO
HINDUISM

*An increasing number of scientists are aware that mystical
thought provides a consistent and relevant philosophical
background to the theories of contemporary science.*
Fritjof Capra

A meeting of two queens

Mrs Vijaya Raje Scindia, a senior parliamentarian, is the
Rajmata (Queen Mother) of what was earlier the Gwalior
state in Central India. Charming and highly disciplined,
the seventy-one year old Rajmata is also the vice-president
of the second largest party in parliament, the Bharitya
Janata party. Beset as it is with nepotism, Indian politics
cannot boast of many fearless politicians like her – she has
virtually disowned her only son due to political differences.
Nor are there many politicians like her, who in spite of
publicly declaring that Mahatma Gandhi was a hypocrite
can still win an election. She draws huge crowds when her
helicopter lands in the rural areas of Madhya Pradesh and
neighbouring states, and she never tires of telling the urban
intelligentsia as well as the illiterate folk that Hinduism
is the answer to India's ills.

To support her claim, the Rajmata often recounts the
story of her meeting with Queen Frederika of Greece at
a reception. Queen Frederika had come to pay homage
to her guru, one of the Shankaracharyas,[1] following his

book on non-dualism – i.e., absolute monism, also called Advaita (or Advaita Vedanta). This book was an exposition of the teachings of the ancient Hindu scriptures called the Upanishads, or Vedanta.[2]

The Queen of Gwalior asked the Queen of Greece what it was that had drawn her to a guru who did not have much of a following even within India. Queen Frederika said that it was her advanced research in physics that had started her on a spiritual quest. It culminated in her accepting the non-dualism or absolute monism of Shankara as her philosophy of life and science. That explanation, though interesting, did not make much sense to the Rajmata, who had often heard that it was drugs and sex that attracted Westerners – initially the hippies – to Hinduism. So she probed deeper. Frederika explained that in the nineteenth century, scientists had thought that the cosmos was made up of ninety-two basic elements, such as hydrogen, oxygen and iron, which were indestructible. This implied that the universe had a diversity of independently existing materials. However, during this century research had revealed that all elements were in fact made up of a single energy. The cosmos was therefore intrinsically one, whether it appeared as a speck of dust, a tree, a Nobel Prize-winning genius or a black-hole beyond the galaxies. The differences were merely appearances. Our senses give us a knowledge of what is apparent, but not of the underlying one reality of the cosmos. This one energy which permeates the whole of creation, Frederika continued, was what Hinduism calls 'brahma'. Long before physics discovered it, Shankara had argued that the world of sense experience, that is the world of matter, was a world of appearance (maya), because at the root of each individual existence is the same energy which forms the cosmos. The human self (atman) is ultimately not distinct from the universal self (brahma). Duality is illusion. Reality is not dual, but one. Science, said Frederika, has yet to catch up with what the seers in India had already understood over 2500 years ago. Therefore, she said to the Rajmata, 'You are fortunate to inherit such knowledge. I envy you. While Greece is the country of my birth, India is the country of my soul.'

Queen Frederika is by no means an oddity. For similar reasons, thousands of PhDs have followed, for however brief a time, a guru like Mahesh Yogi, the populariser of transcendental meditation. Physicists such as Fritjof Capra have seriously argued that the conclusions of the New Physics are best understood in the philosophical framework of Eastern mysticism, such as Taoism, Hinduism and Buddhism. The purpose of this appendix is to examine this claim, with special reference to Hinduism. Before getting into the details of their arguments, it is important for us to grasp the historical significance of the trend which scientists turned-mystics such as Dr Capra and Queen Frederika represent. Many of these people are honest scientists who are no longer willing to silence the voice of their conscience in order to conform to the mainstream philosophy of science (called scientism), which they can no longer accept with intellectual integrity. They have risked their careers in rejecting mechanistic science, because to them its philosophical basis is obviously untrue.

Modern science: The fall of the last citadel of rationalism

Albert Einstein, the greatest scientific genius of our century, said: 'The most incomprehensible thing about the universe is that it is comprehensible.' Not only is there energy, there are also laws that govern it, to give order to the energy; an order that is discoverable by the human mind. This, thought Einstein, was the ultimate riddle of science.

That the human mind can understand something of nature, whether or not it has a proper philosophy of science, is obvious to all. But if you ask the question, what makes our minds capable of comprehending the cosmos? you get at least three completely different answers.

Creation by a rational God: The Judaeo-Christian belief
The founders of what is called 'modern science', such as Francis Bacon, Galileo, and Isaac Newton, were by no means consistently Christian in their thinking or practice. Nevertheless they accepted the biblical view that man can understand nature because the divine mind which created the world also created the human mind in his own image so that we may understand and govern the world on his behalf. In other words, the universe is comprehensible because

there is a given (or divinely ordained) correlation between rationality in nature and rationality in man. Francis Bacon used to be called the father of modern science because he was the first to articulate the 'scientific method' or the 'inductive procedure', which is to make experiments and to draw general conclusions from them, to be tested in further experiments. Bacon is often condemned today for his use of harsh language in describing human authority over physical nature. I sympathise with his critics, but coming as I do from a culture which worships trees, rivers, mountains, rats, snakes, monkeys and cows, I also understand why a person seeking to change his culture's subservient attitude to nature would be tempted to use his kind of extreme language. Be that as it may, the point here is that Bacon believed that the pursuit of science is a theological duty. In his *Novum Organum Scientiarum* (1620), for example, he wrote, 'Man, by the Fall, fell at the same time from his state of innocence and from his dominion over creation. Both of these losses, however, can even in this life be in some parts repaired, the former by religion and faith, the latter by the arts and sciences.'[3]

In Judaeo-Christian culture, scientific investigation proceeded in a systematic rational manner because of what A. N. Whitehead (1904–67) called 'the medieval insistence on the rationality of God' or the confidence 'in the intelligible rationality of a personal being'. In his Harvard University Lowell Lectures, entitled *Science and the Modern World*, Whitehead explained that because of their confidence in the rationality of God, the early scientists had an 'inexpungable belief that every detailed occurrence can be correlated with its antecedents in a perfectly definite manner, exemplifying general principles. Without this belief the incredible labours of scientists would be without hope.'[4]

The biblical revelation gave birth to the scientific method because it taught that man was created to govern nature. Therefore, even though human reason was finite, it could be used to understand and manage nature.

Creation by non-rational chance: Scientism

The Judaeo-Christian belief in a common rationality between the cosmos and man was gradually undercut by rationalism, which began with the French philosopher and mathematician René Descartes (1596–1650). Rationalism dominated philosophy from the seventeenth to the early twentieth centuries. Descartes was a believer in God and considered himself to be a devout Catholic. In his philosophy, however, he rejected 'faith' in God's revelation. He insisted that in searching for truth we must 'reject all knowledge which is merely probable and judge that only those things should be believed which are perfectly known and about which there can be no doubts'. In other words, we should believe that which is discovered and proved by man's reason. Descartes argued that he could doubt everything, but he could not logically doubt that he doubted. That would be self-contradictory and therefore untrue.

Almost as soon as they were put forward, philosophers demolished Descartes' arguments in defence of his faith in reason. His successors in philosophy showed that in order to be truly consistent with his own logic, Descartes could only *believe* that doubting or thinking existed. He could not possibly argue that thinking must be caused by a thinker, without first proving that every effect must have a cause. There is no way we can 'prove' that this law of causation is a universal fact.

Philosophers such as Berkeley and Hume in England and Kant in Germany greatly weakened the logical foundations of the faith in the sufficiency of reason as a means for knowing reality as it really is. The age of scepticism had begun after Kant. But it was Sigmund Freud, the father of modern psychology, who exploded the myth that humans are rational creatures. His discovery of the 'unconscious' mind, and its primacy over the conscious mind, implied that more often than not, the behaviour of human beings is conditioned by irrational drives and biochemical impulses.

Now, of course, not even scientists accept the idea that knowledge comes to us through completely objective observation. We choose what we will observe. The choice is determined by some assumptions of faith. We have to 'believe' in order to know anything.

By presupposing that blind chance was behind creation, scientism had already denied that there was rationality behind nature. The visible order of the universe was understood as the pattern human rationality sees in what is the product of blind chance. But after Freud it became impossible to believe that even human beings were totally rational. However, the philosophers and psychologists were not able to shake the popular faith in reason. The continuing success of the scientific method seemed to vindicate man's confidence in the capacity of human reason to unravel the mystery of life and the universe. Science thus became the last citadel of rationalism. It was only in this century, as we will see later, that the physicists themselves reached what appeared to be a dead end with rationalism. Then the foundations of scientism shook and the citadel began to fall apart. Sensitive individuals such as Queen Frederika saw that even though science works, scientism is intrinsically a self-defeating philosophy. It says that human reason can comprehend the universe, while insisting that there is no rationality behind the universe—which is a product of blind, random chance. How can a universe which is nonrational be understood rationally?

If you compare a painting such as 'The Raising of the Cross' by Rembrandt with modern art such as Jackson Pollock's 'Convergence', which is deliberately painted 'by chance', you can understand the former rationally, but the latter can only be felt. It makes no sense. Or, if you listen to a composer like Bach and compare his music with that of a 'chance' composer such as John Cage, you cannot make sense of the latter, because it is a product not of the rational mind, but of blind chance. The fact that the universe is in fact comprehensible drove scientists like Einstein back to a belief in a rational creation, but scientists such as Capra and Queen Frederika moved towards a third possible answer to the question why the universe is comprehensible.

Creation as consciousness: Mysticism
Put simply, the third answer is that the universe is understandable by the human mind, up to a point, because it is a 'creation' of our mind. That is, consciousness in man is the *universal* consciousness at the root of all reality. Descartes and his successors in science believed that mind and matter are two distinct entities. Mysticism says that they are one and the same thing. It is human ignorance, or what Shankara called *avidhya*, which makes us ascribe an independent and absolute reality to the world. The true

essence of reality, according to this view, is neither matter nor energy, but consciousness.

The ordinary, rational consciousness within our brains, which we experience as a part of our daily life, is said to be a small part of the whole. Through mystical techniques it is considered possible to go beyond the limited experience of rational consciousness and experience universal consciousness, that is, the oneness of everything within our own 'expanded' consciousness.

Why is it that, having rejected scientism, so many scientists prefer to find a new philosophy of science in Hinduism, Buddhism or Taoism instead of returning to the original world-view of modern science? As we shall see at the end of this appendix, the real reason is a negative one. On the surface, however, there do appear to be some attractive and positive reasons for such a choice. Let us examine these first.

Understanding the parallels between the New Physics and mysticism

We can appreciate and evaluate the attraction of a mysticism that seems to follow the rejection of materialistic science if we understand the following concepts: the oneness of the cosmos; the cosmos as appearance; and the limits of logical reason.

The oneness of the cosmos: Non-dualism

While many people feel that through his famous equation $E = mc^2$, Einstein ushered in the terrifying age of nuclear war, oppression and destruction, New Age thinkers maintain that in fact he helped usher in the age of cosmic oneness and harmony by proving the oneness of matter and energy.

The oneness of matter and energy

At the beginning of the twentieth century, when it was demonstrated that X-rays could penetrate matter, it was already understood that the atom was not the solid, indestructible substance that physicists had earlier believed it to be. Einstein's Special Theory of Relativity (1905) was understood to mean that energy and matter were interchangeable.

The energy (E) contained in a piece of matter is equal to its mass (m), times c^2, where c is the speed of light.

The formulation of this theory had two profound philosophical consequences. First, it was no longer possible to be a strict materialist, in the old sense, since matter as such was not the ultimate reality. Second, it was impossible now to believe in the plurality of independently existing material elements. The hundred-odd elements of chemistry had become the one energy of physics in a single stroke of an Einstein equation. As Fritjof Capra puts it,

> This is how modern physics reveals the basic oneness of the universe. It shows that we cannot decompose the world into independently existing smallest units. As we penetrate into matter, nature does not show us any basic building blocks, but rather appears as a complicated web of relations between the various parts of a unified whole.[5]

The relativity of space and time
Nineteenth-century scientists not only believed that the various elements were distinct substances, they also believed that space and time were distinct, absolute and given facts of the universe. This dualism of space and time had been a central pillar of Newtonian physics. Einstein's Theory of Relativity demolished this belief. He showed that space and time were relative to each other and therefore inseparable. Time now became the fourth dimension of the space-time continuum.

The interconnectedness of electrons
The oneness of the cosmos is not simply the potential oneness of elements in their pre-material energy form. Even as 'matter' the cosmos seems to be profoundly interconnected. This interconnectedness is best explained by what is known as the EPR experiment and Bell's Theorem.

It will be easier to understand the problem using an imaginary illustration. Suppose two coins behave in such a way that when they are flipped at the same time, they always fall at the same moment in the opposite way – if A is 'heads', then B will always be 'tails', or vice versa. Suppose now that we separate the coins by thousands of miles and then flip them and they still behave in the same way. We would then naturally ask, How does coin B 'know' the position coin A is taking at that very moment several thousand miles away? Since the theory of relativity assumes that nothing can travel faster than the speed of light, there is no known way through which the information could be transmitted to coin B instantaneously. Therefore, one valid explanation for the phenomenon would be that the two coins, though apparently distinct and spatially separated, may be in some mysterious way a 'single system'.

The EPR paradox was put forward by Einstein and his two young colleagues Boris Podolsky and Nathan Rosen in a joint paper in 1935. Their argument was that the quantum theory is incomplete because it does not explain how two subatomic particles could remain 'correlated' over vast distances without being connected by the law of cause and effect. The following form of this EPR paradox, first proposed by the physicist David Bohm, has become popular in New Age circles.

Imagine two electrons, A and B, are spinning in opposite directions in such a way that the total value of their spin is zero. Before measuring their spin, and without affecting their spin, we separate the two by thousands of miles – say we put one in New Delhi and the other in New York. One special feature of the behaviour of the now distantly separated electrons is that unlike other spinning objects that we normally encounter (such as a spinning-top), we can decide at the last minute whether our axis of measurement will be vertical or horizontal. The instant we perform our measurement on electron A, the second one, electron B, will acquire a definite spin – 'up' or 'down' if we have chosen the vertical axis, 'left' or 'right' if we have chosen the horizontal axis, in the direction opposite to that of electron A. Until 1964 the EPR paradox was only a curious theoretical issue which did not really bother physicists. But in that year John Bell devised a theorem which made it possible to test and confirm the EPR paradox experimentally in a lab. For short distances the paradox has in fact been experimentally confirmed, and if the quantum theory is correct, then the two particles must continue to be 'correlated' even if separated by light years.

Since Bell's Theorem it has become impossible to ignore the question, *What connects the two particles?* Bohm has supported the assumption that some type of field, as yet unexplored, connects the two particles in a single quantum system. While some Christians may be tempted to read into this phenomenon a scientific justification for the New Testament teaching that 'He [Christ] is the image of the invisible God . . . all things were created by him and for him. He is before all things, and *in him all things hold together*' (Col. 1:15–17), the mystics see it as a scientific basis for their world-view. Capra says that the two electrons behave in this manner because even though they are physically separated in space, they are 'nevertheless linked by instantaneous, non-local connections'.[6]

The physicist Henry Pierce Stapp draws even more radical implications from Bell's Theorem. He asserts that it proves 'the profound truth that the world is either fundamentally lawless or fundamentally inseparable'.[7] Another physicist, Nick Herbert, considers this behaviour of the electrons a scientific proof of mysticism. The effect in electron B, he says, is not caused by a transfer of information, at least not in the usual sense. Rather, 'it is a simple consequence of the oneness of apparently separate objects . . . a Quantum loophole through which physics admits not merely the possibility but the necessity of the mystic's unitary vision: we are all one.'[8] Mrs Shakuntala Devi, India's mathematical prodigy, also believes that this interconnectedness of the electrons entails the interconnectedness of the cosmos. She interprets it as a scientific justification for belief in astrology. If the universe is so connected, then it is legitimate to assume that the movement of the stars will affect the destinies of individual lives on this planet.

Most believers in psychic phenomena turn to this aspect of quantum mechanics to explain how extra-sensory perception, telepathy and psychokinesis (e.g., metal spoon-bending) are theoretically possible.

Rupert Sheldrake, a British plant physiologist, postulated in his books *A New Science of Life* and *The Presence of the Past* that all patterns in the universe, from electrons to human minds to galaxies, are linked by 'morphogenetic fields' (M-fields). These M-fields operate without transmitting energy (i.e., instantaneously) on a sub-quantum stratum outside the categories of space and time. These hypothetical M-fields explain how quantum information can get around so fast, why phenomena such as extra-sensory perception and psychokinesis are possible, and how the laws of karma might operate.

Indeed the EPR paradox suggests that quantum mechanics is an incomplete theory and that the quest of physics must therefore continue beyond it. But is it legitimate to build an entire world- and life-view on the strength of an as yet unexplained phenomenon? In a 1988 lecture entitled 'New Physics and Mysticism', an Australian professor of quantum physics, Dr Frank Stootman, rejects as 'unscientific extrapolation' this method of constructing a world-view on such slim and unexplained evidence. Just because two electrons are found to be mysteriously connected, does that give us sufficient reason to assume that everything in the cosmos is connected and is one? Just because a scientist knows that mass and physical energy are two aspects of the same reality, can he then, as a scientist, take a blind leap of faith and assume that physical energy is the same as psychic energy?

Another physicist, Dr Fred Skiff, said in a lecture delivered in June 1990 at St Paul, Minnesota, USA, that the scientific method has been to observe facts, then to construct a theory to explain those facts, and then to deduce logical conclusions from the theory that can be tested experimentally. The theory is modifiable by the experiments and becomes the grid through which we observe facts. Scientists who are propounding mysticism as a world-view on the basis of an as yet unexplained interconnectedness of the electrons are deliberately rejecting the scientific method. Scientists such as Capra can claim to be doing science only if they attempt to come up with an experimentally verifiable theory to explain the puzzling behaviour of electrons. Instead, it seems that they just choose to give up empirical methods of science because a certain phenomenon is not understood at present, preferring to opt for a mystical, unverifiable approach to knowledge. What is often missed by the readers of authors such as Capra is that when he is propounding a mystical world-view, he is not speaking as a scientist at all, but as someone who is denying science and yet invoking his prestige as a scientist to make his readers accept an extra-scientific proposition.

According to the sceptics, the plain truth is that the two identical coins in the earlier illustration, minted at the same time from the same material, do not seem to be interconnected. Nor is our consciousness so connected with them as to enable us to choose, when we flip a coin, whether it will fall 'heads' or 'tails'. We will return to this view again.

The inseparability of the human observer and the observed matter

For centuries a key principle of science was that the researcher (subject) must not influence the facts (objects) he is observing. Science must be based on completely objective observation. This principle assumed that you (the subject) are separate from the physical world (the object). This dualism of subject and object could allow an 'objective' study of the cosmos. It should be obvious, however, that this dualistic assumption on which the scientific method is based undercuts the monism of the mystics which teaches that 'you' and 'the world' are somehow one. Therefore, it is not acceptable to them. Their case against this dualism of subject and object is based on two scientific considerations.

(i) When physicists started studying subatomic particles in a 'cloud chamber' they found that it simply is not possible to observe the experiment without affecting it. The choice of what to observe in and of itself affected the outcome. This suggests that in the final analysis it may not be right to maintain the traditional dualism of subject and object. To quote Capra again:

> The crucial feature of Quantum Theory is that the observer is not only necessary to observe the properties of an atomic phenomenon, but it is necessary to even bring about these properties. My conscious decision about how to observe, say an electron, will determine the electron's properties to some extent. If I ask it a particle question, it will give me a particle answer, if I ask it a wave question, it will give me a wave answer. The electron does not have objective properties independent of my mind. In atomic physics the sharp Cartesian division between the observer and the observed can no longer be maintained.[9]

(ii) A subtler, but in some ways a more fundamental consideration, is that human beings can never experience (see, hear, touch, smell or taste) the world as it *really* is. What our senses receive are waves at different frequencies. These waves are interpreted by our brains as objective realities. We have no means of independently verifying whether or not the image of the world in our mind corresponds to a world actually out there. This, as we saw in chapter 1, leads some mystics to argue that the cosmos does not exist objectively, in its own right, but that 'we create our own reality'.

As we have seen, physicists such as Dr Stootman regard this conclusion as 'sheer extrapolation'. Just because objectivity is restricted at the quantum level, it does not give us the right to assume that an objective reality does not exist at all. While it can be conceded that absolute objectivity is beyond the reach of finite men, it does not follow that we are not capable of a measure of objectivity, and that a scientist should not strive to be at least sufficiently objective for another scientist who may disagree with him to be able to obtain the same results by repeating his experiments. This rejection of objective reality leads us to our second consideration, that is, the view of the cosmos as a projection of the mind – an appearance.

The cosmos as appearance: Maya
Besides non-dualism or 'oneness', the Upanishads also teach the doctrine of maya. That is, the cosmos is ultimately only an illusion. Many serious scientists no longer consider this to be an absurd idea, for the following reasons.

The solidity of the world as an appearance
If an atom could be blown up to the size of a football field, its nucleus would be about the size of a fly in the centre of the field. The electrons would be smaller than the grains of sand on the periphery of the field. This means that atoms are anything but solid substances. Equally important is the fact that even the electrons are not solid substances like a grain of sand. These 'particles' are better described as 'patterns of activity' that have both space and time aspects. Their space aspect makes them appear as objects with a

certain mass. Their time aspect makes them appear as processes involving equivalent energy. The interrelationship
of these energy patterns of the subatomic world is what
finally appears to us as the solid, stable, predictable cosmos. If what is fluid and dynamic only *appears* solid and
stable, then it is indeed tempting to accept Shankara's
concept of maya. Capra says:

> 'Maya' does not mean that the world is an illusion, as it is
> often wrongly stated. The illusion merely lies in our point
> of view, if we think that the shapes and structures, things
> and events, around us are realities of nature, instead
> of realizing that they are concepts of our measuring
> and categorizing minds. Maya is the illusion of taking
> these concepts for reality, of confusing the map with the
> territory.[10]

Simply put, mystics are saying that the next time you hold
your husband or wife in your arms, you must know that it
is not a reality in your arms, but a concept your mind has
fabricated from the raw energy that forms the universe.

The external world as a manifestation of the invisible
The 'peace invocation' that prefaces the Isa Upanishad,
the first of the ten major Upanishads, begins with the
statement:

> Purnamadah Purnamidam
> Purnat Purnamudacyate.

'That (Brahma) is the Full. This (world) is the Full. From
the Full (invisible), the Full (visible) has come.'
     'That' and 'This' are technical terms in Vedanta. 'This'
refers to the cosmos within the grasp of the senses. 'That',
which is the source of 'This' world, is beyond the senses,
known only in mystical experience. This teaching has a
striking parallel in the work of the physicist David Bohm,
a protégé of Einstein. He calls the unmanifest dimension
of the universe 'the implicate order' – that is, the fluid,
interconnected energy patterns which underlie the explicate order of the solid, separate, stable world of matter.
     The earlier scientists had assumed that the manifest
world was the only real world. The first serious challenge

to that assumption came (as we saw in chapter 1) from the palaeontologist and mystic Pierre Teilhard de Chardin. Science, he said, had thus far been preoccupied with the 'without' of things, ignoring the unmanifest dimension or the 'within' of things. In his classic work *The Phenomenon of Man* de Chardin wrote that to ignore the existence of a 'within' was understandable in physics, in bacteriology, and to some extent in botany as well. But

> It tends to become a gamble in the case of a biologist studying the behaviour of insects or Coelenterates. It seems merely futile with regard to the vertebrates. Finally, it breaks down completely with man, in whom the existence of a *within* can no longer be evaded, because it is the object of a direct intuition and the substance of all knowledge.[11]

Commenting on de Chardin, one of the most respected Vedantic scholars in India, Swami Ranganathanda of the Ramakrishna Mission, says that Vedanta also 'speaks of Brahma as the inactive state and Maya or Sakti as the active state of one and the same primordial non-dual reality'.[12] New Age thinkers say that this parallel between New Science and Vedanta is supported by physicists such as David Bohm. Marilyn Ferguson sums up Bohm's view in these words:

> What appears to be a stable, tangible, visible, audible world, said Bohm, is an illusion. It is dynamic, Kaleidoscopic – not really there. What we normally see is the explicate or the unfolded order of things, rather like watching a movie. But there is an underlying order that is father to this second generation reality. He called the other order implicate, or enfolded. The enfolded order harbours our reality, much as the DNA in the nucleus of the cell harbours potential life and directs the nature of its unfolding.[13]

The cosmos as a hologram
Holography is three-dimensional photography using laser beams. When a normal, two-dimensional photograph gets damaged, it is damaged for good. But one characteristic

of a hologram is that if it is broken, any part of it can be used to reproduce the whole image. In a mysterious way, every part of the hologram contains the whole within itself.

This phenomenon is similar to the way our brain seems to function. Neuroscientist Karl Primbram was associated with the attempt to find the precise location of memory in the brain. He learned that the memory is not localised in a particular place. If one part of the brain is damaged, another part takes over the function.

How do we see, hear, taste or smell something? Primbram argues that the brain simply receives the frequencies of the data. It performs complex mathematical calculations on these frequencies and then translates them into hardness or coldness or redness or smell. The hard rock that we see and touch is in fact only a particular frequency mathematically interpreted by the brain to be a rock: 'These mathematical processes have little common sense relationships to the real world as we perceive it.'[14] Thus, according to Primbram, what exist are frequencies which our brain uses to construct a three-dimensional image of the universe, much like a complete holographic picture which is constructed from a tiny fragment of the whole. In Marilyn Ferguson's words, this view implies that, 'If the nature of reality is itself holographic and the brain operates holographically, then the world is indeed, as Eastern religions have said, Maya, a magic show. Its concreteness is an illusion.'[15]

Capra explains this concept with the help of a metaphor:

> In the heaven of (god) Indra, there is said to be a network of pearls, so arranged that if you look at one you see all the others reflected in it. In the same way each object in the world is not merely itself but involves every other object and in fact is everything else. 'In every particle of dust, there are present Buddhas without number'.[16]

The limits of logic
Over two thousand years ago, Hindu seers had rejected faith in human rationality. The Katha Upanishad, which is considered to be the backbone of philosophical Hinduism,

says: *Aaniyan hi atarkyam anupramanat*: '[The illumination is] not a subject to be grasped by logical reason (tarka), because it is subtler than the subtlest.' And *Naisa tarkena matirapaneya*: 'This spiritual understanding cannot be attained by logic (tarka).'

The emerging tradition of scientific mysticism claims that the New Physics has reached similar conclusions. Capra claims: 'Physicists have come to see that all their theories of natural phenomena, including the "laws" they describe, are creations of the human mind: properties of our conceptual map of reality rather than of reality itself.'[17] This is said to be true for a number of reasons.

a) *The law of non-contradiction*. An apple is an apple and cannot be a banana at the same time, says the simplified version of the law of non-contradiction. This has been a basic tenet of logic since the Greek philosopher Aristotle (384–322 BC). Descartes assumed the validity of this law when he said that he could not logically doubt that he was doubting. It would be untrue, because it would be self-contradictory. Since Descartes, the law of non-contradiction was accepted as an a priori truth in the scientific method. An a priori truth is one which has to be assumed before we can prove anything at all. What is a priori cannot be proven itself, but it must be assumed, otherwise no knowledge is possible.

Twentieth-century physics, however, began to raise questions about the absolute nature of the law of non-contradiction when it faced the apparent paradox that light was particles as well as waves. If an apple cannot be a banana, how can a particle appear to be a wave when viewed differently? As Swami Ranganathanda says, 'First fact, then logic, and if fact does not fit into logic, it is logic that has to go.'[18]

b) *The law of causation*. If we cause water to be heated beyond 4 °C it will expand. Every cause has an effect, and every effect has a cause. In identical circumstances a given cause will always have the same effect. This law of cause and effect was another a priori assumption of modern science. If heat will always cause water to expand, then the universe has a uniformity which makes technology such as a steam engine possible. But the discoveries of the New Physics in the twentieth century have raised doubts about the absolute nature of this law as well.

For example, in any one year there is a 1 in 2340 chance that an atom of radium (226 Ra) will undergo radioactive decay by emitting an alpha particle. Thus if we had 2340 atoms of 226 Ra we could expect, on average, to see one radioactive decay event in one year. Or if we had 2340 x 365 atoms of 226 Ra we might expect one decay event each day. But we have no way of knowing which particular atom it might be in any one day, or why it decays.

It has been assumed that the scientist's job is to find out exactly what causes a phenomenon. If we can know the cause, we can predict the effect, such as which atom will emit the particle and when it will do so. Modern science was built on the assumption that every effect must have a cause. Any effect which did not have a knowable cause could not happen, as far as science was concerned. Outside science, it was called 'magic' or 'miracle'. Experimentally and mathematically, physicists became convinced that there were no hidden causes which could not one day be found with more sophisticated techniques.

The rise of modern quantum mechanics, however, has challenged this long-held view. For example, Werner Heisenberg showed in 1927 that in accordance with quantum principles it is impossible to measure simultaneously with precision the position and momentum of a particle. In fact, the uncertainty of the position multiplied by the uncertainty in momentum must always exceed Planck's constant (the ratio between a particle's energy and its corresponding wave frequency); this relationship is known as the Heisenberg uncertainty principle. Thus, for example, if we were to fix the position of an electron beam by passing it through a narrow slit, the result would be diffraction—a sideways spreading of the beam, rendering its direction and momentum uncertain. The implication is that this uncertainty is not due to some hidden cause which one day will be discovered, but rather that the uncertainty is intrinsic to the accepted model of quantum mechanics itself. At the subatomic level, then, a certain randomness or unknowableness is inherent in our understanding of basic reality.

For some thinkers, but by no means all, this has raised the question whether randomness or non-rationality is not the basic truth of the cosmos. If human senses and logic are not reliable means of knowing the truth, perhaps we have to transcend them in a mystical experience to get a direct (non-logical, non-sensory) experience of ultimate reality. But what will that do to science and progress? Will it spell their doom? Gary Zukav, another mystic physicist, whose book *The Dancing Wu-Li Masters* covers the same ground as Capra's *The Tao of Physics,* confesses that one implication of their world-view may be the end of classical 'objective' science. Marilyn Ferguson states his conclusions thus:

> In one sense, Zukav said, we may be approaching 'the end of science'. Even as we continue to seek understanding, we are learning to accept the limits of our reductionist methods. Only direct mystical experience can give a sense of this non-logical universe, this realm of connectedness (of quantum physics). Enlarged awareness – as in meditation – may carry us past the limits of our logic to more complete knowledge.[19]

Will this 'direct experience' or 'complete knowledge' be science? For example, when someone feels 'enlightened' during meditation, will that prove that he did in fact have an experience of the universal divine consciousness? Or will it merely prove that he 'felt' enlightened, with no way of verifying or disproving his experience? It was such considerations that forced Einstein to respond to a lady in Vienna in 1955 with this statement: 'The mystical trend of our times, which is manifested in the rampant growth of the so-called Theosophy and Spiritualism is, for me, no more than a symptom of weakness, confusion and a convenient vehicle for exploitation.'

Be that as it may. Since there are compelling reasons why scientists who reject scientism turn to mysticism in search of a better philosophy of life, we need to examine whether their choice is in fact justified. Or would a return to the original world-view which made science possible be a more sensible alternative?

The parallels: Real or apparent?

In the previous section we looked at the three related concepts of the oneness of the cosmos (non-dualism); the cosmos as appearance (maya); and the unreliability of rationality, which seems to justify mysticism. In this section we will look at these same concepts critically, to examine if the New Physics does lead one towards the mystical non-dualism of Hinduism, or whether the similarities are themselves merely maya, an illusion.

Oneness in physics and non-dualism in Hinduism
Is the energy of physics that permeates the cosmos the same as the One Consciousness of Hinduism which alone is said to be real? Or are the two systems talking about completely different things?

In Vedanta
When the Upanishads say *Tat Tvamasi* ('That thou art') or *Aham Brahmasmi* ('I am Brahma'), they are talking about the oneness of the human self and the divine self. According to Vedanta our experience of finite individuality is our bondage. Liberation means the realisation of our divinity, or the merging of our finite consciousness in the infinite Cosmic Consciousness.

While the Upanishads emphasise the oneness of the human and divine self, they do not teach the oneness of the material body and the conscious self, let alone the oneness of self and the material world. At death, the Upanishads teach, the material body (called *sthula sarira*) remains on the earth, while the subtle body (*suksma sarira*) separates from the former and goes to the astral world. The 'subtle body' is what is called the 'soul' in English. The soul is not the self.

At the 'soul' stage the notion of individuality remains intact. It therefore reincarnates repeatedly in other material bodies until the 'self' is realised. When that happens, we are delivered from bondage to the material world and the subtle astral body (soul) and cease to reincarnate.

The experience of self-realisation is not an experience of the oneness of the material body and the soul. In self-realisation, called *nirvikalpa samadhi*, you experience the oneness of your consciousness with what is called the divine consciousness. However, your consciousness does not merge with the consciousness of others. Even the consciousness of the guru and the disciple do not merge. For example, when Totapuri, a naked guru, helped Ramakrishna Paramhansa to attain *nirvikalpa samadhi*, Ramakrishna sat in his room for three days and nights while Totapuri remained outside, wondering what was happening to his disciple. When he finally entered the room he saw the corpse-like body of Ramakrishna and struggled to bring him back to normal consciousness. The consciousness of the enlightened guru had not become one with the consciousness of the disciple-in-enlightenment.

There is an extreme interpretation according to which non-dualism in Vedanta can mean the oneness of everything, including body, soul and self. That is, if the material world is considered to be totally an illusion – if maya is understood to mean that Brahma (universal consciousness) alone exists, and the rest is its dream. Few modern gurus accept that interpretation of maya, because it completely rules out the possibility of science developing in India. Science can only develop in a culture which has a high view of the material world: its objectivity, rationality and value.

In physics
The discoveries of the oneness of matter and energy, the interconnectedness of electrons, the relativity of space and time, and the inseparability of the subject and object have naturally encouraged scientists to assume that the physical universe is a single system. As such, we should be able to construct one unified theory which will explain all its facets. Many scientists believe that a successful Grand Unification Theory will emerge when relativity and quantum theories are united.

Will such a theory give a unified explanation of the physical universe only, or of its non-physical dimensions as well? For example, will it explain how the one energy functions, and also why it does so? Or why laws that do not exist at an inorganic level of the cosmos appear at the organic level? Indeed, one of the most fundamental problems in science is, where do the laws that govern the energy and give it a definitive force and order come from? Can we believe in laws without a law-giver?

Einstein, who struggled till the end of his life to find the Grand Unified Theory, did not imagine that he was exploring the oneness of the creator and the creation, but only the oneness of the physical order. When he argued against the uncertainty principle of the quantum theorists and said, 'I cannot believe God plays dice with the universe,' he implied that the laws that regulate the cosmos come from outside the physical system itself, and that they are a separate, non-physical realm of reality.

Even if it is taken for granted that physics has already proved the oneness of physical creation, it is at this stage a totally unsubstantiated extension of this belief to imply that 'oneness' means the oneness of creator and creation. Physicists who think that consciousness is both the creator as well as the creation do so purely as a matter of faith. They acknowledge that they do not yet have even a theoretical framework for such an assumption, let alone any experimental justification for it. Capra, for example, hopes that one day physicists will construct a unified theory which may include an explanation of consciousness.[20]

By 'oneness', modern physics generally means the oneness of the physical universe. The question of the oneness of matter and consciousness has not even been studied yet. But consciousness is not the only non-material reality we live with. Normally we consider love, beauty, morals, creativity, freedom, language, the awareness of individuality, etc., to be non-mechanical phenomena, and therefore marks of personality rather than matter. These are not even thought of as a part of consciousness. Insects have consciousness, but we do not normally think of them as persons with moral and aesthetic choices.

Is personality real or illusory? Are love and morals also a part of the physical order physicists talk about? Shirley MacLaine went to meet Professor Stephen Hawking of Cambridge University, seeking to get the approval of one of the foremost physicists of our times for her view that 'oneness' in physics means the oneness of everything, including the oneness of energy and personality. Their conversation specifically considered whether moral behaviour and love are part of the oneness of reality with which physics deals. Ms MacLaine asked Professor Hawking:

'Are we evolving then? . . . Or are we going to destroy ourselves?'

'There is quite a chance we will destroy ourselves,' he
answered . . .
'The universe,' he went on, 'and everything in it, can
be explained by well-defined laws . . .'
'You mean there are no accidents?' I asked.
'Correct.'
'Then is our behaviour also a part of well-defined
laws?' I asked.
'No,' he answered. 'Our behaviour is part of our
human nature . . .'

(Implying that moral behaviour is personal, non-mechanical and therefore unpredictable. Man is free to destroy or
develop himself. Morality or personality is outside the
sphere of mechanical 'oneness' physics talks about.)

Ms MacLaine then turned the discussion to the question of love. She continued:

'You said everything could be explained by laws.'
'Yes.'
'Well then, that means that the universe operates
within a harmony, doesn't it?'
'Yes.'
'Well, isn't harmonic energy loving?'
'I don't know,' he answered, 'that there is anything
loving about energy. I don't think loving is a word I
could ascribe to the universe.'
'What is a word you could use?'
He thought for a moment. 'Order,' he said. 'The uni-
verse is a well-defined order.'[21]

Love and morality are part of personality, not a machine. But are these personal traits part of the oneness of
the physical energy of the cosmos, or are they independent realities? It seems reasonable to think that they are
not part of the cosmic oneness. The oneness of the universe that can be explained by a Grand Unified Theory
will have to be a mechanical oneness. What is non-mechanical cannot fit into mathematical equations. Be that
as it may, the least we can say with total certainty is that,
so far, physics has not even begun to study these questions. By 'the oneness of the universe' physicists mean
only the oneness of the physical, non-personal, mechani-

cal universe. Dr Fred Skiff has argued that 'unification' in physics simply means finding a common basis necessary for communication, while in mysticism it means finding common, undifferentiated unity, thereby erasing all boundaries between things. The two are completely different concepts.

Therefore, the attempt to assert that the interconnectedness of electrons proves the absolute oneness of everything, including the oneness of personality and matter, is at best an unscientific extrapolation. At worst, theologians may be tempted to call it a diabolical deception which makes creation the creator – exactly what Satan said to Eve in the Garden of Eden: 'You will be like God' (Gen. 3:5).

Brahma and maya in Vedanta and physics

It is tempting to see the Brahma of the Vedanta as the equivalent of the 'iniplicate order' of David Bohm or the 'within' of Teilhard de Chardin, for it is indeed conceived of in Vedanta as the unmanifest ground of all the manifest reality. Likewise, it is not difficult to understand why so many are tempted to see maya as the equivalent of the 'explicate order' – or the 'without' of things. Vedanta does say that the visible comes out of the invisible by the power of maya, and is therefore maya. But closer study shows the concepts of Brahma and maya in Vedanta are in fact the opposite of what the New Physics is actually saying.

A major discovery of physics is that the energy which is the unmanifest ground of the material world is dynamic and active. Energy packages are being continuously created and destroyed, though energy itself is not being created or destroyed. They move not at mind-boggling speed, but at a computer-boggling pace. On the other hand, and relatively speaking, the world of matter is stable, solid and predictable.

Vedanta, in contrast, says that the unmanifest Brahma is the unmoved, unchanging stillness, void or nothingness. It is the manifest world of maya that is dynamic and subject to constant change and decay. As Swami Ranganathanda succinctly puts it in his commentary on the Isa Upanishad, 'Vedanta speaks of Brahma as the *inactive* state and Maya or Sakti as the *active* state of one and the same primordial non-dual reality.'[22]

If the mystical experience of an Advaitin Hindu is indeed the experience of the ultimate reality, it is anything but an experience of the implicate order of the physical universe which is dynamic not still. Also, the experience is understood within Vedanta not as getting at the root of the material reality, but as getting away from it.

If a scientist-turned-mystic were able to go to the root or the essence of physical reality in a direct, conscious experience, in such a way that he became one with the universal mind, we would expect him to come up with a Grand Unification Theory as well as a solution to the scientific, technological and ecological problems of the world. Maharishi Mahesh Yogi accepts that the above should be the logical result of an experience of the ultimate reality. But traditionally the logic of mysticism has led mystics to lose interest in physical reality altogether. Totapuri, who guided Ramakrishna Paramahansa in enlightenment, is a typical example. He attained enlightenment after forty years of

unremitting spiritual practice performed on the banks of the sacred Narmada river in Central India. He obtained the fruit of his path of the Advaita Vedanta, the experience of nirvikalpa Samadhi, the impersonal, unconditional state . . . Having achieved this blessed experience, Totapuri wandered from place to place without any aim or purpose of his own . . . realizing Brahma as the one reality, and looking upon the world as an appearance [maya], Totapuri spent his life under the canopy of heaven, alike in storm and sunshine, maintaining himself on alms.[23]

I know personally two physicists who have become mystics – one a Hindu and another a Buddhist. Their life-styles can be described in identical terms to Totapuri's, except that they wear clothes. They admit that it is their mystic experience which leads them away from physical reality and not to its deeper and fuller appreciation.

Whatever a mystical experience may be, it certainly does not appear to be an experience of the essence of the physical reality with which a scientist has to grapple. It has a tendency to take one away from the sphere of scientific investigation. Therefore it is naive to accept the viewpoint which says either that the conclusions of modern science point towards mysticism or that mystical, non-dualistic philosophy provides an intellectual framework for modern science. One can arrive at this conclusion only if one chooses to look at the parallels between physics and mysticism in a superficial way.

Senses and logic in Vedanta and science

It is true that Vedanta teaches categorically that dependence on the senses and logic has to be discarded if we want to know the true nature of the universe. In his authoritative work *Bliss Divine*, Swami Sivananda states unequivocally that the vedantic view is that we must seek to 'consciously destroy the mind by Sadhna and Samadhi'.[24] And again: 'Do not use your reason too much in the selection of your Guru';[25] 'Keep your intellect at a respectable distance when you study mythology. Intellect is a hindrance';[26] 'That which separates you from God [Brahma] is mind.'[27]

Vedanta says that it is the human intellect which is the cause of our ignorance and bondage. The techniques of achieving mystical experience, of seeing the true nature of reality, are techniques of transcending the intellect or 'killing the mind', as the late Osho Rajneesh used to say. The New Physics, on the other hand, has by no means undercut the effectiveness of the scientific method.

The sensory observation of reality

It is true that our senses often deceive us. When we see that each day the sun rises in the east and sets in the west, we infer that the sun revolves around the earth. However, the fact that the truth is the opposite is discovered not by rejecting sensory observation, but by being more meticulous in observing the phenomena of nature.

We observe matter as solid. Therefore it is easy to assume that atoms, or at least subatomic particles, must be solid. We learn that the truth is the opposite not by rejecting our reliance on sense observation, but by being more careful in our observations and their logical inferences.

Logical inferences from observation

It is easy for Swami Ranganathanda to say, 'If facts do not fit logic, it is logic that has to go.' The question is, however, how do we know what the facts are?

Whatever his other mistakes, Kant was right in his insistence that logic is a priori. If we cannot assume the validity of logic, we cannot know any facts. We can see the smoke and the fire, but we cannot conclude that the smoke is caused by the fire without first assuming causation – that an effect must have a cause, which is one of the fundamental laws of logic.

The paradox of light appearing both as a particle and as a wave does not imply that the law of non-contradiction is invalid, that an apple can also be a banana. The fact is that light is neither a particle nor a wave. It is something for which we have no parallel in the macroscopic world, therefore we tend to describe its space dimension as a particle and its time dimension as a wave. Physicists now prefer to call it a wavicle – a name which means nothing concrete to us, because it has no parallel in our macroscopic experience. But it establishes a principle that if at present our language does not adequately describe a particular reality, what we need is not to abolish language, but to coin a new word or phrase.

Likewise, the 'uncertainty' of the behaviour of the electrons is because there are no 'local' hidden variables or causes. It does not prove that there are no 'non-local' hidden causes which could explain the behaviour. Capra himself illustrates this quite simply by differentiating between the concept of probability in classical physics and in quantum physics. When we throw a dice, he says,

> we could – in principle – predict the outcome if we knew all the details of the objects involved: the exact composition of the die, of the surface on which it falls and so on. These details are called local variables because they reside within the objects involved. Local variables are important in atomic and subatomic physics too. Here they are separated by connections between spatially separated events through signals – particles and networks of particles – that respect the usual laws of spatial separation. For example, no signal can be transmitted faster than

the speed of light. But beyond these local connections are other, non-local connections that are instantaneous and cannot be predicted, at present, in a precise mathematical way. These non-local connections are the essence of Quantum reality. Each event is influenced by the whole universe, and although we cannot describe this influence in detail, we recognise some order that can be expressed in terms of statistical laws.[28]

This admission by Capra is a big climbdown from the earlier view, presented in influential books such as Marilyn Ferguson's *Aquarian Conspiracy*. Then, New Age thinkers assumed that the absence of hidden variables proved that the laws of logic, such as causation, were invalid. Therefore, they argued, since we cannot trust our senses and logic, we cannot assume that an objective universe exists outside our consciousness. Ferguson argued that since what the brain receives are frequencies, we cannot assume that the frequencies are caused by a real material world.

Building on the conclusions of the neuro-scientist Karl Primbram and the physicist David Bohm, Ferguson argued that the universe is a hologram or maya. Capra concurred with that view in *The Tao of Physics*. But in *The Turning Point* he drew back from the edge of the precipice to say, 'David Bohm realizes that the hologram is too static to be used as a scientific model for the implicate order at the sub-atomic level. Bohm's theory is still tentative.' And again, 'The universe is definitely *not* a hologram.'[29] In other words, the universe may have a reality, rationality and order of its own, independent of our consciousness, but discoverable by it.

The above discussion brings us back to the basic riddle of science – what makes the universe comprehensible? The New Age rejection of scientism is valid if it is assumed that the universe is a product of blind chance. On the other hand, if we assume the universe to be consciousness, as the New Age claims, then that can be 'realised' only in a mystical experience, by going beyond reason or logic and the very presupposition of science that the physical universe and its laws exist objectively, independent of the human mind. This philosophy, as mentioned earlier, has proved itself historically to be barren as far as its ability to give birth to science and nurture it is concerned. Dr Raimundo Panikkar, famous for his book *The Unknown Christ of Hinduism*, concedes that the concept of cosmic order (*rta*) in Hinduism rules out the possibility of morals, thinking, science and technology. In his foreword to Jeanine Miller's book *The Vision of Cosmic Order in the Vedas*, Panikkar writes:

> There is no law of *rta* [cosmic order]. There is *rta* and *rta* is harmony; but this harmony is not subjected to any ulterior law. There is no mind behind. To live in a *rtic* universe represents a fundamental human experience different from that of believing [we] live in a logical world or in a universe, governed by law ... This is what the upanishads will try to qualify later. Being is free, ultimately even from thinking. No need of ethical norms at the ultimate level. No need of fear, 'Angst', anxiety, regarding ultimate questions. *Rta* is there, but not as a refuge. No need to control everything, to be certain of all things, to know everything.[30]

The above should make it clear that the cosmic order of mystical thought, far from providing a 'consistent and relevant philosophical background to the theories of contemporary science' (Capra), in fact undercuts the very foundation and possibility of science. If this is so, then what attracts some scientists to mysticism?

I suggest that the real attraction is a negative one, as I shall now show.

The relationship between science and the Hindu, Taoist and Buddhist world-views
Puritans and Anglicans played a decisive role in the founding of the Royal Society for Science during 1660–2, in part because of their commitment to the Bible. They believed that God wanted them to understand nature and have dominion over it. George M. Trevelyan writes in *English Social History*:

> Robert Boyle, Isaac Newton and the early members of the Royal Society were religious men, who repudiated the sceptical doctrines of Hobbes. But they familiarized the minds of their countrymen with the idea of law in the universe and with scientific methods of inquiring to discover

truth. It was believed that these methods would never lead to any conclusions inconsistent with biblical history and miraculous religion. Newton lived and died in that faith.[31]

Trevelyan's observations are important to remember, because the conflict between the Church and science had begun long before the founding of the Royal Society. It arose because scientific observations did not fit with specific dogmas of the Church which were not biblical, such as geocentric Aristotelian astronomy. At this stage there was no conflict between science and the biblical worldview itself. For example, when the Roman Church attacked Copernicus and Galileo for teaching that it was not the sun that revolved around the earth, but the earth which revolved around the sun, Galileo (1564–1642) wrote defending the compatibility of Copernicus and the Bible. This was one of the factors which brought about Galileo's trial. But gradually, when the scientists began to give up faith in revelation and believe only what could be proved by the scientific method, it began to be considered unscientific to believe in the creator himself.

An all-out conflict between Christianity and science became inevitable when scientism insisted on completely separating reason from faith. The umbilical cord between the mother (Christianity) and the child (science) was cut and Western Christianity by and large chose faith in the heavenly Father and gave up her loyalty to the rebellious child.

This separation of faith and reason weakened both Christianity and science. The Church isolated itself from the intellectual arena and became preoccupied with faith and personal piety. Reason, cut off from faith in a rational creator, could not stand on its own for long either. If the universe was a product of random chance, how could it be understood by reason? From the beginning scientism was an absurd and self-defeating philosophy. But by the beginning of the twentieth century, science had acquired power and Christianity had become weak. Therefore it could not effectively point out that reason could not possibly comprehend a non-rational universe, and that scientism was an emperor without clothes.

As this inherent contradiction within scientism became

apparent, and it could not logically defend its faith in reason, it was left to Hinduism, Buddhism and Taoism to mount the attack on the absurdity of scientism. Hinduism could attack scientism because it had never had the kinds of problems which Christianity had had with science. In the heyday of science, Hinduism had never had to cross swords with scientism. Thus after science, cut off from its roots, had already become vulnerable, unable to defend its faith in reason, Hinduism could fearlessly attack it and appear as conqueror. The loss of scientism became the gain of Hinduism, Buddhism and Taoism.

But what seems to be overlooked by sincere individuals such as Queen Frederika is that systems of thought such as Hinduism never had a conflict with science, because, as we shall see later, they could never produce and nurture science. To say that Hinduism could not produce science is not the same as saying that India did not have a scientific genius. Indian culture did make a promising start. But it did not result in science for two reasons. First, Hindu polytheism deified natural forces and taught the worship of creation. This made the Indian mind-set too weak to seek dominion over nature. Later, the Hindu monism made the material world unreal (maya), and this undercut the possibility of the pursuit of a systematic study of nature. What is true of Hinduism at this point is also true of Taoism, the Chinese world-view. In spite of a very early and profound understanding of the world, the Chinese could not develop this understanding as full-fledged science. Joseph Needham, well known for his authoritative five-volume study of science and civilisation in China, says in *The Grand Titration* (1969) that there was in their world-view 'No confidence that the code of Nature's laws could ever by unveiled and read, because there was no assurance that a divine being, even more rational than ourselves, had ever formulated such a code capable of being read'.[32]

Buddhism reinforced the anti-scientific stance of Hinduism by seeing the cosmos as intrinsically evil, the source of suffering. For Buddha, enlightenment required that we close our eyes to the world outside and shut the doors of our minds to all physical sensations and intellectual thoughts. For Buddha, bliss was inside human consciousness.

Capra himself admits that modern science became possible because of the biblical mind-set in the West:

> The notion of fundamental laws of nature was derived from the belief in a divine lawgiver which was deeply rooted in the Judaeo-Christian tradition. In the words of Thomas Aquinas: 'There is a certain eternal law, to wit, Reason, existing in the mind of God and governing the whole universe.'
> This notion of an eternal, divine law of nature greatly influenced Western philosophy and science. Descartes wrote about the six laws which God has put into nature, and Newton believed that the highest aim of his scientific work was to give evidence of the six laws impressed upon nature by God.[33]

In contrast to Buddhism, the biblical world-view insists that the physical and social environment of man was intended by God to be the real source of our bliss (Eden). The earth produces 'thorns and thistles' after the fall; but it has to be brought under our stewardship and made useful to us and other creatures, including coming generations.

The recovery of science

Scientism has failed to provide a satisfying philosophy of science, and mysticism is a blind alley which destroys the possibility of science. However, it is possible to go back to the original assumption of the founders of modern science, that the world is comprehensible by human reason because it is created by a rational Being who has also created us in his own image to govern the earth. When our brains receive energy frequencies, we have an adequate basis for assuming that they come from a real world, because God says that he created a world out there. The founders of modern science were able to affirm the reality, rationality and value of the cosmos because they did not hold the humanistic presupposition that man has to find truth either by his own reason or by his sense experience. They believed that ultimately knowledge comes to us by God's revelation. For them the Bible was the book of God's word and nature was the book of God's works. They could trust their senses and their logic because God's word told them that a real world existed which they were created to govern. The universe was not a creation of their consciousness. It had an objective and orderly existence of its own. Objective science was therefore possible.

The one and the many

How are we to account for the oneness that physicists encounter when they investigate the subatomic world? From a biblical perspective the discovery of oneness should not be at all surprising. The biblical world-view insists on the dualism of the creator and his creation as well as on that of the personal and the non-personal, but it does not teach the plurality of eternally existing elements: everything is made by one word (Logos):

> In the beginning was the Word, and the Word was with God, and the Word was God. He was with God in the beginning.
>   Through him all things were made; without him nothing was made that has been made. (John 1:1–3)

The Bible also affirms that the one reality that underlies the universe (the implicate order?) is not open to observation by the senses: 'By faith we understand that the universe was formed at God's command, so that what is seen now was not made out of what was visible' (Heb. 13:3).

The real scientific problem is not how to explain the oneness of the cosmos, but its diversity. Why does one undifferentiated energy, call it Brahma if you like, appear as completely different objects – from atoms of hydrogen to the molecules of heavy water, from single-celled bacteria to people of different languages – so that even though they are supposed to share a common consciousness, they cannot understand each other? What are the laws that ensure that on this planet energy forms x amount of hydrogen and y amount of oxygen, and that ensured that all oxygen does not react with hydrogen to form water or with carbon to form carbon monoxide – that enough free oxygen remains to make life possible?

The passage quoted above says that the laws that regulate the one energy are the commands of the creator. No explanation of why one energy exists in such diverse and well-balanced forms surpasses the biblical explanation given in the Genesis account of creation, where the act of creation is often described as the separation of one into many at God's command:

> In the beginning God created the heavens and the earth [time-space and matter]. Now the earth was formless and empty, darkness was over the surface of the deep, and the Spirit of God was hovering over the waters.
>
> And God said, 'Let there be light,' and there was light. God saw that the light was good, and he separated the light from the darkness. God called the light 'day', and the darkness he called 'night'. And there was evening, and there was a morning – the first day.
>
> And God said, 'Let there be an expanse between the waters to separate water from water. So God made the expanse and separated the water under the expanse from the water above it. And it was so . . . (Gen. 1:1–7).

It is important to repeat that the real marvel in the universe is not the oneness of creation. The oneness is given. What demands an explanation is why the one appears as separate entities.

Physicists acknowledge that one dynamic, fluid, ever-changing energy forms stable and solid elements in just the right proportion on the planet to make life possible, because the behaviour of the energy is governed by strong conservation laws. Where do these laws come from? A dream? Human imagination? No. Science is possible because the creation obeys the commands of its creator. Some of these laws do not appear at the nuclear level, where the reality is 'formless' and 'void', that is, devoid of the 'shapes' and 'forms' that fill the earth. But at the atomic and molecular levels some of the previously non-existent laws become operational, just as the moral (or aesthetic) laws do not appear at non-human levels, but they make an appearance at the human level, where God commanded them.

Again it is energy's obedience to the creator's command which gives it uniformity, predictability and rationality at atomic and molecular levels – which makes the universe comprehensible to us, who are also made from the earth, yet separated from it by virtue of the fact that we bear the image of the personal creator. This makes science or a study of natural laws not only possible, but our religious duty as

well. As Francis Bacon put it, 'Let no man out of weak
conceit or sobriety, or in ill-applied moderation, think or
maintain that a man can search too far or be too well
studied in the book of God's words, or in the book of God's
works.' For Bacon, the book of God's words was the Bible
and the book of God's works was the cosmos which God had
made. To the physicists who cannot find an explanation for
what causes certain aspects of the behaviour of electrons,
Bacon would say, do not give up the study of the book
of God's works for mysticism. To assume that you have
already reached the limits of knowledge is either 'weak
conceit' or 'ill-applied moderation'. True humility is to go
on asking questions of the book of God's works as well as
of the book of God's words.

The biblical world-view which says that behind the visible
universe is the invisible Word of God not only explains the
one and the many (unity and diversity); it also gives a high
view to the world of senses. When the universe is seen as
the creative work of a great designer, rather than a mere
appearance, dream, or illusion, we have a basis for affirming
not only its rationality, but its intrinsic goodness as well.
The creation account in Genesis 1 repeatedly says that God
looked at what he had 'made' (separated out of the previous
oneness), and 'saw that it was good'. When creation on this
planet had been completed, the Bible says, 'God saw all that
he had made, and it was very good' (Gen. 1:31). God was
pleased with the results of his creative act.

Creation is neither eternal nor infinite. Yet it is real
and good. This high view of the physical universe is a
necessary presupposition of science. Men and women can
find their true self, their identity, not by getting away from
the physical world through mystical experience, but in a
creative relationship with the world, as its manager.

NOTES

1 The Universe in the Human Mind: The Background to New Age Thought

1   Shirley MacLaine, *Going Within* (New York: Bantam Books, 1990), pp. 270, 211, 314.
2   Joseph Chilton Pearce, *The Crack in the Cosmic Egg: Challenging Constructs of Mind and Reality* (New York: Julian Press, 1971).
3   MacLaine, *Going Within*, pp. 45–6.
4   Quoted in P. A. Schlipp (ed.), *Albert Einstein: Philosopher Scientist* (Evanston, IL: The Library of Living Philosophers, 1949), p. 248.
5   Arthur Stanley Eddington, *The Nature of the Physical World* (Cambridge: Cambridge University Press, 1928), p. 332.
6   ibid., p. 338. According to the Bible the universe was created by the Logos – the Word of God – which was incarnated as Jesus Christ; see John 1:1–14.
7   René Descartes (1596–1650), the father of Western philosophy, assumed mind and matter were separate physical entities that interact in the human pineal gland.
8   Marilyn Ferguson, *The Aquarian Conspiracy* (Los Angeles: J. P. Archer, 1987).
9   Teilhard de Chardin, *The Phenomenon of Man* (New York: Harper & Row, 1975), p. 71.
10 Omega is the last letter of the Greek alphabet, alpha the first. The New Testament describes Jesus Christ, the Word of God, as both 'the Alpha and the Omega', the beginning and the end of the universe (Rev. 1:8; 21:6; 22:13).
11 Jean-Paul Sartre, Karl Jaspers and Martin Heidegger are among the better-known figures of the existential movement.

12   Charles Reich, *The Greening of America* (Harmondsworth: Penguin Books, 1970), p. 15.
13   Robert Bellah, et al., *Habits of the Heart* (London: Hutchinson, 1988), p. 29.

2 'Let Us Make Man in the Image of His Stars': Astrology and the New Age

1   Tracy Marks, *The Astrology of Self-Discovery* (Sebastopol, CA, 1985), p. 3.
2   Dr A. P. Stone, unpublished notes from Workshop on Astrology, Bolton Regional Seminar, 1990. The diagram that follows is also from Dr Stone's notes.
3   A. P. Stone, *Hindu Astrology* (New Delhi: Select Books, 1981), p. 191.
4   Michel Gauquelin, *Astrology and Science* (London: Mayflower Books, 1972) and *The Cosmic Clock* (London: Granada, 1980).
5   See J. A. West and J. G. Toonder, *The Case for Astrology* (Harmondsworth: Penguin Books, 1973).
6   Quoted in Arthur Koestler, *Janus: A Summing Up* (London: Picador, 1983), p. 263.
7   Carl Jung, *Memories, Dreams and Reflections* (New York: Vintage Books, 1965), p. 441.
8   Quoted by A. P. Stone from R. Wilhelm and C. Jung, *The Secret of Golden Flower* (London, 1942).
9   Anon, *The Revelation of Ramala* (Glastonbury: The Ramala Centre, 1978), pp. 47–8.
10   Donna Cunningham, *Astrology and Vibrational Healing* (San Rafael: CA: Cassandra Press, 1988), p. 150.
11   Marks, *The Astrology of Self-Discovery*, p. 235.
12   Wim Rietkerk, *The Future Great Planet Earth* (Mussoorie, India: Nivedit Good Books Distributors, 1989), p. 20.

3 Spiritism: A Balance Sheet

1   Bernie Siegel, *Love, Medicine and Miracles* (New York: Harper & Row, 1986), p. 20.
2   Carl G. Jung, *Psychology and the Occult* (London: Ark Paperbacks, 1987), p. 125.
3   ibid., footnote on p. 125.
4   Siegel, *Love, Medicine and Miracles*, p. 218.
5   Dan Korem, *Powers: Testing the Psychic and Supernatural* (Downers Grove, IL: InterVarsity Press, 1988).

6 Shirley MacLaine, *Dancing in the Light* (New York: Bantam Books, 1986), p. 338.
7 V. K. Sethi, *Kabir – The Weaver of God's Name* (Beas, Punjab: Radha Soami Satsang, 1984), pp. 25–6.
8 Francis A. Schaeffer, *Trilogy* (Westchester, IL: Crossway Books, 1990), p. 340.
9 David Icke, *The Truth Vibrations* (London: The Aquarian Press, 1991), p. 120.
10 ibid., p. 124.
11 Shirley MacLaine, *Out on a Limb* (New York: Bantam Books, 1984), p. 48.
12 ibid., p. 233.
13 ibid., see ch. 14.
14 MacLaine, *Dancing in the Light*, p. 342.
15 Steven Lee Weinberg (ed.), *Ramtha* (Eastbound, Wash.: Sovereignty Inc., 1986), quoted by Ted Schultz in Robert Basil (ed.), *Not Necessarily the New Age* (New York: Prometheus Books, 1988), p. 348.
16 MacLaine, *Dancing in the Light*, p. 307.
17 ibid., p. 341.
18 ibid.

4 UFOs – A Religious Experience?
1 Arthur Koestler, *Janus: A Summing Up* (London: Picador, 1983), p. 284.
2 ibid., p. 321.
3 Richard Hall, *Uninvited Guests: A Documented History of UFO Sightings, Alien Encounters and Coverups* (Santa Fe, New Mexico: Aurora Press, 1988), p. 235.
4 Carl G. Jung, *Flying Saucers: A Modern Myth of Things Seen in the Sky* (London: Ark Paperbacks, 1987), p. 2.
5 Quoted in Koestler, *Janus*, p. 319.
6 Hall, *Uninvited Guests*, p. 327.
7 David Icke, *The Truth Vibrations* (London: The Aquarian Press, 1991), pp. 64–5.
8 Jung, *Flying Saucers*, p. xiii.
9 Quoted in Koestler, *Janus*, p. 319.
10 Hall, *Uninvited Guests*, p. 91.
11 Shirley MacLaine, *Going Within* (New York: Bantam Books, 1990), p. 22.
12 Koestler, *Janus*, p. 325.
13 Shirley MacLaine, *Out on a Limb* (New York: Bantam Books, 1984), p. 211.

14 ibid., p. 347.
15 Koestler, *Janus*, p. 284.
16 Icke, *The Truth Vibrations*, p. 117.
17 Anon, *The Revelation of Ramala* (Glastonbury: The Ramala Centre, 1978), p. 232.
18 ibid., p. 233.
19 ibid.
20 ibid.

5 Tantric Sex – A Celebration of Life?

1   Fritjof Capra, *The Tao of Physics* (London: Flamingo, 1990).
2   ibid., p. 322.
3   Quoted in Shirley MacLaine, *Going Within* (New York: Bantam Books, 1990), p. 187.
4   Amaurey de Riencourt, *The Soul of India* (Honeyglen Publishing, 1986).
5   S. Radhakrishnan and Charles A. Moore, *A Source Book in Indian Philosophy* (Princeton University Press, 1957).
6   Capra, *The Tao of Physics*, p. 338.
7   See Vishal Mangalwadi, *The World of Gurus* (Landour, Mussoorie: Good Books, 1987), ch. 7.
8   Capra, *The Tao of Physics*, p. 322.
9   Brooks Alexander, 'Tantra: The Worship and Occult Power of Sex', *SCP Newsletter*, vol. 2, no. 2 (Summer 1985).
10 ibid.
11 ibid.
12 Capra, *The Tao of Physics*, p. 322.
13 MacLaine, *Going Within*, p. 187.
14 Rajneesh, *Neo-Sannyas*, vol. 2, no. 4 (1975), p. 2.
15 Riencourt, *The Soul of India*, p. 140.
16 Amma, *Swami Muktananda Paramhamsa* (Ganeshpuri, 1971), pp. 32–43.
17 ibid., p. 35.
18 ibid., p. 36.
19 Charles S. J. White, 'Swami Muktananda and the Enlightenment Through Sakti Path', *History of Religions*, vol. 23, no. 4, p. 319.
20 Quoted in R. C. Zaehner, *Mysticism: Sacred and Profane* (London: Oxford University Press, 1961), p. 91.
21 ibid., p. 96.
22 ibid., p. 92.

23 Alexander, 'Tantra: The Worship and Occult Power of Sex'.
24 Mangalwadi, *The World of Gurus*, pp. 209–11.
25 Riencourt, *The Soul of India*, pp. 139–40.
26 Alexander, 'Tantra: The Worship and Occult Power of Sex'.
27 MacLaine, *Going Within*, p. 195.

6 Doing Ecology is Being Human

1   Fritjof Capra, *The Turning Point* (London: Flamingo, 1990), p. 462.
2   ibid., p. 308.
3   Machaelle Wright, *Behaving as if the God in All Life Mattered* (Perelandra, 1987).
4   Quoted in Paul Hawken, *The Magic of Findhorn* (London: Fontana/Souvenir Press, 1988), pp. 48ff.
5   ibid., p. 144.
6   David Icke, *The Truth Vibrations* (London: The Aquarian Press, 1991), p. 133.
7   James Lovelock, *Gaia* (Oxford: Oxford University Press, 1979).
8   See, for example, Lovelock's chapter 'God and Gaia' in his later book *The Ages of Gaia* (Oxford: Oxford University Press, 1988).
9   Capra, *The Turning Point*, p. 316.
10 Fritjof Capra and Mike McGrath, 'Zen and the Art of Changing the World', *Express*, Berkeley, California, 16 February 1990.
11 Fritjof Capra, *The Tao of Physics* (London: Flamingo, 1990).
12 Robert Bellah, et al., *Habits of the Heart* (London: Hutchinson, 1988), p. 72.
13 Capra, *The Turning Point*, p. 302.
14 ibid.
15 ibid. p.463
16 ibid., pp. 325–6.
17 Arthur Koestler, *Janus: A Summing Up* (London: Picador, 1983), pp. 9–11.
18 See the chapter entitled 'The Sadness of Successful Women' in Shirley Nicholson's anthology, *The Feminine Principle Today: The Goddess Reawakening* (Wheaton, IL: The Theosophical Publishing House, 1989).
19 Sondra Ray, *Loving Relationships* (Berkeley, CA: Celestial Arts, 1980), pp. 115–16.

7 Vegetarianism – Self and Selfishness

1 Howard Williams, *The Ethics of Diet*, p. 38. Tolstoy's preface to this book is entitled 'The Morals of Diet or the First Step'. The preface seems to have first appeared in a Russian edition of the book in 1892. An acquaintance kindly lent me a photocopy of the preface. I have not been able to discover the name and year of the publication of the preface in English.

2 J. de Marquette, 'The Supreme Value of Vegetarianism', in *The Vegetarian Way* (Madras: Indian Vegetarian Congress, 1977), p. 110.

3 Williams, *The Ethics of Diet*, pp. 45–7.

4 M. K. Gandhi, *The Story of My Experiments With Truth* (Ahmedabad: Navjian Publishing House, 1927). (All quotations are taken from the 1976 edition.)

5 ibid., pp. 13–14.

6 Swami Satyananda Saraswati, 'Vegetarianism a Culture', in *The Vegetarian Way*, p. 51.

7 Quoted by M. P. Vaidehi, 'Vegetarianism – The Trend', in *The Vegetarian Way*, p. 113.

8 J. M. Jussawalla, 'All Life is Sacred', in *The Vegetarian Way*, p. 47.

9 The widow of the late Sri Sanjay Gandhi, no relation of Mahatma Gandhi.

10 Richard Wagner, in *The Vegetarian Way*, p. 107.

11 Gordon Lotto, 'Medical Aspects of Vegetarianism', in *The Vegetarian Way*, p. 13.

12 M. M. Bhamgara, 'Yoga and Diet', in *The Vegetarian Way*, p. 137.

13 Quoted in *The Vegetarian Way*, p. 2.

14 Shirley MacLaine, *Dancing in the Light* (New York: Bantam Books, 1986), p. 346.

15 C. W. Leadbeater, 'Vegetarianism and Occultism', in *The Vegetarian Way*, p. 165.

16 Quoted in *The Vegetarian Way*, p. xxi.

17 ibid., p. xix.

18 V. K. Sethi, *Kabir – The Weaver of God's Name* (Beas Punjab: Radha Soami Satsang, 1984), p. 145.

19 Fred C. Whittle, in *The Vegetarian Way*, p. 108.

8 The Reincarnation of the Soul

1 Arthur Koestler, *Janus: A Summing Up* (London: Picador, 1983).

2 Alister Hardy, *The Divine Flame* (London: Collins, 1966); *The Spiritual Nature of Man* (Oxford: Clarendon, 1979).
3 Shirley MacLaine, *Out on a Limb* (New York: Bantam Books, 1984).
4 Raymond A. Moody, *Life After Life* (New York: Bantam Books, 1976).
5 Ian Stevenson, *Twenty Cases Suggestive of Reincarnation* (New York: American Society for Psychical Research, 1966), p. 353.
6 ibid., p. 13.
7 ibid., p. 381.

The case of Sri Satya Sai Baba also presents strong evidence that the so-called cases of reincarnation are in fact cases of spirit-possession. On 8 March 1940, at about 7 p.m., Satya Narayan Raju leapt into the air with a loud shriek, holding one toe of his right foot. Everyone present thought that he had been 'stung by a big black scorpion'. He writhed in pain for some time, but slept soundly during the night. The next evening he became unconscious and his breathing became difficult. When he regained consciousness the following morning, his behaviour had changed. His Australian biographer and devotee, Mr Howard Murphet, writes:

The boy was by no means normal in behaviour, he seemed at times to be a different person. He seldom answered when spoken to, he had little interest in food. He would suddenly burst into song or poetry, sometimes quoting long Sanskrit passages far beyond anything learned in his formal education and training. Off and on he would become stiff, appearing to leave his body and go somewhere else. At times he would have the strength of ten, at other times he was as weak as a lotus stalk. There was much alternate laughter and weeping but occasionally he would become very serious and give a discourse on the highest Vedanta philosophy. (Howard Murphet, *Sai Baba: Man of Miracles* [New Delhi: Macmillan, 1972], p. 54.)

This abnormal behaviour convinced his parents and neighbours that some evil spirit had possessed him. Prof. Gokak, his well-known Indian disciple, writes: 'He was subjected to great suffering by the family because they called in an exorcist to treat him, believing that he was possessed by the devil.' (V.K. Gokak, *Bhagvan Sri Sathya Sai Baba* [New Delhi: Abhinar Publications, 1975], p. 4.)

The torture inflicted by one of the exorcists was so horrible that the parents decided that it was better for the boy to live and be possessed than for him to die at the hands of the exorcists. So they took him home. Two months later Satya Narayan Raju began to perform miracles and claimed, 'I am Sai Baba.'

8   Some Jews in Christ's time thought that a foetus could sin, therefore it is not necessary to assume that the disciples had reincarnation in mind when they asked the question. They may have been asking if a foetus could sin.

9   Joseph Head and S. L. Cranston (eds), *Reincarnation: An East-West Anthology* (Wheaton, IL: Theosophical Publishing House, 1968), back cover.

10   Elizabeth Kübler-Ross (ed.), *Death – The Final Stage of Growth* (New York: Simon & Schuster, 1975).

11   Leslie Weatherhead, *The Christian Agnostic* (London: Hodder & Stoughton, 1965).

12   It also creates more difficulties than it resolves. If child prodigies bring their special skills from a previous life, why don't all souls bring with them their learning and experiences from past lives? Why do most of us have to begin learning from scratch as infants?

Tertullian, an early church Father (ad 160–220), asked in his 'Treatise on the soul', 'How happens it that a man who dies in old age returns to life as an infant?' Tertullian's simple but profound objection has never been answered by the reincarnationists. Should the explanations for child geniuses be sought in genetic, cortical and environmental factors, or should we just accept a metaphysical assumption that they bring their genius from another life?

If the 'love-at-first-sight' phenomenon is due to relationships in a previous life, then why does it happen only after puberty?

It has been shown that *déjà vu* experiences are a result of having seen pictures, paintings or movies. Arthur Reber, in the *Penguin Dictionary of Psychology* (1985) suggests that the *déjà vu* experiences are 'due to a kind of momentary neural short circuit so that the impression of the scene arrives at the memory store (metaphorically speaking) before it registers in the sensorium'. Obviously it is proper to explore such natural explanations first before settling for a metaphysical answer for apparently unusual happenings.

13 Romila Thaper, *A History of India* (Harmondsworth: Penguin Books, 1975), p. 46.
14 See for example Paul de Parrie and Mary Pride, *Unholy Sacrifice of the New Age* (Westchester, IL: Crossway Books, 1988).
15 MacLaine, *Out on a Limb*, p. 347.
16 Shirley Maclaine, *Dancing in the Light* (New York: Bantam Books), p. 347.
17 Maclaine, *Out on a Limb*, p. 363.
18 ibid., p. 199.
19 ibid., p. 220.
20 Richard Lannoy, *The Speaking Tree: A Study of Indian Culture and Society* (Bombay: Bhartya Vidhaya Bhawan, 1971), p. 168.
21 ibid., p. 169.
22 Stevenson, *Twenty Cases Suggestive of Reincarnation*, p. 33.

9 My Course in Miracles

1 Bernie Siegel, *Love, Medicine and Miracles* (New York: Harper & Row, 1986), p. 8.
 2 Marilyn Ferguson, *The Aquarian Conspiracy* (Los Angeles: J. P. Archer, 1987), pp. 241–2.
 3 ibid., p. 277.
 4 George Vithoulkas, *Homeopathy: Medicine of the New Man* (Northamptonshire: Thorsons, 1985), p. 19.
 5 David Icke, *The Truth Vibrations* (London: The Aquarian Press, 1991), p. 83.
 6 ibid., p. 82.
 7 Ferguson, *The Aquarian Conspiracy*, p. 262.
 8 ibid., p. 276.
 9 ibid., p. 249.
10 ibid., p. 277.
11 Matthew Manning, *Matthew Manning's Guide to Self-Healing* (Northamptonshire: Thorsons, 1989), p. 21.
12 ibid., pp. 53–4.
13 ibid., pp. 68–9.
14 *A Course in Miracles* (London: Arkana, 1985), Teacher's Manual, p. 23 (see also p. 31), p. 16 and pp. 16–17.
15 Shirley MacLaine, *Going Within* (New York: Bantam Books, 1990), p. 103.

16 ibid., pp. 264–6.
17 ibid., p. 268.
18 William Nolen, *Healing: A Doctor in Search of a Miracle* (New York: Random House, 1974).
19 *A Course in Miracles*, Student's Work Book, p. 3.
20 ibid., p. 4.
21 ibid., Introduction.
22 MacLaine, *Going Within*, p. 262.
23 ibid., p. 264.
24 Allegra Taylor, *I Fly Out With Bright Feathers* (London: Fontana, 1987).
25 Bernie Siegel, *Love, Medicine and Miracles* (New York: Harper & Row, 1986), p. 20.
26 ibid., p. 218.

Epilogue: Finding Ourselves

1 Carl Jung, *Memories, Dreams and Reflections* (New York: Vintage Books, 1965), p. 325.
2 John Calvin, *Institutes of the Christian Religion*, edited by John T. McNeill, translated by Ford Lewis Battles (Philadelphia: Westminster Press, 1960), vol. 1, p. 37.
3 Shirley MacLaine, *Dancing in the Light* (New York: Bantam Books, 1986), pp. 334–9.

Appendix: From the New Physics to Hinduism

1 Adi Shankaracharya (AD 785–820), who interpreted the Upanishads as a philosophy of absolute monism, established four centres in India. Later a fifth one was also added. The head of each centre is called Shankaracharya.
2 The Upanishads are the last part of the Vedic literature written as philosophic discourses by the hermit gurus before the Christian era.
3 Quoted in Francis A. Schaeffer, *How Should We Then Live?* (Old Tappan, NJ: Fleming M. Revell, 1976), p. 134.
4 ibid., pp. 132–3.
5 Fritjof Capra, *The Turning Point* (London: Flamingo, 1990), p. 70.
6 ibid., pp. 73-5.
7 ibid., p. 75.
8 Quoted by Marilyn Ferguson, *The Aquarian Conspiracy* (Los Angeles: J. P. Archer, 1987), p. 172.
9 Capra, *The Turning Point*, p. 72.
10 Fritjof Capra, *The Tao of Physics* (London: Flamingo, 1990), p. 100.

11 Teilhard de Chardin, *The Phenomenon of Man* (New York: Harper & Row, 1975), p. 55.
12 Swami Ranganathanda, *The Philosophy of the Upanishads* (Bombay: Bharitya Vidhya Bhawan, 1971).
13 Ferguson, *The Aquarian Conspiracy*, p. 150.
14 ibid., p. 17.
15 ibid., p. 180.
16 Capra, *The Tao of Physics*, p. 328.
17 ibid., p. 317.
18 Ranganathanda, *The Philosophy of the Upanishads*, p. 172.
19 Ferguson, *The Aquarian Conspiracy*, p. 172.
20 Capra, *The Turning Point*, p. 87.
21 Shirley MacLaine, *Going Within* (New York: Bantam Books, 1990), pp. 304–5.
22 Ranganathanda, *The Philosophy of the Upanishads*, p. 65.
23 ibid., pp. 226–7.
24 Swami Sivananda, *Bliss Divine* (Divine Life Society, 1974), p. 106.
25 ibid., p. 206.
26 ibid., p. 236.
27 ibid., p. 392.
28 Capra, *The Turning Point*, p. 71.
29 ibid., pp. 88, 329.
30 Raimundo Panikkar, 'Foreword', Jeanine Miller, *The Vision of Cosmic Order in the Vedas* (London: Routledge & Kegan Paul, 1985), p. xix.
31 Quoted in Schaeffer, *How Should We Then Live?*, p. 136.
32 ibid., p. 142.
33 Capra, *The Tao of Physics*, p. 317.